中国文化精粹丛书

中国成语故事

Stories of Chinese Idioms

（汉英对照）

杨振刚　郑分　译
孙毅　译审

西南交通大学出版社
·成都·

图书在版编目（CIP）数据

中国成语故事 = Stories of Chinese Idioms：汉英对照 / 杨振刚，郑分译. —成都：西南交通大学出版社，2020.9
（中国文化精粹丛书）
ISBN 978-7-5643-7586-7

Ⅰ. ①中… Ⅱ. ①杨… ②郑… Ⅲ. ①汉语－成语－故事－汉、英 Ⅳ. ①H136.31

中国版本图书馆 CIP 数据核字（2020）第 167044 号

中国文化精粹丛书

Zhongguo Chengyu Gushi

中国成语故事 Stories of Chinese Idioms（汉英对照）

杨振刚　郑　分　译

责任编辑	赵玉婷
特邀编辑	任　乐
封面设计	GT 工作室
出版发行	西南交通大学出版社 （四川省成都市金牛区二环路北一段 111 号 西南交通大学创新大厦 21 楼）
发行部电话	028-87600564　028-87600533
邮政编码	610031
网　　址	http://www.xnjdcbs.com
印　　刷	四川煤田地质制图印刷厂
成品尺寸	170 mm × 230 mm
印　　张	29.25
字　　数	432 千
版　　次	2020 年 9 月第 1 版
印　　次	2020 年 9 月第 1 次
书　　号	ISBN 978-7-5643-7586-7
定　　价	88.00 元

该丛书译著受西安翻译学院2019年度双一流建设项目资助

The translation works in the series are funded by the Double A-class Development Project of the Xi'an Fanyi University, 2019

序

『中国文化精粹丛书』

今天，在全院努力建设“一流专业”—— 翻译专业的时刻，在全院全力以赴申请“硕士点授予权”的时刻，人人都在拼搏，要么进言献策，要么集思广益。“尽心尽力尽责”成了西译人的箴言。这种苦干、实干、巧干的精神对翻译学院今后的发展，对翻译专业未来的建设以及对翻译专业学生未来的实训、就业具有现实意义。

由于每个国家有着不同的社会制度、宗教信仰和历史背景，一种文化所包含的信息并不存在于另一种文化之中。英、汉两种语言都有着悠久的历史，它们在各自民族、各自文化、各自政治、各自经济、各自科学等的发展过程中，都积累和创造了很多具有各自民族风格和鲜明文化知识内涵特色的语言，这就给汉英-英汉翻译带来了一定的困难。语言是文化的载体，翻译不仅是语言的转换，还是文化的传真。译者应当有强烈的文化意识，不仅应该熟悉两种语言，了解相关专业知识，还应该熟悉两种文化，并在翻译中充分考虑两种文化的差异，让翻译在促进科学技术、商贸往来和文化交流中真正起到作用。

文化的交流以语言为媒介，翻译是跨文化交流的桥梁。翻译研究作为一个新学科，在 20 世纪 70 年代就已经开始文化层面的探索，但我们对中国翻译传统的研究，到目前为止仍未实现真正突破性的发展。传统的翻译研究历来比较重视语言分析和文本对照，而对语言翻译过程中所涉及的文化现象则研究不够。鉴于此，我们必须摆脱传统的教学模式，即从词到句，从句到篇章的句法或语法教学方式。为了更好地传播中国文化，弘扬中国精神，讲好中国故事，在学好、用好中文的基础上，我们必须大量阅读外文书籍。中国文化是中华民族在长期历史发展中的伟大创造，是中华民族勤劳和智慧的结晶。数千年来，它不但在中国历史上光彩夺目，惠及历代中华儿女，还影响过周边各国文化的发展，特别是自汉代开辟“丝绸之路”、明代郑和七下西洋，对西方乃至世界的历史和文明的进程产生过巨大而深远的影响。然而，在汉英文化翻译方面，我们目前还做不到水乳交融，炉火纯青，其主要原因是我们在译入语中找不到相对应的词语。分析其原因：一是我们的阅读量不够；二是跨文化意识不强；三是对汉英两种文化背景、思维方式、语言结构和表达习惯注重不够，研究不足。鉴于此，我们欲将几部有关中国文化方面的著作翻译成英文，整合为“中国文化精粹丛书”，其中包括《中国神话故事》（*Chinese Mythological Stories*）、《中国十大古典喜剧故事》（*Ten Chinese Classic Comedies*）、《中国十大古典悲剧故事》（*Ten Chinese Classic Tragedies*）、《中华国学经典选读》（*Selected Readings of Chinese Classics*）、《中国成语故事》（*Stories of Chinese Idioms*）。

这些著作将作为翻译学院高年级英语翻译专业学生翻译实训的项目。希望通过分析对比汉英-英汉民族不同的文化心理、文化观念和文化习俗，着重探讨文化与翻译之间的关系，特别是我国国情文化对汉英翻译的影响以及相应的翻译策略，这项工程能够有利于培养和增强学生译者和教师译者在翻译过程中的跨文化意识，提高译者的文化修养和译文质量，以便更好地为中国文化外译服务。我们愿意为此尽绵薄之力，做出点滴贡献。

丁晶

（西安翻译学院董事长）

Foreword

Today, everyone of the University is striving to make translation major a first-class major and apply for the qualification to grant the MA degrees. “Try our best and perform our duty” has become the maxim of all XFU (Xi’an Fanyi University) staff members. This kind of hard-working, steadfast and ingenious spirit will, undoubtedly, prove its realistic significance for the future development of the university, for the future course design of the translation major and the practical training of the students.

Due to different social systems, religious beliefs and historical backgrounds, the information contained in one culture doesn’t exist in other cultures. Both English and Chinese languages are proud of a long history throughout which they have accumulated and created many peculiar verbal wisdom that carries their own ethnic styles and cultural connotations with the development of their ethnics, cultures, politics, economy and science, which make English-Chinese and Chinese-English translation tough and testing. Language is the carrier of culture. Translation is not only a language transfer but also cultural transition. A translator should have a strong cultural awareness. When translating, he/she should not only be familiar with the two languages, have a sound understanding of the related information, but also be familiar with the two cultures and fully consider the cultural differences so as to help his/her translation play a real role in pushing forward science and technology, commerce and trade, and the communication and development of both cultures.

Language usually serves as a medium of cultural communication and translation the bridge of cross-cultural communication. Translation studies, as a new subject, began to explore at the cultural level in 1970s. However, we haven't made any real breakthroughs in the study of Chinese translation tradition up till today. Traditional translation studies have been stressing language analysis and text contrast all along, but insufficient studies have been done on cultural phenomena involved in the process of language translating. In view of this, we must break away from the traditional pedagogy, which is often referred to as a grammatical teaching method or syntactical method that starts from words, moves on to sentences and ends in texts. In order to spread Chinese culture with better effects, expand Chinese spirit, tell well the Chinese stories, we must read extensively in both the target language and the source language on the basis of learning and using both languages proficiently.

Chinese culture is a great creation of Chinese people in its long historical development. It is also a crystal of wisdom and industry of the Chinese nation. For thousands of years, it has not only been dazzling in the Chinese history and of benefits to all the Chinese descendants, but also has great impact on the development of neighboring cultures. Especially since the opening of the silk-road in the Han Dynasty and Zheng He's seven voyages to the West in the Ming Dynasty, Chinese culture has had profound and far-reaching effect on the progress of the history and civilization of the west, even on that of the world. But we still can't be highly proficient and get perfect harmony in Chinese-English cultural translation due to our helplessness of not finding exact equivalents due to three reasons, namely, an inadequate amount of reading; a weak cross-cultural awareness; and insufficient attention to and research on the cultural backgrounds, the ways of thinking and expressing, and the linguistic structures. In this respect, we are making great efforts to translate five classic Chinese works concerning Chinese culture into English. They are: *Chinese Mythological Stories*, *Ten Chinese Classic Comedies*, *Ten Chinese Classic Tragedies*, *Selected Readings of Chinese Classics*, and *Stories of Chinese Idioms*.

These translated works will be used in translation training programs designated for seniors of translation majors of XFU in the hope of developing and strengthening both students' and instructors' cross- cultural awareness in the process of translating, enhancing cultural accomplishment of translators and the quality of their translations in order to enable them to better translate the Chinese culture through analysis of and comparison between the cultural phycology, cultural concepts and conventions of the two peoples reflected in the Chinese- English and English-Chinese. Instructors and students alike ought to focus on probing into the relationship between cultures in their translation, especially on the influence of Chinese national culture on Chinese-English translation and seemingly the relevant strategies. We are willing to try our best to make contributions to this noble and honorable cause.

Ding Jing

(President of Xi'an Fanyi University)

前言

成语，一般是指某种通用语言文字中人们长期以来习用的、简洁精辟的定型词组或短句。在欧美、西方称俗语、谚语、格言、警句，而在中国，则多以“成语”二字加以概括，统称中国成语。

中国成语源远流长，可以说从中国古代语言文字诞生之时起就开始形成了，其具有鲜明的中国特色，是中国传统文化中特有的语言文字现象，是华夏语言文字中一颗璀璨的明珠。“成语，众人皆说，成之于语，故成语”，这就是成语一词的由来。极多数中国成语来源于古汉语或曰古华夏语。

中国成语一般由四字构成，多出自经典记载或世传谚语，一般都含有极其丰富的哲理启示，许多成语本身就是一个完整美丽、蕴涵丰富的故事。如“鹬蚌相争”“狐假虎威”“狼狈为奸”“画蛇添足”“刻舟求剑”“自相矛盾”“掩耳盗铃”“郑人买履”“完璧归赵”等。还有许多的成语直接摘自古代典籍、名篇名作，如《尚书》《论语》《左传》《庄子》等，如“水落石出”出自苏轼《后赤壁赋》。人们口头常说的“别开生面”“车水马龙”“同舟共济”“一鸣惊人”之类俗语，因言简意赅、生动形象，以极其凝练的文字表达非常丰富的内容，也被划入成语之列。

前言

中国成语浩如烟海，无从胜计。因篇幅所限，《中国成语故事》一书仅收集翻译了两百则最为流行的四字成语。这些成语，每一个背后都有一个寓意深刻、富含哲理，既幽默风趣又发人深省的美丽故事。我们把它们一道奉献给您，就是希望您能够“尝一脔而知鼎调”，从中领略中国成语的迷人魅力，增进对中国传统文化精髓的认知，也理解中国人民真诚期望与地球村的所有居民友好往来的一片盛情。

译者

2020 年 3 月

Preface

Idioms generally refer to the conventional and brief linguistic units of a fixed format that have been used repeatedly for a long time in a certain language. In western countries, idioms are collectively referred to as slang, proverbs, aphorisms, or mottoes, while in China, they are generally called idioms (*chengyu*).

The origin of Chinese idioms can be dated back to ancient times when ancient Chinese language and writings were first created. As a unique language phenomenon in traditional Chinese culture, they have distinctive Chinese characteristics, and are considered a shining pearl of Chinese culture. "Idioms are sayings widely used by people. Due to their being widely used, these sayings are called 'Chengyu' with its equivalent in English as Chinese idioms and allusions, meaning generally-accepted phrases." This explains how Chinese idioms were created and developed. Most of the Chinese idioms originated from classic Chinese. Classic Chinese is also referred to as ancient Huaxia language.

Chinese idioms, normally phrases of four Chinese characters, mostly originated from classical legends or fable stories. These legends and stories are complete, beautiful and philosophically deep in meaning, making the idioms of aesthetic and philosophic value. Examples can be taken easily such as “A Struggle Between a Snipe and a Clam”, “The Fox Borrowing the Tiger’s Terror”, “A Wolf Working Hand in Glove with a Jackal”, “Drawing a Snake and Adding Feet to It”, “Notching the Boat to Retrieve the Sword”, “Self-contradiction”, “To Plug One’s Ears While Stealing a Bell”, “To Buy Shoes Like the Man from Zheng Did”, “To Return the Jade Intact to the State of Zhao”, and so on. Besides, some idioms are sayings excerpted from ancient books and writings, such as *The Book of History, The Analects of Confucius, The Spring-Autumn Annals* and *Chuang-tsu*. For example, “When the Water Subsides, the Rocks Emerge” is excerpted from *The Second Ode for the Red Cliff*, a famous writing by Su Shi. In addition, some idioms stemmed from people’s daily speaking are also included for their concision and vividness, such as “Opening Up a Fresh Outlook”, “Endless Stream of Horses and Carriages”, “Crossing a River in the Same Boat”, and “Startling the World with a Single Cry” and so on.

There are a tremendous amount of Chinese idioms and allusions. It is, therefore, impossible for us to list all of them and their English versions here. So we chose the most popular 200 idioms to share humorous and meaningful stories with you. We hope to make you have a brief knowledge and great interest in Chinese idioms, so that you may further your study about Chinese idioms and Chinese culture. We also hope to make you feel Chinese people’s sincere expectation to communicate with people all over the world in a friendly way.

March 2020

目录

『中国文化精粹丛书』

A

B

C

D

J

K

L

M

N

P

目录

W

X

Y

Z

Contents

CONTENTS

CONTENTS

成语故事

A

按图索骥

秦国有个人叫孙阳，他一眼就能认出好马和坏马，人们把他叫“伯乐”。伯乐把自己认马的本领都写到叫《相马经》的书里，并画上了各种马的图。伯乐的儿子很笨，却希望自己也能像父亲那么厉害。伯乐的儿子把《相马经》背得很熟，以为自己也有了认马的本领。一天，伯乐的儿子在路边看见了一只癞蛤蟆。他想起书上说额头隆起、眼睛明亮、有四个大蹄子的就是好马。“这家伙的额头隆起来，眼睛又大又亮，不正是一匹千里马吗？”他想。他非常高兴，把癞蛤蟆抓回了家，对伯乐说：“快看，我找到了一匹好马！”伯乐哭笑不得，只好说：“你抓的马太爱跳了，不好骑啊！”

这个故事比喻不灵活变通，缺乏实践经验的做事方式。

Looking for a Fine Horse with the Aid of Its Picture

In the Spring-Autumn Period (770–476 BC), there was a man named Sun Yang in the State of Qin, who was an expert at judging horses, so people called him Bo Le. Based on his experience and knowledge of horses, he wrote a book named *How to Judge Horses* in which he introduced fine horses with description and illustrations. His son, having a simple mind and no factual knowledge about horses, thought that it was easy to judge a fine horse after having learnt the book by heart. One day, he set to look for fine horses and saw a toad by the roadside. According to the instructions in the book, a fine horse has a raised forehead, bright eyes and four big hooves. He was so excited that the toad matched all the criteria. He took it home, saying to Bo Le, "Look, what a good horse!" Amused and sadden, Bo Le said, "Your horse is jumping up and down and will give a bumpy ride".

This idiom is used to indicate lacking practical experience and handling a matter in a mechanical way.

A

安步当车

战国时，齐国有位高士，名叫颜斶。齐宣王知道后，便把他召进宫来，想委以官职。宣王见了颜斶，就呼唤说："颜斶，过来！"不料颜斶一步不动，呼唤宣王说："齐王，你过来！"宣王听了很不高兴，左右的大臣见颜斶目无君主口出狂言，都说："齐王是君主，你是臣民，怎能这样无礼呢？"颜斶说："正是如此，我才叫他过来。否则，别人就说我羡慕权势了；如果大王走过来，才能说明君王礼贤下士。"齐宣王恼怒地说："到底是君王贵，还是士人尊贵？"颜斶不假思索地说："当然是士人尊贵，君王并不尊贵！从前秦国进攻齐国的时候，秦王曾经下过一道命令：有谁敢毁坏高士柳下季坟墓五十步以内一草一木的，格杀勿论！他还下了一道命令：有谁能砍下齐王的脑袋，封他为万户侯，赏金千镒。可见，一个活着的君主的头，竟然不如一个死去的士人之墓尊贵。"

Strolling Around Instead of Riding in a Carriage

In the Warring States Period (457–221 BC), there was a noble man named Yan Chu in the State of Qi. Hearing about him, King Xuan of Qi sent for him and intended to appoint him a post. Meeting with Yan Chu, the King said in contempt, "Chu, come here!" Yan stood still and replied, "Your Majesty, come here!" The King became angry. The surrounding attendants told Yan Chu, "You are nobody and you can by no means be so impolite to the King of Qi." Yan Chu said, "It is because he is the King that I asked him to come over to me. Otherwise, I would be thought to butter up the King for his power. Only if he comes over to me will people know he is courteous to those who are humble." Hearing that, the King argued with rage, "who is more respectable, a scholar or a king?" Without hesitation, Yan Chu answered with a story, "Long ago, the State of Qin attacked the State of Qi. To protect the tomb of Liu Xiaji, a famous scholar, the King of Qin gave an order that whoever destroyed anything within fifty steps near the tomb would be beheaded. After the army of Qin entered the State of Qi, the King issued another order that whoever handed in the head of the King of Qi would be awarded the title of duke and large quantities of gold. So the answer is quite clear."

齐宣王无言以对，心想有才德之人毕竟得罪不得，便改换笑脸说："颜先生果然名不虚传，我要向您请教，请多多帮助我。今后您就住在我这里，我保证您饮食有肉吃，出门必有车乘，您夫人和子女个个会衣着华丽。"颜斶却辞谢说："玉，原来产于山中，如果一经匠人加工，就会被破坏；虽然仍然宝贵，但毕竟失去了本来的面貌。士人生在穷乡僻壤，如果选拔上来，就会享有利禄；不是说他不能高贵显达，但他外来的风貌和内心世界会遭到破坏。所以我情愿大王让我回去，每天晚点吃饭，也像吃肉那样香，安稳而慢慢地走路，足以当作乘车；平安度日，并不比权贵差。清静无为，纯正自守，乐在其中。"颜斶说罢，向宣王拜了两拜，就告辞前去。

The King had nothing to say in reply, thinking that it was no good offending a man of integrity, so he smiled, "Mr. Yan, as we all know, you have a well-deserved reputation. I need your advice and you will serve me at my side from now on. I can guarantee you refined wine and meat and carriages, and your wife and children beautiful clothes. Your family will lead an honorable life." However Yan Chu refused and said, "Jades are from mountains. Though they are precious, jades lose their natural appearance after being refined. A scholar from a remote and poor village will be well-paid and respected after he has been appointed an official position, but his mind will change. So I'd rather go back home to lead a simple life. I can postpone meal time until I am hungry so the dishes will taste as good as meat. I can walk on foot in a leisure way, a state outweighing carriage-riding. Leading a simple and noble life, I feel happier and more satisfied than those officials who are going after fortune and higher position." After saying that, Yan Chu showed deep appreciation and left.

B

拔苗助长

孟子是战国时期著名的教育家、思想家和政治家。公孙丑是他的学生，有一次，他为弟子讲了一个故事：宋国有一个农夫，他担心自己田里的禾苗长不高，就天天到田边去看。可是，一天、两天、三天，禾苗好像一点儿也没有往上长。他在田边焦急地转来转去，自言自语地说：我得想办法帮助它们生长。一天，他终于想出了办法，急忙奔到田里，把禾苗一棵棵地拔，从早上一直忙到太阳落山，弄得筋疲力尽。他回到家里，十分疲劳，气喘吁吁地说："今天可把我累坏了，力气总算没白费，我帮禾苗都长高了一大截。"他的儿子听了，急忙跑到田里一看，禾苗全都枯死了。

这个故事告诉我们要遵循事物发展的自然规律。"拔苗助长"与"欲速则不达"含义相同。

Helping the Crops Grow by Pulling Them Upwards

Mencius was a famous statesman, educator and thinker during the Warring States Period (457–221 BC). Gongsun Chou was one of his disciples. One day, he told his students a story. There was a peasant in the State of Song. When he found that the crops in his field grew too slowly, he said to himself, "I have to do something to help the crops grow faster and stronger." Finally, he came cross an idea and pulled the crops upwards a bit until sunset. Returning home exhausted, he said proudly, "I spent the whole day helping the crops grow taller." His son heard about this and ran out to the field, hoping to find out what magic had been done by his father. To his surprise, all the crop began to wither.

This idiom indicates that we should let things go in its natural course, which coincides with the proverb "Haste makes waste."

B

百步穿杨

春秋时代，楚国有一个名叫养由基的人。擅长射箭的他能在距离柳树一百步的地方放箭射击，每箭都射中柳叶的中心，百发百中，左右看的人都说射得好，可是一个过路的人却说：“我擅长射箭，可以教他该怎样射箭。”

养由基听了这话，心里很不舒服，就说：“大家都说我射得好，你竟说可以教我射箭，你为什么不来替我射那柳叶呢！”

那个人说：“我不能教你伸左臂屈右臂的射箭本领。不过你有没有想过，你射柳叶百发百中，但是却不善于调养气息，等一会疲倦了，弓便拉不开了，箭便歪斜了，一箭射不中，就会前功尽弃。”

后用“百步穿杨”形容箭法或枪法非常高明，并引申为本领非常高强。

A Hundred Shots, a Hundred Bull's Eyes

In the Spring-Autumn Period (770–476 BC), there was an expert archer in the State of Chu named Yang Youji, who could hit the willow tree leaves right in the center standing more than one hundred paces away. All the crowds applauded his performance, while a passer-by said, "I'm an excellent archer, so it's time for me to teach him how to shoot."

Yang Youji was annoyed by the passer-by's comments and said, "Everybody here agrees that I am an expert archer, but you said you could teach me how, so why don't you shoot the leaves in front of us?"

The man said, "In fact, I can't teach you how. Have you considered that even though you can hit the target with every shot, you're not good at conserving strength and storing up energy? When you are exhausted, all that has been achieved is spoiled."

This idiom describes excellent marksmanship. Later it is used to indicate great precision and perfect assurance.

班门弄斧

春秋末期的鲁班是一个善于制作精巧器具的能手，木匠行里把他奉为祖师。传说他曾用木头制作了一只五彩斑斓的凤凰，能够在空中飞翔三天不掉下来。谁敢在鲁班门前卖弄使用斧子的技术，也就是说，想在大行家面前显示自己的本领，这种太不谦虚的可笑行为，就叫作“鲁班门前弄大斧”，简称“班门弄斧”。

明代诗人梅之涣到采石矶凭吊诗仙李白，在李白墓旁观看一番之后心中大为不满，因为他见墓前可以写字的地方，都被人题上了诗句。那些附庸风雅的游人，竟在“诗仙”李白的墓上胡乱题诗，那些拙劣诗句的作者，有什么资格在李白面前舞文弄墨呢？真是可笑至极，荒唐至极！

梅之涣感慨之余，也挥笔题下了一首诗，用来讽刺那些不自量力的诗人：

“采石江边一堆土，李白之名高千古。

来来往往一首诗，鲁班门前弄大斧。”

这句成语有时也用作自谦之词，表示自己不敢在行家面前卖弄自己的小本领。

Showing Off One's Proficiency with an Axe Before Lu Ban

Lu Ban was the master carpenter at the end of the Spring-Autumn Period (770–476 BC). It is said that he once carved a wooden phoenix that was so lifelike that it actually flew in the sky for three days. The idiom "Showing off one's proficiency with an axe before Lu Ban" is used to describe those who display their skill in front of experts.

In the Ming Dynasty, a poet named Mei Zhihuan once travelled to Caishiji to visit the grave of Li Bai, who was one of the famous poet in the Tang Dynasty. Irritated by clumsy poems scribbled on the grave, Mei Zhihuan felt that these so-called poets overrated their attainment. So he inscribed a satirical poem, sneering at those poets who dared to show off on Li Bai's grave, "Under a pile of earth at the river side quarry buried the remains of Li Bai, a great poet with everlasting fame. Visitors have left one poem after another, not knowing they are just like showing off their skills with axe before Lu Ban the master carpenter."

The idiom is sometimes used as a self-modest word to describe those who are afraid of showing off their skills in front of experts.

B

半途而废

东汉时期有个叫乐羊子的人，他的妻子非常贤惠。一次乐羊子在外面捡到一块金子，高兴地拿回家去。谁知妻子见了却说："一个有志气的人是不食嗟来之食的，又怎么会去捡不属于自己的东西！"乐羊子听了非常羞愧，赶紧把金子放回去。

后来，乐羊子告别妻子去远方求学，一年后又回到家中。妻子问他为什么回来，乐羊子说："我一个人在外面，很想念家中的你。"妻子听了，默默地拿起剪刀来到织布机前，说："这些丝织品都是从蚕茧中一根一根抽出来，再一寸一寸慢慢织成的。如果我现在把丝割断，就不可能织出布来。你做学问也是一样，应该每天不间断地学习积累，要是中途跑回来，不是半途而废了吗？那和我现在割断这些丝又有什么不同呢？"

乐羊子听了大受启发，于是出门继续修完自己的学业，七年都没有再回家。

该成语指做事不能坚持到底，中途停顿，有始无终。

Giving Up Halfway

In the Eastern Han Dynasty (AD 25–220), there was a man named Yue Yangzi who married a virtuous wife. One day he saw a piece of gold in the street and took it home. When he gave it to his wife, she said, “A man of virtue and ambition, who never accepts handout offered contemptuously, will never bring home things belonging to other people and accept them.” Feeling ashamed, Yue Yangzi put the gold where it was.

Later, Yue Yangzi left home to study afar. A year later, he returned home to see his wife. “Why do you come back so soon?” asked his wife. Yue Yangzi answered, “It has been a while since I left home and I miss you so much.” With a pair of scissors, his wife took him to the loom and said, “One thread after another, I managed to weave inches and meters long brocades. Now if I cut them in the middle, all my previous work will be in vain. If you give up study halfway, isn’t it just like cutting the thread in the middle?”

Yue Yangzi suddenly realized his wife’s words. The next day he left home to continue his study until he finished seven years later.

The idiom means doing something inconsistently and giving up halfway.

抱薪救火

战国后期，秦国渐渐强大，它取用远交近攻的策略，不断向邻近的国家扩张。从公元前 276 年到公元前 274 年，秦国连续三次进攻魏国，占去魏国许多土地。公元前 274 年，秦国又向魏国出兵。魏国有许多人给打怕了，不敢抵抗。大将段干子建议魏王将南阳的地方割让给秦国，向秦国求和。谋士苏代反对说："割地求和很危险啊！魏国的地不割完，秦国的野心就不会灭。用土地来侍奉秦国，就好比拿着柴草去救火一样，柴草不用尽，火是不会灭的。"魏王不听，将南阳割给了秦国。

秦国得了南阳，并不收手，在以后的三四十年，仍不断夺取魏地，魏国越来越弱小，在公元前 225 年，终于被秦国灭了。

"抱薪救火"是形容用错误的方法去化解矛盾。

Carrying Faggots to Put Out a Fire

During the end of the Warring States Period (457–221 BC), Qin was the most powerful state. In terms of the strategy for dealing with other seven states, Qin made friends with distant states while attacking those nearby. From 276 BC to 274 BC, Qin waged three wars on the State of Wei. As a result, Wei suffered heavy casualties and loss of territories. When Qin attacked Wei in 274 BC, Wei was too terrified to resist the aggression of Qin. In this case, Duan Ganzi, a general of Wei, suggested ceding the area of Nanyang to Qin for peace. Su Dai, the minister of Wei, opposed that Duan's proposal was dangerous. Qin wanted to get the territory of Wei and they would never be satisfied until Wei had nothing to cede. He persuaded the King by saying, "It is just like carrying faggots to put out the fire, only to make the situation even worse. The fire will never extinguish until all the faggots are burnt." Unfortunately, the King ceded Nanyang to Qin.

After occupying Nanyang, Qin never stopped. In the following thirty to forty years, Qin continued attacking Wei to occupy even more territories. In 225 BC, the State of Wei was totally occupied by Qin in the end.

The idiom means adopting a wrong measure to save a desperate situation only to make it even worse.

B

杯弓蛇影

晋朝时候，有一个叫乐广的人，请一位朋友到家里喝酒。那位朋友很高兴，可是当他端起酒杯一饮而尽的时候，突然看见酒杯里有一条游动着的小蛇，他还是勉强把酒喝下去了。喝完酒他很难受，总觉得肚子里有一条小蛇，因此回到家中就病倒了。

乐广知道后，就把朋友再次请来，并让他坐在原来的地方喝酒。那位朋友这才弄明白，原来杯中的蛇影是墙上挂着的一张弓映照出来的。事情弄明白了，他的病也就好了。

该成语比喻疑神疑鬼，自相惊扰。

Mistaking the Reflection of a Bow in the Cup for a Snake

In the Jin Dynasty (AD 265–420), a man called Yue Guang once invited a friend to have a drink at home. When the friend lifted his cup, he saw a small snake in the cup, yet he forced himself to gulp down the wine. The friend felt very queer, thinking that there was a snake in his stomach. Back home, the friend recalled the incident, and felt so disgusted that he fell ill.

Hearing about this, Yue Guang invited his friend again. He asked him to sit in the same place and drink. Then his friend saw that the image of the snake in the cup was actually the reflection of a bow hung on the wall. Realizing this, the friend recovered quickly.

This idiom indicates a condition of being over-suspicious bringing trouble to oneself.

背水一战

楚汉相争时，韩信率军数万攻打赵国。他探得对方在井陉布置了二十万重兵，便连夜精选两千名轻骑，每人持一面小红旗，火速赶到赵军营地。

次日天明，韩信亲率一万人背对大河列阵。赵军见此大笑不止，认为背水列阵是犯了兵家之大忌，不啻是自断退路，一旦败退就无处可走。于是，人人摩拳擦掌，想讨个便宜仗打。谁知韩信用的是诱兵之计，且战且退，一直退到大河边上。先前派去的两千名轻骑，趁赵兵出营追赶之机依计占领了赵营，竖起了汉军小红旗。赵兵继续追击，汉军因退到河边，无路可走，便奋勇反击。赵军抵挡不住，准备掉头逃跑时，才发觉自己的营地早已落入汉军之手。

原来，韩信早想好了背水布阵使士兵置之死地而后生的战略方案，派两千名轻骑偷袭敌军，只是为了使这一方案实施得更完满而已。赵兵不知有时犯兵家之忌反而可以险中求胜的道理，产生轻敌思想，终于一败涂地。

“背水一战”比喻处于绝境之中，为求生路而决一死战。

Fighting with One's Back to the River

During Chu-Han War period (206–202 BC), Han Xin led tens of thousands of troops to attack the State of Zhao. He found out that the enemy had deployed 200,000 troops in Jingxing, so he selected 2,000 light fighters overnight, each holding a small red flag, and rushed to areas adjacent to Zhao's camp.

The next morning, Han Xin had 10,000 soldiers arrayed with their back to the river. Zhao's army laughed at them because arraying with back to the river was a big taboo in fighting, which actually left no way for retreat in case of defeat. As a result, everyone in the Zhao' camp thought that it was an easy fight. However, Han Xin used the tactic of inducing troops and he retreated to the riverside. The pre-arranged 2,000 light fighters took advantage of Zhao's departure to capture Zhao's camp and put a small red flag for the Han army. Zhao' soldiers were still pursuing till the riverside. As the Han army retreated to the river and there was no way out, they fought a life-and-death battle. When Zhao' army was about to lose, they turned around to withdraw, but only found that their camp was under the control of the Han's army.

It turned out that Han Xin had long thought of a strategic plan to lay out the army with their back to the river. The 2,000 light fighters' attack was to make the plan more complete. Zhao's army failed to realize that Han Xin took the risk to seize the chance of winning among dangers appearing one after another, so they underestimated the enemy and suffered a crushing defeat.

The idiom means fighting a life-and-death battle.

别开生面

曹霸是唐代著名的画家，特别擅长画人物和马匹。他的名声很大，就连居住在深宫里的玄宗皇帝也知道他的名字，经常把他召进宫，让他当面挥笔作画。

长安城里的太极宫中，有一座著名的凌烟阁。凌烟阁四壁画着二十四幅唐朝开国功臣的肖像。七十多年过去了，凌烟阁中的功臣像大部分已经剥落，失去了原有的光彩。有一天玄宗想起了曹霸，就派人召他进宫，让他重新画功臣的肖像。几天后，二十四幅功臣肖像就全部画好了，曹霸把他们画得神采飞扬、英姿飒爽。唐玄宗非常满意，给了曹霸很多赏赐，并且封他当左武卫将军。

后来，曹霸因为一件小事没有办好，被削职为民，离开了长安。“安史之乱”爆发后，为了躲避战乱，曹霸流落到成都，靠给过路的行人画像勉强维持生活。这时，著名的大诗人杜甫也避乱来到成都，住在城郊浣花溪畔的草堂里。有一天，杜甫在朋友家中看到曹霸的《九马图》，就进城去四处寻访他，终于在街头见到了曹霸。杜甫十分同情他的不幸遭遇，就写了一首《丹青引》，称颂他：“凌烟功臣少颜色，将军下笔开生面。”

后来，“笔开生面”演化为成语“别开生面”，比喻另外开辟一种新局面或创造出一种新的风格。

Opening Up a Fresh Outlook

Cao Ba was a famous painter in Tang Dynasty (AD 618–907) who specialized in drawing figures and horses. Even the Emperor Xuan Zong knew him and often asked him to the palace to paint in person.

There was a pavilion named Lingyan Pavilion in Tai Chi Palace, where 24 portraits of the dynasty founders were painted on the walls. Over 70 years, the paint had mostly fallen off and lost their original brightness. Emperor Xuan Zong thought of Cao Ba and sent for the famous painter to repaint all the portraits.

A few days later, all 24 portraits of the heroes were finished and became extremely lifelike. Emperor Xuan Zong was very satisfied and granted his the title of general with plenty of rewards.

Later, Cao Ba left Chang'an because he hadn't handled a trifling matter well and was stripped off his title. During the Rebellion of An Lushan and Shi Siming, he drifted about to Chengdu and made a living by painting for passer-by.

At the same time, the famous poet Du Fu also came to Chengdu to avoid chaos and lived in a thatched cottage in the suburb. One day, Du Fu saw Cao Ba's painting named *Nine Horses* in his friend's home and decided to look for him. He finally found Cao Ba in the street. Du Fu was very sympathetic to him and wrote the poem for him: "Portraits of founders in Lingyan Pavilion faded, they took on a new look under the general's brush."

Later, the "brush creates a new look" became the idiom "opening up a fresh outlook" to indicate breaking new ground or creating a new style.

B

闭门造车

在古时候，山里有个老头，以砍柴为生，每天都是日出时去砍柴，太阳快要下山的时候，再背回家，第二天背着柴去镇上卖。

一路上，他走得满头大汗，正在这时，一辆独轮车从他身边经过，他见了心想：这东西好，用上了就省力多了，于是用木条把车辙的宽度量好，带回了家中，开始闭门造车。邻居见他拿着木头又锯又刨，问他干什么，他就说我在闭门造车。很快，老头就把车做好了，推出去一看，车辙竟严丝合缝，小车飞快地跑了起来。

“闭门造车”本来的意思是，只要按照同样的规格，就算是关起门来造的车子，用起来也能合辙，比喻想法和做法一致，并没有贬义。可是到了现代，却被断章取义，理解为完全相反的意思，比喻只凭主观想象办事，不顾客观实际，结果总是碰壁。

该成语现喻义为开展一个项目时将自己与实际情况割离。

Make a Cart Behind Closed Door

In ancient times, there was an old man in the mountain who cut firewood for a living. Every day he went out at sunrise to cut firewood and carried it home when the sun was going down. The next day he sold it in the town.

The other day, he was on his way back home with heavy firewood on his back and saw a cart passing by. The old man said to himself, "This cart will greatly save me efforts." He measured the width of it with branches and began to make it accordingly. His neighbors saw him working on wood, sawing and planning, and asked him why. He said, "I am making a cart", and closed the doors. Soon, the old man got the cart ready and took it out. The cart perfectly matched the ruts and ran smoothly.

The original meaning of "make a cart behind closed doors" is that even a cart built behind closed doors can be used in the same way as long as it conforms to the same specifications. It means the concept and practice can be a perfect match without any derogatory meaning. However, in modern times, it has been taken out of context and interpreted as its opposite meaning: being too subjective and working without any knowledge of the actual process.

The idiom now means divorcing oneself from reality in carrying out a project.

病入膏肓

春秋时期，晋景公得了一个非常严重的疾病。后来他听说秦国有一个医术非常了得的大夫，于是他就专门派人去请那个大夫来为自己看病。

在大夫没有来到之前，他还是心事重重，后来周围的人都劝他先好好休息。病中他梦到自己的疾病变成两个小人，在他的旁边悄悄说着话。其中一个人说："那个医术高明的大夫马上就要来了，看来我们这一次在劫难逃了。"可另一个小人仿佛很有自信地说："不要怕。我躲到肓的上面，你躲到膏的下面，这样大夫就奈何不了我们了。"古人把心尖脂肪叫"膏"，心脏与膈膜之间叫"肓"。

大夫赶过来诊断后，语重心长地说："您的病在肓之上，膏之下，用灸法攻治不行，扎针又达不到，吃汤药，药效力也达不到。这病实在没法子治了。"

这个成语比喻病情或事情已经非常严重，到了不可挽救的地步。

Suffering from Incurable Diseases

In the Spring-Autumn Period (770–476 BC), Duke Jing of the State of Jin suffered from a very serious disease. Later he heard of a miracle-working doctor in the State of Qin, so he sent a servant to invite that doctor.

Before the doctor came, he was still preoccupied. Later, he was advised to have a good rest. One night he dreamed that the disease turned into two figures whispering beside him. One said, "I'm afraid the doctor will hurt us." The other said, "Don't worry. We can hide below *gao* and above *huang*. Then the doctor will be able to do nothing to us." In ancient times, people called the apical fat as *gao* and the part between the heart and diaphragm as *huang*.

After diagnosis, the doctor said earnestly, "Your Majesty, I'm afraid your disease is incurable. It's below *gao* and above *huang,* and neither medical treatment of moxibustion and acupuncture nor herbal medicine can exert effect."

This idiom indicates being at death's door from illness or a hopeless condition.

B

博士买驴

古时候有个博士（古时官名），熟读四书五经，满肚子都是经文。他非常欣赏自己，做什么事都要咬文嚼字一番。

有一天，博士家的一头驴子死了，就到市场上去买一头。双方讲好价后，博士要卖驴的写一份凭据。卖驴的表示自己不识字，请博士代写，博士马上答应。卖驴的当即借来笔墨纸砚，博士马上书写起来。他写得非常认真，过了好长时间，三张纸上都是密密麻麻的字，才算写成。卖驴的请博士念给他听，博士干咳了一声，就摇头晃脑地念了起来，过路人都围上来听。

过了好半天，博士才念完凭据。卖驴的听后，不理解地问他说："先生写了满满三张纸，怎么连个驴字也没有呀？其实，只要写上某月某日我卖给你一头驴子，收了你多少钱，也就完了，为什么唠唠叨叨地写这么多呢？"在旁观看的人听了，都哄笑起来。这件事传开后，有人编了几句讽刺性的谚语："博士买驴，书券三纸，未有驴字。"

该成语形容写文章或讲话不得要领。

An Ancient Academician Buying a Donkey

In ancient times, there was a knowledgeable official holding the title of academician who had read the four books and five classics. He swelled with pride and seized every chance to show off.

One day, the academician's donkey died and he went to the market to buy one. After making a bargain, he proposed to write a receipt. The seller said, "I could not read nor write, so could you please write it for me?" The academician was happy to help the seller. He started immediately after the seller borrowed the brush, ink and paper. The academician was very engaged and didn't stop writing until three sheets of paper were full of words. The donkey seller asked the doctor to read it. The academician cleared his throat and began to read while wagging his head, which attracted widc public attention.

It took a long time for the academician to finish. After hearing this, the seller did not understand and asked, "Sir, you have written three full sheets, but why haven't I heard a word of donkey? In fact, it will be OK to include the date, our deal and the price. But why do you make it so complicated by writing such a wordy piece? The bystanders all laughed. Later, people made up a few lines of sarcastic proverbs about what happened.

The idiom indicates someone who fails to grasp the main point when writing or making a speech.

B

不寒而栗

汉武帝时，有一个人名叫义纵，因为他的姐姐受到太后的恩宠，义纵便做了县令。上任以后，公务办得很出色，案子处理上敢作敢为，不论是有钱有势的豪绅，还是平民，只要犯了法，义纵即秉公审办，皇帝很赞赏他，调他做河内郡都尉。一到任，他立即把祸害一方的豪门大族穰氏满门抄斩，河内郡的治安和社会风气大有好转，有人不慎把东西失落在道路上，也没有人抢走据为己有。

后来，汉武帝又任命义纵做定襄太守。当时定襄的社会治安混乱。义纵到任以后，把押在狱中的二百多名重犯，以及为重犯开脱罪责进行贿赂的二百多名门客亲属，一律严加追究，拘捕治罪，一天之内处死的就有四百多名。从此以后，定襄的人一听到义纵的名字就“不寒而栗”。

“不寒而栗”指即使并不寒冷也让人因恐慌而战栗的情形。

Shivering All Over Though Not Cold

In the reign of Emperor Wu of the Han Dynasty (202 BC–AD 220), there was a man named Yi Zong, who was appointed as a county magistrate just because the Empress was very fond of his elder sister. After he took office, he did a very good job by taking impartial measures handling public affairs, regardless of social status, rich or poor, a despotic gentry or a commoner. The Emperor appreciated his ability and promoted him to the military commander of Henei Commandery. Upon arrival, he wiped out a rich and powerful Rang clan who had oppressed the local people. At that time, the local public security and social atmosphere had greatly improved. The things lost accidentally by people on the road would remain there, and no one would take possession of them.

Latcr, he was appointed Prefecture Chief of Dingxiang. To put out the riot and chaos, he killed 200 criminals indiscriminately right after his arrival. In addition, the criminals' relatives and friends who tried to defend or offer a bribe were arrested for severe punishment. Within one day, 400 people were killed. Shocked at the miserable massacre, the Dingxiang people panicked into shivering though not feeling cold.

The idiom indicates a situation which makes the local people live in extreme horror and shiver all over though not cold.

不合时宜

苏东坡做了官之后，不为名誉所累，一心一意为国家效力。无论是朝廷在治理国家时存在的弊端，还是皇帝本人的错误，苏东坡都直言不讳地指出来，时常惹得皇帝和官员们十分不高兴。

这天早晨，苏东坡吃完饭后，边拍着自己的肚子，边缓步走出了房门。走到门口，他随口问自己的侍童："你们猜猜，我这肚子里边都是什么东西？"侍童蛮有情趣地回答说："大人的文章名扬天下，当然是满肚子文章了。"苏东坡听罢，摇了摇头。另一个侍童接过话头说："既然不是满腹文章，那就一定是满腹见识了。"苏东坡听了，只是苦笑着摇摇头。

这时，恰巧苏东坡的侍女走了过来。她悟性极高，跟随在苏东坡左右，也学到了不少的知识。她非常了解苏东坡这时的心情，于是风趣地回答道："依我看，学士整天上书、进策，一心为朝廷，可人家连理睬也不理睬，四处碰壁，回家就发牢骚……所以我看哪，学士是一肚子不合时宜！"

苏东坡听后，拍着肚皮爽朗地笑了："真让你说中了，我真是不合时宜啊！"

"不合时宜"指不适合社会潮流或时代需要。

Being Incompatible with Present Needs

After Su Shi became an official, he didn't strive to achieve fame but devoted himself to serving the country. He pointed out bluntly both the shortcomings of the government in governing the country and the Emperor's own mistakes, which often made the Emperor and officials annoyed.

One morning after breakfast, he walked slowly out of his room with hands on his belly and asked his servant in a casual way, "Can you guess what is in my belly?" They answered with wit and humor, "Your Excellency, your articles are famous all over the world, so your belly is full of articles for sure." Su Shi shook his head. Another servant said, "Since article is not the right answer, your belly is full of knowledge!" Su Shi shook his head again with a wry smile.

Su Shi's maid happened to come across. With a quick comprehension, she understood Su Shi's mood quite well and replied in a witty way, "Your Excellency, you often submit written statements and advice to the court, but no one takes notice of them. As a result, you grumble about that at home. So I think your belly is full of stuff totally incompatible with present needs."

Su could not help laughing and said, "You got it, and I'm incompatible with the present needs."

The idiom describes the condition of being out of accord with the social trend or present needs.

不拘一格

晚清思想家、文学家龚自珍曾在道光年间中进士，担任礼部主事。当林则徐赴广东查禁鸦片时，龚自珍就预见到英国可能发动侵略战争，建议加强战备。

后来，龚自珍被迫辞官归隐，离京返乡。途经镇江时，恰好赶上庙会，参加这次庙会的有好几万人，十分热闹。有位道士便请求龚自珍代自己写一篇“青词”。青词是人对神的祈求，写在青色的纸上，供奉在神像面前。

忧国忧民的龚自珍很希望有英雄人物降世，打破这万马齐喑的可悲景象。于是，他挥笔在青纸上写道：

九州生气恃风雷，
万马齐喑究可哀，
我劝天公重抖擞，
不拘一格降人才。

该成语告诉我们要有创新的勇气，而非局限于一种规格或方式。

Not Stick to One Pattern

Gong Zizhen, a famous thinker and writer of the late Qing Dynasty (AD 1644–1911), held the post of the Ministry of Rites in the court. When Lin Zexu, a Chinese scholar-official of the Qing Dynasty, went to Guangdong Province to ban opium trade and consumption, Gong Zizhen advised the court to strengthen the national defense for he had foreseen the possibility of British aggression, which was the later Sino-British Opium War.

Later, upon his dismissal from office, he left the capital city Beijing. When he passed Zhenjiang on the way to his hometown, tens of thousands of people were attending a temple fair. A Taoist priest asked Gong to write a "Qing Ci", a poem written on cyan-paper which was presented in front of the statue of the God.

Being a patriot, Gong Zizhen hoped that a national hero would come to reverse the situation. So he wrote the following: Only by wind and thunder can China show its vitality, it is after all mournful that ten thousand horses were all muted. O Heaven! I beseech you to rouse, and not stick to one pattern in selecting elites.

The idiom indicates that we should have the courage to innovate and not stick to one pattern.

C

草木皆兵

公元 383 年，十六国之一的前秦国王苻坚带了 80 万大军攻打东晋。在淝水一带，被晋朝大将谢玄的前锋部队打得大败。苻坚夜登寿阳城楼，看见晋军阵容严整，心里害怕起来。再远望八公山上长着许多草和树木，也以为是东晋的士兵，更加惊恐万分。后来苻坚终于全军覆没，带着少数残余的队伍逃了回去。

该成语形容人在极度紧张、慌张时，神志过敏、极其疑惧、惊恐的心理状态。

Every Bush and Tree Looks like an Enemy

In 383 AD, Fu Jian, the King of the Former Qin, led a huge army consisting of eight hundred thousand soldiers to attack the Eastern Jin. He was defeated at Feishui of Anhui Province by the vanguard led by Xie Xuan, a general of the Eastern Jin. Fu Jian ascended the city wall of Shouyang at night to observe the enemy. He was terrified when he saw the formidable battle army of the Eastern Jin. And then looking at the mountains around, he mistook the grass and trees for enemy soldiers. As a result, when the nervous Fu Jian led his army into battle, he suffered a crushing defeat.

The idiom is used to describe a mental state of extreme nervousness, over-sensitiveness and apprehension.

沉鱼落雁

春秋的时候，有一个叫西施的美女，她每天都会到溪边去浣纱，溪中的鱼看到西施，觉得自己长得比西施丑，都羞愧得不敢浮上水面，全沉到水底去。

汉朝的时候，也有一个美女叫王昭君，她要出塞去嫁给番王的时候，天空飞过的雁，看到王昭君长得那么漂亮，都惊讶得忘记该怎么飞了，全坠落到树林里面。

庄子的本意是雁鱼不辨美色，只知道见人躲避。后来意义转变，人们用“沉鱼落雁”称赞女人的容貌美丽无比。

Breath-Taking Beauty

During the Spring-Autumn Period (770–476 BC), there was a beautiful woman named Xi Shi. When she went to the stream to do the laundry every day, the fish in the stream saw Xi Shi and felt that she was extremely beautiful, so they were too ashamed to stay just above the surface of the water and sank to the bottom.

During the Han Dynasty, there was also a beautiful woman named Wang Zhaojun. On her way to Tubo (minority nationality in ancient China inhabiting the Qinghai-Tibetan plateau) to marry the King, the geese flying in the sky were surprised to see how beautiful she was and they all flew into the woods.

According to Zhuang Zi, the original expression indicated that fish and goose can never appreciate beauty but only to escape. Later, the idiom is used to describe surpassing feminine beauty.

城下之盟

春秋时期，有一次楚武王率军攻打绞国，楚军节节胜利，一直打到绞国都城的南门。绞国军队凭借高大坚固的城墙，顽强抵抗，死守城池。楚将向楚武王献计说："绞国弱小，处理事情缺少计谋，我们可以利用他们的弱点，以诱敌之计取胜。"

第二天，楚国派出几十个化装成樵夫的士兵，分散到绞国都城四周的山上伐木砍柴。绞国将领发现楚人在山上打柴，山下没有楚军保护，就派兵出城围追抓捕，结果抓了 30 个楚人。这个意外的胜利，使绞军官兵非常得意。

隔了一天，又有一批楚兵改扮的樵夫上山砍柴。绞兵发现后，不等将领发令，就乱哄哄地拥出城来，都想捉楚人回去邀功请赏。正在这时，预先埋伏在城北的楚军一齐出击，截住绞军退路。绞军溃不成军，很快就被打垮了。绞军遭到致命打击，眼看都城难以保住，没有办法，只得被迫同意在绞国城下与楚国签订了屈辱的城下之盟。

该成语比喻在武力逼迫下和敌人订立的不平等条约。

Signing a Treaty Under Coercion

During the Spring-Autumn Period (770–476 BC), the King Wu of the State of Chu once led his army to attack the State of Jiao. The Chu army won one victory after another until it reached the south gate of the capital of the State of Jiao. The stranded army, relying on the tall and strong city wall, fought tenaciously to defend the city. A general of Chu offered the King of Chu an advice and said, "The State of Jiao is weak and lacks strategies to deal with the war. We can win by using their weakness to lure the enemy. "

The next day, the state of Chu sent dozens of soldiers disguised as woodcutters to cut wood on the mountains around the capital of Jiao. The generals found that the Chu people were collecting firewood on the mountain, but there was no protection from the Chu army at the foot of the mountain. They sent troops out of the city to chase and captured 30 woodcutters, which made the soldiers very proud.

One day later, another group of woodcutters of the State of Chu went to the mountain to cut wood. Without any orders, the soldiers of the State of Jiao rushed out of the city to capture the woodcutters and would take credit for reward. At that moment, the Chu troops ambushed in the north of the city attacked together in advance to block the retreat route of the enemy troops. The enemy troops were soon defeated. Seeing that the capital city was about to lose and there was no chance to withstand, the State of Jiao had to agree to sign a humiliating treaty of peace with the State of Chu at their city gates.

The idiom indicates a humiliating treaty of peace signed under force threat with the invader.

C

程门立雪

杨时是宋代著名的理学家，被东南学者誉为“程学正宗”。据说他从小就聪明伶俐，四岁入村学，七岁就能写诗，八岁就能作赋。因此，当时许多人都称他为“神童”。

有一年，杨时拜师程颐，以求学问上进一步深造。有一天，杨时与他的学友游酢因对某问题有不同看法，为了求得一个正确答案，就一起去老师家请教。

Standing in the Snow to Wait for Master Cheng Respectfully

Yang Shi, a well-known Neo-Confucianist in the Song Dynasty (AD 960–1279), was recognized by the Southeast Scholars as scholar of "The Authentic Cheng School". He was said to be talented since he was a little child because he went to school at four, wrote poems at seven, and a year later, he could write poetic essay. Therefore, he was called "child prodigy" by many people at that time.

For further study, Yang Shi came under Cheng Yi's tutorship. Once, Yang Shi visited his teacher with his schoolmate You Zuo for consultation on academic dispute. It snowed heavily on that day with dark clouds over the sky. The temperature was extremely low. They held their coats tightly to hurry to their teacher's house no matter how fiercely the rain and snow shaved their faces and how cold the wind ran into their collars. When they reached the gate of the house, their teacher was taking a afternoon nap. In order not to interrupt the teacher, they stood outside of the gate respectfully and piously. They waited for such a long time that Yang Shi's feet were frozen, his body was shaking, but he still stood there respectfully, without any tiredness or impatience. When Cheng Yi woke up, he found Yang Shi standing outside in the heavy snow, covered with snow more than one foot thick. Cheng Yi hurried to welcome them into the house. Moved by them, Cheng Yi answered their questions carefully and meticulously.

时值隆冬，天寒地冻，浓云密布。他们行至半途，朔风凛凛，瑞雪霏霏，冷飕飕的寒风肆无忌惮地灌进他们的领口。他们把衣服裹得紧紧的，匆匆赶路。来到程颐家时，适逢先生坐在炉旁打坐养神。杨时二人不敢惊动打扰老师，就恭恭敬敬侍立在门外，等候先生醒来。这时，远山如玉簇，树林如银妆，房屋也披上了洁白的素装。杨时的一只脚冻僵了，冷得发抖，但依然恭敬侍立。过了良久，程颐一觉醒来，从窗口发现侍立在风雪中的杨时，只见他通身披雪，脚下的积雪已一尺多厚了，赶忙起身迎他俩进屋。程颐被他们感动了，耐心地回答了问题。

从那以后，程颐更加用心地向他们传授知识，并悉心指导。后来，杨时和游酢没有辜负人们的期望，成为著名的理学家。

这个成语告诉我们，求学时不仅要虚心，也要尊师重教。这是中华民族的传统美德。

Since then, Cheng Yi imparted knowledge to them with much more attention and instructed them with the utmost care. Living up to people's expectations, Yang Shi and You Zuo finally gained the true essence of the Cheng School of Neo-Confucianism and became well-known Neo-Confucianists.

The idiom tells us that we should not only seek knowledge modestly, but also respect and honor our teachers, which is a traditional Chinese virtue.

C

唇亡齿寒

春秋时候，晋献公想消灭虢国。可是在晋国和虢国之间隔着一个虞国，讨伐虢国必须经过虞国。大夫荀息建议，把献公的美玉和宝马，送给虞国国君，请求借道。晋献公接受了。

虞君见礼物，很高兴，答应借道。大夫宫之奇阻止说：“不行啊！虞国和虢国就像牙齿和嘴唇的关系，没有了嘴唇，牙齿就会感到寒冷。我们两个小国相互依存，有事可以彼此帮助，万一虢国被消灭了，我们虞国也就难保了。借道给晋国万万使不得。”虞君不听。

果然，晋国军队借道虞国，消灭了虢国。回来时顺便又消灭了虞国。

“唇亡齿寒”比喻双方关系密切，相互依存。

Share a Common Lot

During the Spring-Autumn Period (770–476 BC), Duke Xian of the State of Jin wanted to occupy the State of Guo, but the State of Yu located in the middle, through which the army of Jin had to pass. Xun Xi, a senior official of the State of Jin suggested Xian Gong presenting the King of the State of Yu precious jade and fine horse for passing through, and Xiangong accepted his suggestion.

The King of the State of Yu was very happy to see all the presents and agreed. Gong Zhiqi, a senior official dissuaded and said, "This is not feasible! The relationship between the State of Guo and us is like that between the teeth and lips. If the lips are gone, the teeth will suffer the coldness. Our two small countries depend on each other and can help each other if things go wrong. The occupation of the State of Guo by the State of Jin will endanger us. It is absolutely not feasible to let the army of the State of Jin pass through our territory." The King of the State of Yu ignored his suggestion.

As a result, the army of the State of Jin took the geographical advantage of the State of Yu to occupy the State of Guo. When they returned, the State of Yu was occupied as predicted.

The idiom indicates that if one of the two interdependent things falls, the other is in danger.

车水马龙

东汉明帝的皇后姓马，是伏波将军马援的小女儿，非常有德行。明帝去世后，章帝即位，尊马皇后为皇太后。

章帝即位之初，想封赏自己的几位舅舅，但皇太后不同意。第二年夏天，又有官员建议封赏，于是皇太后下诏说："凡是上奏说封赏外戚的大臣，都不过是想谄媚我以求取福禄罢了。不久前我回家，看见几个舅舅都阔绰得很，拜候请安的人，络绎不绝，车子来往如同流水，马匹走动如同游龙，还看到他们家的佣人们带着绿色的袖套，衣服的领子和袖口干净洁白。回头再看看我的车夫，他的穿戴比那些奴仆们差远了。我之所以对他们没有加以谴责怒斥，仅仅断绝了每年对他们的赏赐，是希望以此暗示他们自己醒悟改过。朝廷如果再给他们封官授爵，那怎么能行呢？"马太后的言行传出后，受到广大官民的好评。

现在，该成语用来形容来往不断的车马，或街上拥堵的交通。

Endless Stream of Horses and Carriages

In the reign of Emperor Ming of the Eastern Han Dynasty (AD 25–220), the daughter of Ma Yuan, a famous general, entered the palace as an imperial concubine and later became the Empress. After Zhang, son of Emperor Ming, succeeded to the throne, she was called Empress Dowager Ma.

Emperor Zhang intended to give his uncles title of nobility, while the Empress Dowager disagreed. The next summer, some officials suggested granting the Emperor's uncles title of nobility. Empress Dowager Ma said, "Those who fawn on me have their own purposes. Last time when I returned home, several uncles became extravagant and visitors come in an endless stream. Carriages and horses line up out of their houses. Their servants are even better dressed than my grooms. But I controlled myself and neither was angry nor blamed them. Since then, I haven't given them subsidies, hoping they would correct their way of life. How can the court give them title of nobility now?" What she said was spread and praised by officials and common people.

Nowadays, the idiom means the endless stream of horses and carriages, or the congested traffic in the street.

尺短寸长

屈原是战国时代楚国的伟大诗人和爱国主义者，曾经多次向楚王提出忠告，但昏庸的楚王不仅不接受，反而听信谗言，把他逐出都城，流放远方。

屈原因无法报答祖国和人民而心烦意乱。在无可奈何的状况下，请人卜卦。他对占卜人说：“对君王应该是真诚直言呢，还是虚假应酬？应为真理正义牺牲一切呢，还是奴颜婢膝、苟且偷生呢？应当与天鹅比翼双飞呢，还是和鸡鸭去争食吃呢？……”他感叹道：“这个世界如此污浊，我该如何是好？谁了解我的廉洁忠贞！”

占卜人很是同情屈原，坦诚地对屈原说道：“对不起，尺有所短，寸有所长，物有所不足，智有所不明，我也无法解释你的疑虑啊！”

该成语比喻人或事物，在不同场合各有短处，也各有长处，不能一概而论。

Sometimes a Foot May Prove Short While an Inch May Prove Long

Qu Yuan was a great poet and patriot of the State of Chu during the Warring States Period (457–221 BC). Being honest and upright, he was driven out of the capital city and sent into exile because the fatuous King of Chu believed crafty, fawning calumny about him.

He was terribly upset because he could not serve the country and people. He went to a fortune-teller and asked, "Should I tell the truth to be punished or pursue honor to seek temporal ease? Should I be indomitable to keep loyalty or be a follower of crafty sycophants due to my fear and dread? Should I fly wing to wing with the swan in the sky or compete for food with hens and ducks on the ground? And then he continued, "Well, what should I do in such a dirty world? Who knows that I'm upright and loyal?"

The fortune-teller felt very sympathetic towards him, so he said honestly to Qu Yuan, "I'm sorry, but I can't help you. Just as a foot may prove short while an inch may prove long, divination sometimes doesn't work like the god. I can't help you and it depends on yourself."

The idiom "sometimes a foot may prove short while an inch may prove long" indicates that different people or things have their own good qualities and shortcomings, so we could not treat them as the same.

出尔反尔

战国时，有一年邹国与鲁国发生了战争。邹国吃败仗，死伤了不少将士。邹穆公很不高兴，问孟子道："在这次战争中，我手下的官吏被杀死了三十三个，可是老百姓却没有一个为他们去拼命，他们眼看长官被杀，而不去营救，可恨得很。要是杀了这些人吧，他们人太多，杀也杀不完；要是不杀吧，却又十分可恨。您说该怎么办才好呢？"

孟子回答说："记得有一年闹灾荒，年老体弱的百姓饿死在山沟荒野之中，壮年人外出逃荒的有千人之多，而大王的粮仓还是满满的，国库也很充足，管钱粮的官员并不把这严重的灾情报告给您。他们高高在上，不关心百姓的疾苦，而且残害百姓。"

孟子在回顾了这辛酸的往事后，接着又说："您记得孔子的弟子曾子说过的话吗？他说，要警惕呀！你怎样对待别人，别人也如何对待你。如今百姓有了一个报复的机会，就要用同样的手段来对待那些长官了。"孟子最后告诉邹穆公说："所以，大王不要去责怪他们、惩罚他们。如果实行仁政，您的百姓就会爱护他们的长官，并且愿意为他们献出生命。"。

出尔反尔这个成语原指你怎样对待别人，别人就会怎样对待你。现多指言行自相矛盾，反复无常，说话不算数。

Promise and Then Renege

In the Warring States Period (457–221 BC), the State of Zou and the State of Lu went to war. The State of Zou was defeated and lost many soldiers. Duke Mu of Zou was angry and asked Mencius, "There were more than thirty officials killed by the people of Lu. There were many Zou people on the spot, but none was brave enough to protect them. So I want to kill all the lookers-on, but I dare not to do it ruthlessly and mercilessly. But if I don't punish them, who else will then protect the officials in the future? Could you tell me what to do?"

After hearing that, Mencius replied, "When the State of Zou was hit by a calamity years ago, the old and weak starved to death on the side of the road. The young and vigorous all fled away. But the state is wealthy and your warehouses were full of grain at that time. This situation was not because you didn't want to take out the grain and cloth to save the people but because local officials didn't report to you. They enjoyed their superiority and deceived higher authorities to harm the common people".

Mencius continued, "Zeng Shen, one disciple of Confucius, once said, 'Be careful! People will treat you as you treat them.' He was reasonable, wasn't he? The common people suffered a lot at peacetime, and they would never save them at risk." At last, Mencius said to Duke Mu, "There is no need to blame or even punish them. If we treat them mercifully, they would sacrifice themselves to show loyalty to their emperor."

The idiom indicates that people will treat you as you treat them. Nowadays, it indicates self-contradiction or people who do not keep their promise.

出其不意

东汉末年，曹操打败了袁绍，平定了北方。不久，原袁绍势力重要人物高干在并州据地反抗曹操。此时河东的卫固、范先也表面上要求任为太守，实际上是与高干暗通。没多久，曹操任杜畿为河东太守，打算把这些地方稳住。

杜畿被曹操任为河东太守后，便带了几千人去赴任。当队伍走到陕津渡口时，队伍被河水阻挡无法过河。曹操见无法过河，就要派大部队去围剿。杜畿说："没有这个必要。卫固这个人虽然多计，却不能决断，而且他表面上还是表示服从的。我看他并不是真的要跟着高干闹事，只不过要讨一个太守当当而已。如果这时我一个人前去，会使卫固感到出乎意料。我去后只要一个月的时间，就能把他手下一些人争取过来，使卫固势单力孤，到那时就容易收拾了。"

后来，杜畿果然孤身一人前往河东赴任。不久，真的如他所料，河东很快就稳定了下来。杜畿在河东当了十六年的太守，由于他体察民情、鼓励农桑，深受当地百姓的爱戴。

"出其不意"指行动出乎对方的意料，使之没有思想准备。

Go Beyond All Expectations

At the end of the Eastern Han Dynasty (AD 25–220), Cao Cao defeated Yuan Shao and unified the north. Soon, Gao Gan, a key subordinate of Yuan Shao, held sway over Bingzhou. At this time, Wei Gu and Fan Xian in Hedong also claimed to be prefecture, but in fact they were in secret communication with Gao Gan. Before long, Cao Cao appointed Du Ji prefecture of Hedong and planned to stabilize these places.

After Du Ji was appointed prefecture of Hedong, he took thousands of people with him to assume the post. When the team reached the Shanjin Ferry, the team was blocked by the river and could not cross the river. Seeing that they could not cross the river, Cao Cao determined to send large troops to encircle and destroy the enemy. Du Ji said, "This is not necessary. Although Wei Gu is very tricky, he makes decisions hesitatingly, and he still shows obedience to you. He just wants to win a post. If I go alone at this moment, Wei Gu will be surprised. Within a month, I can win over some of his men and isolate Wei Gu to bring about a radical change in the situation."

Later, Du Ji went to Hedong to assume his post alone. As he expected, Hedong was under control soon. Du Ji remained prefecture of Hedong for 16 years and was deeply honored by the local people.

The idiom means attacking the enemy where they are unprepared and unexpected.

出人头地

苏轼，宋朝著名文学家。苏轼在二十一岁时参加礼部举办的考试，当时社会上流行奇谈怪论、不合正道的文风，主考官大文学家欧阳修希望通过主持考试选拔人才的方式来挽救这种弊病。苏轼在文章中提出不仅要惩治腐恶，更要奖赏忠厚。欧阳修看过后非常惊喜，把这篇文章评为第一，但又怀疑它可能是自己的学生曾巩所作，为避嫌疑最终将其评为第二名。

后来苏轼给欧阳修写信，感谢他的知遇之恩。欧阳修看完信后对梅圣俞说："我读到苏轼的来信，不觉汗出，非常痛快。我不应该挡着他，应给他让开路，让他比众人高出一头。"当时听到这话的人并不信服，欧阳修仍然坚信自己的看法，认为只要假以时日，苏轼的文章一定会名满天下。果然，随着时间的推移，苏轼的文章渐渐出名，他也成为一代文豪。

"出人头地"喻义高人一等。

Rise Head and Shoulders Above Others

Su Shi was a remarkable prose writer and poet in the Song Dynasty (AD 960–1279). When he attended the examination organized by the Board of Rites at the age of 21, the harmful trends and corrupted practices prevailed in the society. Ouyang Xiu, the examiner and also a man of letters, intended to change the situation through the selection of talents. In Su Shi's article, he proposed that the criminal law shall not only punish the corrupt and the evil but also reward the honest and the upright. Ouyang Xiu was surprised at Su Shi's article and complemented it highly, so he wanted to mark it as the top. But he thought it was written by his student Zeng Gong. To avoid arousing suspicion, he made Su Shi's article number two.

Later, Su Shi wrote a letter of appreciation to Ouyang Xiu to extend his sincere thanks for Ouyang Xiu's recognition. After reading the letter, he said to Mei Shengyu with a knowing smile on his face, "This is a promising young man and he will rise head and shoulders above others in the future." Other people doubted the compliment, but Ouyang Xiu believed without a shadow of doubt. As time went by, Su Shi became a man of letters.

The idiom means going beyond the common people or cutting above other people.

出奇制胜

齐泯王是个骄傲、喜欢享乐的人，因此人民生活得很苦，于是齐国的邻国燕国便派大将联合另外几个国家一同进攻齐国。齐国百姓恨透了齐泯王，因此都无心抗敌，士气也非常低落。后来，他们看到燕兵掳掠百姓，心里非常难过，于是逃往莒城和即墨誓死抵抗。

燕军攻了几年，一直都没有攻下莒城，于是只好转攻即墨城。即墨城中的守军知道大将田单是位足智多谋的勇士，于是就推举他为守城的大将军。聪明的田单想出了一个新的计谋，叫“火牛阵”。他先叫城内的商人，拿着金银珠宝偷偷送到燕军将领手中，并且要他们假装投降，并且说：“即墨城的守军兵力不够快要投降了，这些珠宝献给你们，请求大人您入城之后千万别杀我们！”燕军一听，以为即墨城里已经准备投降，一高兴就放松了警戒。

Defeat the Enemy by a Surprise Move

King Min of the State of Qi was a proud and hedonistic ruler, and the people led a miserable life. The State of Yan, a neighboring state, united other states to go to war against the State of Qi. The people of Qi hated their King so much that they did not intend to resist the enemy. Later, when they saw Yan soldiers plundering the people, they fled to Jucheng City and Jimo City to fight to the death.

After several years, Yan army failed to occupy Jucheng City, so they had to turn to Jimo City. The garrison in Jimo City knew that Tian Dan was a resourceful warrior, so they elected him as the general. The clever Tian Dan came up with a new scheme called "Fire Ox Array". He first asked merchants in the city to smuggle gold, silver and jewelry to the generals of Yan army. They pretended to surrender and said, "The garrison in Jimo City is not strong enough and will soon surrender. These jewelry are for you. Please don't kill us after you enter the city!" Hearing this, the Yan army felt relaxed and thought that Jimo City was within their reach.

没想到田单从城里收集来一千多头牛，并且将这些牛都披上五彩龙纹衣，双角上绑着尖刀，尾巴上绑着草，在一个月黑风高的夜晚，他一声令下，部署们将火把点上牛尾巴上的草，牛被火烫到之后，就拼命往前跑。燕军从睡梦中惊醒，看到这一大群五彩怪兽，吓得惊慌失措，四处乱逃。田单又乘胜追击，最后收复了被燕军占领的七十多个城邑。

“出奇制胜”意为用出人意料的方法取得了胜利。

Unexpectedly, Tian Dan made a special operation. More than 1,000 oxen in colorful dragon stripes were collected from the city with sharp knives tied to their horns and grass tied to their tails. One night, he commanded to light the grass on the oxen's tails. After the oxen were scalded by fire, they ran forward as fast as they could. The Yan army woke up from sleep in affright and was terrified at the sight of a large group of colorful monsters. They were soon defeated and fled away. Tian Dan followed up the victory with hot pursuit and finally recovered more than 70 cities occupied by Yan army.

The idiom means applying unexpected plan for victory.

打草惊蛇

唐朝的时候，有一个名叫王鲁的人，他在衙门做官的时候，常常接受贿赂、不遵守法规。有一天，有人递了一张状纸到衙门，控告王鲁的部下违法、接受贿赂。王鲁一看，状纸上所写的各种罪状，和他自己平日的违法行为一模一样。王鲁一边看着状纸，一边发着抖：这……这不是在说我吗？

王鲁越看越害怕，都忘状纸要怎么批，居然在状纸上写下了八个大字：汝虽打草，吾已蛇惊。意思就是说你这样做，目的是打地上的草，但我就像是躲在草里面的蛇一样，可是被大大地吓了一跳了！

这个成语比喻做机密的事行动不小心，使对方觉察后有所防备。

Beating the Grass and Flushing Out the Snake

In the Tang Dynasty (AD 618–907), a county magistrate named Wang Lu took bribes and accumulated wealth by immoral measures. One day, somebody sent him a written complaint accusing his secretary of practicing graft and taking bribes. The magistrate trembled when he read it, because he found that he was involved in all crimes mentioned. With it in hand, Wang Lu said to himself, "Are you accusing me?"

He failed to properly handle the case and couldn't help writing on it: You have beaten the grass and frightened a snake. It indicated that he was the frightened snake in the grass who committed crimes even more serious than his subordinate.

This idiom refers to an embarrassing situation in which people alert the opponent by being incautious, thus making things become more difficult to handle.

大腹便便

东汉时期，有个读书人名叫边韶，字孝先。他很有些文才，在没有当官的时候，教了几百名学生。

边韶很有口才，说起话、讲起课来头头是道，从没有回答不出问题来的。不过他有个毛病，就是爱打瞌睡。因为他人胖，肚子大，打起瞌睡来，学生看他的模样很好笑。

有一天，他又和衣打瞌睡。他的学生就私下编了句顺口溜嘲笑他："边孝先，腹便便；懒读书，但欲眠。"意思是：边孝先是个大肚皮，懒得读书，只想睡觉。不料边韶醒来后，很快知道了这个顺口溜，于是马上编了几句顺口溜作答："边为姓，孝为字。腹便便，王经笥。便欲眠，思经事。寐与周公通梦，静与孔子同意：师而可嘲，出何典记？"它的意思是：边是我的姓，孝是我的字，大肚皮，是装着五经的竹箱子。只想睡觉，去思考五经的事。老师可以嘲笑，这规矩出自哪家经典？

该成语现用来形容肚子肥大的人。

Potbellied

In the Eastern Han Dynasty (AD 25–220), there was a scholar named Bian Shao (styled Xiaoxian). Before he was appointed as an official, he was a teacher of hundreds of students.

Bian Shao was a knowledgeable and eloquent speaker and seemed to know everything. But he had such a big belly that he had difficulty moving around, so he was accustomed to lie all day long. When he fell asleep, he was funny in his students'view.

One day, he fell asleep again. Several naughty students made doggerel to jeer at him, "Bian Xiaoxian is potbellied; he is so lazy that he doesn't read but sleeps." Unexpectedly, Bian heard about the doggerel and made a new one to response, "Bian is my surname and Xiao the style; the potbelly is loaded with the Five Classics; I was pondering over the Classics and communicating with Zhou Gong and Confucius when sleeping." "How dare you and what etiquette do you follow to laugh at teachers?" he continued.

The idiom means potbellied man at present.

倒屣相迎

东汉献帝时，左中郎将蔡邕是一位博学多闻的文学家、书法家，很受朝廷器重，在当时很有名气，家里经常高朋满座。有一天，蔡邕正在家里陪几位客人习诵诗经。一位仆人通报王粲来访。蔡邕迫不及待地出迎，竟然把鞋子穿倒了。

蔡邕以很高的礼节，非常客气地把王粲迎请进来。当时众宾客皆好奇是什么人物会让蔡邕如此尊敬。原来竟是个年幼瘦弱的孩子，满屋子的人都觉得惊异。蔡邕说："这位是王府公子，天赋异禀，我自叹不如，我家收藏的书籍文章，都应该赠给他。"

王粲的确是智力超群，问无不对。他可以过目成诵，并且倒背如流，可以把搞乱的棋局一点不错地重新摆好，而且他的文章诗赋写得特别好，后成为东汉末著名的文学家。

"倒屣相迎"指倒穿着鞋迎接客人，形容迎客的急迫，或形容对来客的热情欢迎。有时也用来比喻客人的尊贵。

Greeting a Guest with Shoes Reversed

During Emperor Xian's reign in the Eastern Han Dynasty (AD 25–220), general Cai Yong was an erudite writer and calligrapher. He was highly valued by the court and was very famous at that time, so he usually welcomed friends and guests at home. One day, when Cai Yong was studying *the Book of Songs* with several guests at home,a servant reported Wang Can's visit. Cai Yong couldn't wait to rush out and put on his shoes reversed.

Cai Yong welcomed Wang Can in with great courtesy. At that time, all the guests were surprised and curious about what made Cai Yong so enthusiastic. It turned out to be a small and thin child, and the whole house was amazed. Cai Yong said, "He is a gifted and talented child from palace. I feel inferior to him. He deserves all books and articles I collected."

Wang Can was indeed a man of extraordinary intelligence and knew everything. He could read and recite articles after a glance. He could restore the messed-up checkerboard as its former arrangement. Moreover, his articles and poems were among the top, which made him a man of letters at the end of the Eastern Han Dynasty.

"Greeting a guest with shoes reversed" refers to an enthusiastic welcome. It is also used to indicate the honor of the guest.

道听途说

艾子，是春秋战国时的人。有一次他刚从楚国回到齐国，一个叫毛空的人告诉他说："有个人家的 1 只鸭子生了 100 个蛋。"

艾子不相信，问道："哪有这样的事呢？"

毛空自己想想不对，改口说道："那么是 2 只鸭生的蛋。"

艾子还是不相信。

毛空又改口说："那么是 3 只鸭生的蛋。"

后来毛空见艾子总是不相信，就一次又一次地把鸭子的数目增加到 10 只。

艾子问他道："你为什么总是增加鸭子的数目，不减少蛋的数目呢？"

毛空说："我宁愿增加鸭子的只数，也不减少蛋的数目。"

Spread Hearsay Overheard

In the Spring-Autumn Period (770–221 BC), Ai Zi returned to the State of Qi from the State of Chu, and a man named Mao Kong told him, “A duck laid 100 eggs at a time.”

Ai Zi did not believe it and asked, “How could that be?”

Mao Kong thought it was impossible and changed his mind and said, “Then two ducks laid the 100 eggs.”

Ai Zi still didn’t believe it.

Mao Kong changed again and said, “Then three ducks laid the eggs.”

Later, Mao Kong increased the number of ducks again and again to 10.

Ai Zi asked him, “Why do you always increase the number of ducks instead of decreasing the number of eggs?”

Mao Kong said, “I would rather increase the number of ducks than decrease the number of eggs.”

艾子见他如此固执己见，自己便无话可说。

毛空却接着说："上个月天上掉下 1 块肉来，有 30 丈长，10 丈宽。"

艾子说："没有这个道理。"

毛空改口说：那么就是 20 丈长。"

艾子还是不相信，毛空又说是 10 丈长。

艾子忍不住了，问他："你看见这个世界上有 10 丈长、10 丈宽的大块肉吗？"毛空也觉得这事似乎荒唐，艾子接着又问，"你刚才说的鸭子是哪一家的？ 那块肉又掉在什么地方？"

毛空老老实实地回答道："我是听别人说的。"

艾子马上转过脸对他的学生们说："你们可不要像他这样'道听途说'啊！"

该成语喻指没有根据的传闻。

Ai Zi had nothing to say because he was so stubborn.

Mao Kong went on to say, "Last month, a piece of meat, 90 meters long and 30 meters wide, dropped from the sky."

Ai Zi said, "It's ridiculous."

Mao Kong corrected and said, "Then it was 60 meters long."

Ai Zi still didn't believe it. Mao Kong said it was 30 meters long.

Ai Zi could not help but asked him, "Have you ever seen a large piece of meat that is 90 meters long and 30 meters wide in this world?" Mao Kong felt that it seemed absurd. Ai Zi then asked, "Whose duck has laid 100 eggs at one time? Where did the meat fall on the ground?"

Mao Kong replied honestly, "I overheard them from others."

Ai Zi turned to his students immediately and said, "You should never spread what is heard on the road like Mao Kong!"

The idiom indicates hearsay that is overheard on the road.

得过且过

五台山有一种鸟，名叫寒号鸟。它长着四条腿，两只肉翅，但不能飞翔。

每年到了炎热的夏天，它的身上便长满了色彩鲜艳、花纹美丽的羽毛。每当这个季节，它便四处走动，不管碰到飞禽还是走兽，它都得意地对它们说："看到了吗，我比凤凰漂亮多了！"

可是，到了深冬严寒之际，它身上华丽的羽毛逐渐褪完，光秃秃的身子像初生的小鸟，那样子十分难看。它怕别的动物发现自己丑陋的模样，便躲在石缝中不敢外出一步。它可怜地安慰自己说："得过且过。"太阳出来时，得到片刻温暖的寒号鸟便忘记了寒冷，叫道，"得过且过，太阳旮旯里真暖和！"

"得过且过"用以形容做事没有进取心、马马虎虎混日子的人。

Get by However One Can

There was a bird named Hanhao in Wutai Mountain. It had four legs and two meaty wings, but it could not fly.

Every hot summer, it grew colorful feathers with beautiful patterns. So the bird walked around with wide open wings and said to other birds and animals in a proud way, "How beautiful I am! I am much more beautiful than the phoenix! "

However, when winter came, its luxuriant feathers faded and lost gradually, and its ugly bare body looked like a newborn bird. So it hid in the gaps between the rocks and did not dare to go out. It comforted itself piteously and said, "Get by however I can." When the sun came out, the Hanhao Bird got warmth for a while. It forgot the cold and sang, "Muddle along, it's still warm in the sun!"

The idiom is used to satirize those who perform their duty in a perfunctory manner without aggressive spirit.

得陇望蜀

东汉时期，有一位大将名叫岑彭。岑彭不仅作战勇敢，而且会用计谋，收罗了不少人才。

光武皇帝建武八年（公元 32 年），岑彭领兵去攻打天水，当时隗嚣占据着西城，公孙述占据着四川。岑彭军队将隗嚣包围了，公孙述派兵帮助隗嚣把守上邽。这时，皇帝给岑彭下了一道诏书说："这两处攻下来以后，你可派兵去攻打四川。"皇帝是不知足的，既然平定了陇地，还想得到蜀地（得陇望蜀）。

岑彭得到皇帝的诏书，就用灌水的办法攻打西城，可是，水深还没有达到一丈，救兵就来了，把隗嚣救走了。岑彭看看自己的粮草已经不足，也就只好领兵回去。

该成语比喻人心不足，贪得无厌。

To Have Insatiable Desires

During the Eastern Han Dynasty (AD 25–220), there was a general named Cen Peng. As he was both resourceful and brave, he recruited many talents.

In the eighth year of Emperor Guangwu's reign, Cen Peng led an army to attack Tianshui. At that time, Wei Ao occupied Xicheng and Gongsun Shu occupied Sichuan. When Cen Peng's army surrounded Wei Ao, Gongsun Shu sent troops to help Wei Ao to guard Shanggui. At that time, the Emperor issued a letter to Cen Peng, "After you occupied the two cities, go to attack Sichuan." The Emperor was greedy because he wanted not only Long but also Shu.

Upon the order from the Emperor, Cen Peng used watering to attack Xicheng. However, before the water depth reached 3 meters, reinforcements arrived and rescued Wei Ao. As a result, Cen Peng had to withdraw for the lack of sufficient supply.

This idiom refers to being greedy for gain.

得心应手

春秋时期，齐桓公有一天坐在宫殿上读书，正在宫殿下制作车轮的木匠轮扁突然放下手中的工具，来到齐桓公面前问道："请问您读的书里面都讲些什么啊！"

桓公说："都是圣人说的话。"

轮扁说道："圣人已经死了，您所读的，有可能不过是古人的糟粕而已。"

齐桓公厉声喝道："你如果能把刚才说过的话讲出道理，我就饶了你，如果讲不出道理，我就把你处死！"

轮扁说："我就以我做车轮这件事做例子来说一说吧。用斧头、刨子、锯将木头做成车轮，只有不慢不快，得之于手而应于心，才能做出不宽不紧、不大不小、正合适的车轮。我虽然说不出其中的道理，但是这里却有一定的技术和经验。我无法把这技术单靠嘴说教给我的儿子，我的儿子也无法仅仅听我讲，就能把技术学到手。所以，我虽然已近 70 岁了，还是一个人在这里制作车轮。古人的技术不可言传，因为人死了无法亲授。因此，只读古人的书本是不够的，何况现在情况不一样，古人的东西现在不一定适用了。"

"得心应手"指心里怎么想，手就能怎么做，比喻技艺纯熟。

Suite One's Mind and Hand

In the Spring-Autumn Period (770–476 BC) there was a carpenter named Bian. He was called Wheel Bian because of his skilled workmanship in making wheels. When King Huan of Qi was sitting in the palace reading a book one day, Wheel Bian, who was making wheels outside the palace, put down his tools and came to the King and asked, "Your Majesty, what are you reading? "

The King said, "It's all the words of sages."

Wheel Bian said, "The sages died long ago. What you are reading may be the least valuable idle words left by them. "

The King raged against him and shouted, "How dare you say that? If you can make sense of what you've just said, I will spare you. If not, you will be executed! "

Wheel Bian said, "Let me take the wheel-making as an example. I make wheels out of wood with my ax, plane and saw. With a well-balanced pace, I feel the whole in my heart and my hands respond to it. Only through this way, I can guarantee a perfect match among all the parts to make a wheel perfect. Although I can't explain in detail, my skill comes from practice but not books by the past sages. I can't teach my son how to make it by merely explaining to him, and my son can't learn it only by listening to me. Therefore, although I am nearly 70 years old, I still make wheels here alone. The ancient skill and truth cannot be taught in person because people passed away. Therefore, it is not enough to read ancient books, and the situation is different now. The ancient things may not be applicable now. "

The idiom, which means skilled workmanship, describes someone whose hands accomplish what his heart wishes.

地利人和

有一回有人问孟子："先生以为怎样做才算是圣主明君呢？"

孟子说："我认为圣主明君是用仁政来治理天下的，这样顺从、支持他的人就多，反对他的人就少。我的意思是说天时不如地利，地利不如人和。举个例子说吧，比如有座小城，敌人多次进攻失败后是一定会利用适合作战的阴晴、寒暑、风雨等有利天时的，但它不能获胜。因为这座小城占有地形上的优势，城高池深，这种地利超过了敌方的天时。

同样的一座山城，城墙很牢固，兵力也强，兵器也锐利，粮食充足，可是敌人来了，城内守兵弃城逃跑，这又是什么原因呢？这说明地利不如人和呀！这就证明了我的主张：靠疆界是无法限制百姓的；守卫家园依靠山川险阻也是靠不住的；同样，仰仗武力也是不能长久地威行天下的。如果你不施行仁政，人们就离你远远的，会搞得众叛亲离，那么你不是注定要垮台吗？"

"地利人和"意为有良好的地理条件和广泛的群众支持。

Geographical Advantages Plus the Support of the People

Once Mencius was asked, "How can one be a wise king in your opinion?" He answered, "In my opinion, a wise king should administer the country benevolently. As a result, more people support him while few oppose. I mean that the favorable climate isn't as important as the geographical condition, but the geographical condition isn't as important as the unity and support of the people. Taking a small city for example, after several failures in capturing the city, the enemy will surely take advantage of climatic conditions as cold and hot, and wind and rain. The effort still end in vain because the high walls and deep moat of the small city outweigh the advantage of favorable climate conditions used by the enemy.

For the same city with high and firm walls, sharp weapons and sufficient supply, the soldiers on guard fled without resistance when the enemy came. Why is it so? This is definitely because the geographical condition isn't as important as unity of the people. The two examples fully support my viewpoint that the people cannot be confined by the boundaries and the country cannot be safeguarded relying on geographical condition. Resorting to force is not a long term policy to manage a country. Without the adoption of the benevolent policy, the ruler is doomed to lose power because people will no longer offer their support. "

The idiom means advantageous geographical conditions plus the support of the masses.

点石成金

传说晋朝初年，许逊被朝廷任命为旌阳县县令。此人道术高深，能施符作法，替人驱鬼治病，百姓们见他像见仙人一样。

当时年成不好，农民缴不起赋税，一年一年越欠越多，许逊非常同情。他叫大家把石头挑来，然后他施展法术，用手指一点，使石头都变成了金子。这些金子补足了百姓们拖欠的赋税。

“点石成金”现在比喻将文字稍加改动，使其成为上乘之作。

Turn a Stone into Gold by Touching It

Legend has it that in the early years of the Jin Dynasty (AD 265–420), Xu Xun was appointed by the court as the magistrate of Jingyang County. He had profound Taoist skills and could perform magic tricks to drive away ghosts and cure diseases. People regarded him as a celestial being.

At that time, the year's harvest was not good and the peasants could not afford to pay taxes. Their debt accumulated year by year, so Xu Xun became even more sympathized with them. Xu Xun asked everyone to pick up and collect the stones. Then he cast spells and turned the stones into gold, which made up for the taxes owed by hundreds of people.

The idiom now means turning a crude essay into a literary gem.

调虎离山

东汉末年，孙坚之子孙策，继承其父之基业时年仅十七岁，年少有为，势力逐渐强大。公元 199 年，孙策欲向北推进，准备夺取江北卢江郡。卢江郡南有长江之险，北有淮水阻隔，易守难攻。

占据卢江的军阀刘勋势力强大。孙策知道，如果硬攻，取胜的机会很小。他和众将商议，定出了一条调虎离山的妙计。针对刘勋极其贪财的弱点，孙策派人给刘勋送去一份厚礼，并在信中把刘勋大肆吹捧一番。

Luring the Tiger Out of the Mountains

At the end of the Eastern Han Dynasty (AD 25–220), Sun Ce, the son of Sun Jian, was only 17 years old when he inherited the peerage and army of his father. He was young and promising, and his power grew enormous. In 199 AD, Sun Ce wanted to push northward and was ready to capture Lujiang County north of the Changjiang River. With the dangerous Changjiang River in the south and Huaishui River in the north, Lujiang was easy to defend and hard to attack.

Liu Xun, the warlord occupying Lujiang, was powerful. Sun Ce knew that the chance of winning by storm was very slim. He consulted with the generals and worked out a plan to lure the tiger out of the mountains. In response to Liu Xun's weakness of being extremely greedy for money, Sun Ce gave him a generous gift and flattered him in the letter.

孙策信中表示要与刘勋交好，还以弱者的身份向刘勋求救。他说，上缭经常派兵侵扰我们，请求将军发兵降服，我们感激不尽。刘勋见孙策极力讨好他，万分得意。上缭一带，十分富庶，刘勋早想夺取，今见孙策软弱无能，免去了后顾之忧，决定发兵。

孙策见刘勋亲自率领几万兵马去攻上缭，城内空虚，心中大喜，说："老虎已被我调出山了，我们赶快去占据它的老窝吧！"于是立即率领人马，水陆并进，袭击卢江，几乎没遇到顽强的抵抗，就顺利地控制了卢江。

这个成语常常用来比喻使用计策，引诱人离开有利的环境，以便于控制或消灭他们。

Sun Ce said in his letter that he was among the weak and would form union with Liu Xun for help. He said that Shangliao often sent troops to stir up trouble and asked the general to send troops to capture Shangliao. Liu Xun was extremely proud to receive Sun Ce's appreciation. Shangliao area was very rich and Liu Xun wanted to capture it. Seeing that Sun Ce was weak and incompetent, he relieved himself of worries and decided to send his troops.

Liu Xun led tens of thousands of military forces personally to attack Shangliao, leaving Lujiang empty. Sun Ce was overjoyed and said, "The tiger has been lured out of the mountains. Let's seize the chance to occupy its habitat!" Deploying forces immediately via land and water, Sun Ce captured Lujiang without any stubborn resistance.

The idiom is used metaphorically to mean luring an enemy away from his safe place in order to put him at a disadvantage by schemes.

东施效颦

西施是春秋时期越国的一个美女，她的一举一动都十分吸引人。只可惜她的身体不好，有心痛的毛病。

有一次，她在河边洗完衣服准备回家。就在回家的路上，突然胸口疼痛，所以她就用手扶住胸口，皱着眉头，但是见到她的村民们却都称赞说她这样比平时更美丽。

同村有位名叫东施的女孩，长相并不好看。她看到村里的人都夸赞西施用手扶心口的样子很美丽，于是也学着西施的样子扶住胸口，皱着眉头，在人们面前慢慢地走动，认为这样就有人称赞她。可是有人看到之后，赶紧关上大门；有些人则是急忙拉妻子和孩子躲得远远的。

该成语比喻盲目地去模仿别人，效果适得其反。

An Ugly Woman Aping the Beauty's Frown

In the Spring-Autumn Period (770–476 BC), there was a beauty in the State of Yue called Xi Shi, but she often suffered from pains in her chest.

One day, after doing her laundry by the riverside, Xi Shi had a sudden pain in her chest and knitted her brows. Even though, people said that her posture of knitting brows was feminine and beautiful.

There was an ugly girl in the village called Dong Shi who admired Xi Shi's appearance. Striving to copy Xishi, she walked in front of people with hands pressing her chest and brows knitted. She thought that this made her elegant, but in fact, her strange appearance only made her uglier. So some shut doors and some ran away at the sight of her.

The idiom is used to indicate improper imitation that produces the reverse effect.

东食西宿

齐国有个姑娘，有两家人来求婚。东家的男子长得丑但是很有钱，西家的男子长得俊美但是很穷。

父母犹豫不决，便征询女儿意见，要她自己决定愿意嫁给谁："你要是难于启齿，不便明说，就袒露你的胳膊，愿意嫁哪一家就袒露哪只胳膊，让我们知道你的意思。"

没想到女儿袒露出两只胳膊。父母亲感到奇怪就问其原因。女儿说："想在东家吃饭，在西家住宿。"

"东食西宿"比喻贪婪的人各方面的好处都想要。

Dine in One Family and Sleep in Another

There was a beautiful girl in the State of Qi and two young men went to propose to her. The ugly young man from a rich family lived in the eastern village and the other handsome young man from a poor village lived in the western village.

The parents didn't know how to choose, so they asked their daughter to make a decision, but they were afraid that she was too shy to tell her real thoughts. So they asked the girl to bare one arm to indicate her idea.

To their surprise, she bared both of her arms. The parents asked, "What do you mean?" The girl said, "I want to dine in the eastern village and sleep in the western village."

The idiom indicates that greedy people want to get both the fish and the bear's paws.

D

对牛弹琴

战国时期，有一个叫公明仪的音乐家，擅长演奏。一次，他对着牛弹了一段曲子，希望牛也来欣赏他的技巧。曲子虽然很好听，但是牛却丝毫不理会，只顾埋头吃草。公明仪没办法，只好摇摇头叹了口气。人们对他说:”你不要生气了！不是你弹的曲子不好听，是你弹的曲子不对牛的耳朵啊！”

“对牛弹琴”这个成语，比喻对不懂道理的人讲道理，也用来讥笑说话的人不看对象。

Play a Tune to a Cow

In the Warring States Period (457–221 BC), there was a musician named Gongming Yi who played the zither very well. Once, he played a tune in front of a cow, hoping that the cow would appreciate it. The tune was melodious, but to his disappointment, the cow showed no reaction, and just kept on eating grass. Gongming Yi sighed with anger. The people there told him, "Your performance is excellent, but you've chosen a wrong audience."

This idiom, which shares the same meaning with "casting pearls before swine", is used to indicate reasoning with stubborn people or talking to the wrong audience.

对症下药

华佗是东汉时期著名的医学家。一天傍晚，他正忙着为病人诊症开方，这时，大门外进来两个人：一个是府吏倪寻，一个是商人李延共。

华佗热情地走过去，问有什么病情。两人指着对方，异口同声说："我俩都感到头痛身热。"华佗一言不发，分别给他们切脉后，说："倪寻先生应当服药通畅肠胃，李延共先生应当服药使身体发汗。"

两人感到奇怪，提醒说："医生，我们两人病情相同，服用的药怎么能不一样？"华佗笑道："倪寻身体外部无病，病因是内部伤食；李延共内部无病，病因是外部受了寒。你们两个虽然病情相同，但病因不同，因此药方也应该不同，这叫对症下药。"

两人按照药方取了药，回家后服下，病就都痊愈了。

"对症下药"比喻针对事物的问题所在，采取有效的措施。

Suite the Medicine to the Illness

Hua Tuo was a splendid doctor and medical scientist in the Eastern Han Dynasty (AD 25–220). One day at dusk, he was busy prescribing when two men came to see him. Ni Xun was the state official and Li Yangong was a businessman.

Hua Tuo came to them and asked about their illness. The two men said, "We both suffer from headache and fever." After pulse feeling, Hua Tuo said, "Ni Xun should take the purgative while Li Yangong should take medicine to sweat out the cold."

The two men were surprised and asked why they had to take different medicine while they suffered the same illness. Hua Tuo smiled and explained, "Ni Xun is well externally, and his illness resulted from excessive dining; Li Yangong is well internally, but he caught a cold. Although you share the same state of illness, the causes are different. So the prescription and treatment are different."

After taking the prescribed medicine, both of them recovered from illness.

The idiom means taking the correct actions to solve a problem.

E

尔虞我诈

春秋时期，楚王派遣大臣申舟出使齐国。从楚国到齐国，要途经宋国，申舟出使时，楚王跟他说不用向宋国借道。申舟说："如果不借道，我就一定会被杀掉。"楚王说："如果你被杀，我就出兵灭了宋国。"于是申舟不借道而行，后来果然被宋国杀掉。

楚王于是发兵进攻宋国，围困宋国九个多月还没有攻下，楚王就想退兵。申舟的儿子说："先父甘冒杀身之祸而不敢放弃您不借道的命令，现在君王您却放弃了自己以前的诺言。"楚王哑口无言。这时楚王的车夫申叔出主意说："在阵地上修建房屋，并让逃亡的人来这里种田，宋国就会认为我们要打持久战，就一定会屈服。"楚王听从了这一建议，宋国果然非常害怕。

Trying to Cheat Each Other

In the Spring-Autumn Period (770–476 BC), the King of the State of Chu sent his minister Shen Zhou to the State of Qi. But the State of Song was in the middle. When Shen Zhou was about to leave, the King of Chu told him there was no need to inform the State of Song when passing through. "If I don't inform them in advance, I will definitely be killed," said Shen Zhou. The King of Chu said: "If you were killed, I will send troops to destroy the State of Song." As a result, Shen Zhou was killed.

The King of Chu then sent troops to attack the State of Song and besieged it for more than nine months. The King of Chu wanted to withdraw his troops. Shen Zhou's son said, "My father risked his life and did not dare to give up your order. Now, Your Majesty, you are going to break your previous promise." The King had nothing to reply. At this moment, Shen Shu, the King's coachman, came up with an idea and said, "Why not build houses in the battle field and let the fugitives come here to farm? Then the State of Song will give in for being afraid of a protracted war." The King of Chu accepted this suggestion.

于是宋国派遣勇士华元趁夜潜入楚军，直接跑到宰相子反的床边，对他说："实话告诉你，我们城里已经断粮，大家交换儿子当粮吃，拿死人骨头当柴烧。尽管这样，我们也宁愿与国同亡，而不会接受屈辱的条约。假如你们现在退军三十里，双方便可签订和约。"子反害怕了，便同意撤退三十里然后结盟。宋楚结盟时在盟约中写道："我无尔诈，尔无我虞"，意思是我不欺骗你，你也不要欺骗我。

该成语形容互相欺诈。

So the State of Song sent the general Hua Yuan to sneak into the camp of Chu army at night and ran directly to the tent of Zi Fan, the prime minister of Chu. Hua Yuan said to him, "To tell you the truth, our city has run out of food. People in the city exchanged children for food and burnt the bones of the dead for firewood." Even though, we would rather die with our country than accept a humiliating treaty. If you withdraw 30 li (15 kilometres) now, and we can sign a peace treaty." Zi Fan was afraid and then agreed to retreat for 30 li. When Chu made peace with Song, they wrote, "We are not cheating you just as you are not cheating us."

The idiom means each trying to cheat or outwit the other.

返老还童

相传汉朝时候的淮南王刘安专好求仙学道。他昼思夜想，到处寻问，想知道哪里有长生不老之术。由于他求仙心诚，一天，果然来了八个老翁请求拜见他。来者声称有使人延缓衰老、防止早衰或能促使生命逆转、使人返老还童的长生不老之术，愿当面奉献给他。可刘安见他们均已老态龙钟，心想哪里还会有什么长生不老之术啊！觉得分明是骗局，一气之下就叫人把他们赶走了。

八个老翁听说淮南王嫌他们太老而不相信长生不老术是真的，就说："好吧，等着瞧吧，看看我变！变！变！"说着说着就真的"返老而为少"，变成儿童了。

该成语形容上了年纪却像年轻人一样充满活力的人。

Recover Youthful Vigor

During the Han Dynasty (BC 202–AD 220), Liu An, the King Huainan, wanted to live forever. So he tried hard to find ways to be an immortal. One day, eight old men came to visit him. They said that they were immortals and they could teach Liu An how to keep from aging. Liu An said, "Why are they all old if they know how to keep from aging? They must be telling lies." He ordered his servants to send them away.

The old men smiled and said, "It is very easy to regain youthful appearance from old age. Just wait and see!" Several minutes later, they all became children.

The idiom is used to describe the old who are very energetic.

F

负荆请罪

战国时，廉颇和蔺相如同在赵国做官。蔺相如因为“完璧归赵”有功而被封为上卿，位在廉颇之上。廉颇很不服气，扬言要当面羞辱蔺相如。蔺相如则处处避让，不与他相斗。

蔺相如的门客以为他畏惧廉颇，然而蔺相如说：“秦国不敢侵略我们赵国，是因为有我和廉将军。我对廉将军容忍、退让，是把国家的危难放在前面，把个人的私仇放在后面啊！”

这话传到了廉颇耳朵里，廉颇十分感动，便光着上身，背负荆杖，来到蔺相如家请罪。两个人终于结成誓同生死的朋友。

“负荆请罪”这个成语用来表示向别人赔礼、认错。

Bring the Birch and Asking for Punishment

In the Warring States Period (457–221 BC), Lian Po and Lin Xiangru were both officials of the State of Zhao. Lin Xiangru accompanied the King of Zhao to the State of Qin and successfully got the jade intact to the State of Zhao. Lin Xiangru was promoted one of the highest-ranking officials, which was above Lian Po. Disgruntled, Lian Po announced that he intended to humiliate Lin when he met him. Hearing about that, Lin Xiangru maintained a low-key attitude to avoid any conflict with Lian Po.

Lin Xiangru brought opprobrium on himself and his servants felt ashamed. Lin Xiangru said, "The reason why the powerful State of Qin dare not invade us lies in both me and general Lian. I put the benefit of our country first and personal feelings behind."

Hearing about these words, Lian Po realized his mistake. He was so ashamed that he went to Lin's residence with birch on his naked back for punishment. From then on, they became close friends and united to guard their country.

This idiom indicates acknowledging one's mistake and offering a sincere apology.

负隅顽抗

战国时，有一年齐国发生饥荒，许多人饿死。孟子的弟子陈臻听到这个消息，急忙来找老师，心情沉重地说：“老师，您听说了吗？齐国闹饥荒，人都快饿死了。人都以为老师您会再次劝说齐王，请他打开谷仓救济百姓。”

孟子回答说：“我不能再这样做了，你听说过冯妇的故事吗？”

冯妇是晋国的猎手，善于和老虎搏斗。后来他成为品行端正的士人，不再做打虎之类不符合身份的行为了。有一年，某座山里出现了一只猛虎，常常伤害行人。几个年轻猎人联合起来去打虎，他们把老虎追至山的深处，老虎背靠着一个山势弯曲险要的地方，面向众人。它瞪圆了眼睛吼叫，没有人敢上前去捕捉。

就在这时，冯妇坐车路过这儿。猎手们见了他，都快步上前迎接，请他帮助打虎。冯妇下了车，挽起袖子与老虎搏斗起来，经过一场拼搏，终于打死了猛虎，为民除了害。年轻的猎手们高兴地谢他，可是一些读书人却讥笑他，认为他又从善士做回了猎人。

该成语指残敌守住一角或险要之地顽固抵抗，拒不投降。

Put Up a Desperate Resistance

During the Warring States Period (457–221 BC), a famine occurred in the State of Qi and many people starved to death. Hearing the news, Chen Zhen, a disciple of Mencius, hurried to Mencius and said with a heavy heart, "Master, did you know there was a famine in the State of Qi and people were starving. Everyone thought that you would try to persuade the King of Qi again to open the granary to help the people. "

Mencius replied, "I can't do this again. Have you heard the story about Feng Fu?"

Feng Fu was a hunter in the State of Jin and was good at fighting tigers. Later he became a kind-hearted man and didn't hunt anymore. Years later, a tiger appeared in a mountain and hurt pedestrians. Several young hunters went together to capture the tiger. They chased the tiger to the depth of the mountain until the tiger leaned against a corner. It widened its eyes and roared, and no one dared to go forward.

At this moment, Feng Fu passed by. When the hunters saw him, they rushed forward to meet him and asked him to help fight the tiger. Feng Fu got out of the carriage, rolled up his sleeves and fought with the tiger. After a struggle, he finally killed the tiger. He did a good thing for the people. The young hunters thanked him sincerely, but some scholars laughed at him, considering that he became a hunter again .

The idiom indicates that the remnants of enemy troops put up a stubborn resistance at a strategic position or corner and will not give in.

F

覆水难收

姜太公在辅佐周文王之前，一直过着贫困潦倒的生活。妻子马氏不愿与他生活，离他而去。后来，姜太公得到周文王的重用，又帮助周武王联合各诸侯攻灭商朝，建立西周王朝。

马氏见其执掌西周王朝大权，懊悔当初离开了他，便找到姜太公请求与他恢复夫妻关系。姜太公已看透了马氏的为人，不想和她恢复夫妻关系，便把一壶水倒在地上，叫马氏把水收起来。马氏赶紧趴在地上去取水，但只能收到一些泥浆。姜太公冷冷地对她说："你我已不能复合，这就好比倒在地上的水难以再收回一样。"

该成语比喻事已成定局，难以挽回。

Spilt Water Can't Be Gathered up

Before Duke Jiang assumed the military counselor of the State of Zhou, he led a miserable life for a long time. His wife left him because she couldn't endure the extreme poverty. Afterwards, Duke Jiang was put in an important position by the King Wen of Zhou Dynasty and later, he helped the King Wu of the Zhou Dynasty unite all the dukes to destroy the Shang Dynasty and establish the Western Zhou Dynasty.

Jiang's ex-wife knew that he became a dignitary. She regretted having left him, so she went to Duke Jiang, in the hope of becoming his wife again. Understanding her thoroughly, Jiang split a bottle of water on the ground and said, "Try to gather up the water!" She bent down to gather the water and found nothing but slurry. Jiang said indifferently, "Since you left me, it is impossible for you to come back just like the spilt water couldn't be gathered up."

The idiom means what's done can't be undone.

改过自新

西汉初年，有个名叫淳于意的人，年轻却喜好医术。后拜阳庆为师，三年之后为人治病，预断生死，多能应验。可是后来他经常出游，不常在家，有时不肯为别人治病，因此许多病家怨恨他。于是有人上书朝廷控告他，当地的官吏判他“肉刑”。

淳于意的小女儿缇萦替父申冤，上书汉文帝为父求情，阐述肉刑的残酷。她说：“我父亲得过人们的好评，现在却要受刑。人死了不能复活，手脚被砍了不能接上。这样一来，即使受刑的人愿意改过自新，也没有机会了。”

汉文帝看过上书很受感动，于是赦免了淳于意的罪过。

该成语指认识到做了错事之后，决心改正。

Making a Fresh Start

In the early Western Han Dynasty (202–8 BC), a young man named Chunyu Yi adored the art of healing. So he was apprenticed to Yang Qing and after three years, he became a miracle-working doctor. Later, he went on sightseeing tours frequently and sometimes he refused to cure patients, so many patients had a grudge against him. At last, the local authority arrested him and sentenced him "corporal punishment" because someone accused him of his irresponsible behavior.

Chunyu Yi's youngest daughter, Tiying, wrote a letter to intercede Wendi Emperor of the Han Dynasty for his father, explaining the cruelty of corporal punishment. She wrote in the letter, "My father was upright and has won praise from people, but now he would be punished. If a person dies, there is no way to return to life; if his feet are cut off, he will be disabled. As a result, the punishment will deprive him the chance of correcting his mistake."

Emperor Wendi was very moved, so he remitted Chunyu Yi's punishment.

The idiom means one will correct the mistake and make a fresh start after one has done something wrong.

高枕无忧

春秋时代，有一个名叫冯谖的人，在齐国相国孟尝君门下做食客。有一次孟尝君派他到薛地去讨债，他到达薛地后，不仅不讨债，反而把借契全烧掉了，并在薛地设宴招待欠债之人，以此说明孟尝君是很好的主人，他不在乎这些钱，所以借钱给大家，主要是帮助大家过上好的生活，故没钱的人就不需还钱。这样，薛地的人民大为高兴，对孟尝君非常感激。

Sleep Without Fear of Any Disturbance

In the Spring-Autumn Period (770–476 BC), a man named Feng Xuan was a dependent of Lord Mengchang, the grand chancellor of the State of Qi. Lord Mengchang once sent him to Xuedi to collect payment for debts. When he arrived in Xuedi, he not only demanded no payment, but also burnt all the receipts. What's more, he hosted a banquet in Xuedi to entertain the debtors. The practice showed that Lord Mengchang was a good host and didn't care about the money, so he lent money to people in need to help them lead a good life. Those who had no money didn't need to pay back. As a result, the people in Xuedi were very happy and grateful to Lord Mengchang.

后来孟尝君被齐王解除相国的官职，前往薛地闲居，受到薛地人民热烈的欢迎。这时冯谖对孟尝君说："狡兔三窟，只能免除一死。现在你才有一窟，还不能把枕头垫得高高地睡觉，我再替你筑两窟。"于是他去游说梁惠王，说是若能请到孟尝君治理国事，定能国富兵强。梁惠王被说动了，便用重金去请孟尝君，请了三次，冯谖都叫他不要去。这事给齐王知道了，怕孟尝君为梁国所用，急忙用更隆重的礼节再请他做相国。冯谖又劝孟尝君向齐王请求赐给先王传下的祭器，放在薛地，建立宗庙，以保证薛地的安全。当宗庙建成时，冯谖对孟尝君说："现在三个窟已经建成，你可以'高枕为乐'了。"

后来，人们就用"高枕无忧"来形容做任何事情准备周全，感觉很安心、不用害怕。

Later, Lord Mengchang was removed from his official position by King Qi and he came back to live in Xuedi. He was warmly welcomed by the people there. At this moment, Feng Xuan said to Lord Mengchang, "With three caves, a smart rabbit will have one chance to avoid the hunter. Now that you have only one cave, you can't sleep without anxiety. I'll build two more caves for you." So he went to the State of Liang and said to the King, "The king who invited Lord Mengchang to govern the affairs of state would make the state prosper. So the King of Liang wanted to appoint Lord Mengchang as prime minister with high reward. The King invited him for three times but Lord Mengchang didn't accept the invitation as Feng Xuan told him not to. After hearing about that, the King of Qi hurried to invite Lord Mengchang to resume the former post, because the King of Qi was afraid of brain drain. Feng Xuan urged Lord Mengchang to ask the King of Qi for the sacrificial utensil handed down by the former king and then built a temple at Xuedi to ensure the safety of Xuedi. When the ancestral temple was built, Feng Xuan said to Lord Mengchang, "Now that three caves have been built, you can enjoy your sleep without anxiety."

The idiom is used to describe the state of being well prepared for everything and being without anxiety.

G

割席分坐

有两个读书人，一个叫管宁，一个叫华歆；他们的感情很好，不仅在同一个地方读书，而且形影不离。

有一次，管宁和华歆一起到院子里锄草，忽然发现了一块金子。当时，管宁视若无睹，仍旧挥动锄头，而华歆却动心了，立刻就拾起了金子，放在一边。

又有一次，管宁和华歆正一同坐在席上读书，忽然有坐着轿子的官员从门前经过，管宁照常读书，华歆却忍不住放下了书本，跑出去看。管宁见华歆这样不专心，又羡慕做官的人，再想到他见到了金子动心的事，就坚决地割断了并坐的席子，把座位分开，面色严肃地对华歆说：“从现在开始，你不再是我的朋友了。”

“割席分坐”是指朋友之间志趣不合，感情破裂，以致断绝往来。

To Cut the Mat and Break Off Friendly Relations

Guan Ning and Hua Xin were two scholars. They maintained sound relations with each other, not only reading books in one place but also staying together all the time.

One day, Guan Ning and Hua Xin went weeding in yard together and suddenly found a piece of gold. At that time, Guan Ning turned a blind eye and still worked his hoe, while Hua Xin was tempted and immediately picked up the gold and kept it.

Another day, Guan Ning and Hua Xin were sitting on a mat reading together. At the moment, thc officials in sedan chairs passed by the door. Guan Ning was reading as usual, but Hua Xin could not help but put down his books and ran out to see. Seeing that Hua Xin was so inattentive and envious of being an official, and days before he was tempted by gold, Guan Ning resolutely cut off the mat and separated the seats. He said solemnly to Hua Xin, "From now on, you are no longer my friend."

The idiom refers to casting off one's friend who has proved unworthy or dishonest.

各自为政

春秋时期，郑国出兵攻打宋国。宋国派华元为主帅，统率宋军前往迎战。两军交战之前，华元为了鼓舞士气，杀羊犒劳将士。忙乱中忘了给他的马夫羊斟分一份，羊斟便怀恨在心。

交战的时候，羊斟对华元说："分发羊肉的事你说了算，今天驾驭战车的事，可就得由我说了算了。"说完，他就故意把战车赶到郑军阵地里去。结果，堂堂宋军主帅华元，就这样轻易地被郑军活捉了。宋军失掉了主帅，因而惨遭失败。

该成语喻义各自按照自己的意见去办事，指行动不统一，不配合。

Each Administers in His Own Way

During the Spring-Autumn Period (770–476 BC), the State of Zheng sent troops to attack the State of Song. Song State sent Hua Yuan as its commander in chief to lead troops to defend. Before the war, Hua Yuan slaughtered sheep and divided mutton to reward the soldiers. In the bustle, he forgot to keep a piece of meat for his chariot driver Yang Zhen. Yang Zhen thought that he was looked down upon and intended to revenge.

During the war, Yang Zhen said to Hua Yuan, "You have the final say in the distribution of mutton. But I have the final say in the control of chariots today." Soon he deliberately drove the chariot out of his army and rushed into the enemy's troops. As a result, Hua Yuan, the commander in chief, was captured alive so easily by Zheng's troops. Then Song's troops suffered a terrible defeat.

This idiom means lacking coordination and consistent cooperation.

功亏一篑

周武王任用能人治理国家，周朝很快强大起来。四方各国都来朝拜，甚至离周朝很远的小国西戎也派使臣来朝贺，还带来了西戎特产的一种大狗献给武王，武王很高兴。

太保召公对武王说："这是您的圣德，四方都归服于您，无论远近，都把当地的土特产贡献给您。您也应该对他们分封赏赐，以表示信诚。赏赐的物品是无所谓贵贱的。无德，物也不值钱；有德，物才显得贵重。德行要靠自己修养，圣主不可以沉浸在声色之中。把人当作玩物加以戏弄，会丧失德行；把稀罕物件当作玩物加以赏玩，会丧失志气。犬马这类东西不是本地所产的，不应畜养它；珍禽异兽没有什么用途，也不该养它；远来的宝物不要那么珍爱它，不收人家的东西，人家才会归服你。最要紧的是珍爱能人，这是国家安稳的根本大计！明主应该随时积累德行，大德都是从小德积累而来的。比如筑一座九仞高的土山，如果最后一筐土没有加上去，这座山就没有堆成。您如果从这些方面加以注意，就可以世代稳坐天下了。"

该成语比喻做事情只差最后一点而没能完成。

Fail to Build a Mound for the Lack of One Final Basket of Earth

The Zhou Dynasty (1046–256BC) became strong very quickly because King Wu of Zhou put talented people in important positions, so countries around it all came to make obeisance to it. Even Xirong, a small country that was far away from Zhou, sent special envoys to present their special local product—a kind of big dog. King Wu was very pleased.

Duke Zhao said to King Wu, "All countries submit to you and all of them pay tribute to you with their special local gifts no matter how far away they are, so you should grant rewards to them in return. It makes no difference whether the rewards are valuable or not. Without moral integrity, the rewards will not be honorable. Moral integrity depends on self-cultivation, and wise monarch should not be immersed in sensual pleasures. If you make fun of people as if they are toys, you will lose moral integrity; if you play with rare things, you will lose aspiration. Dogs and horses should not be raised because they are not locally born or bred. Don't be very fond of jewels that were paid tribute by people. People will submit to you if you don't accept others' gifts. The most important thing is to treasure talented people, because they are key to a strong and powerful country. Wise monarch should accumulate virtues from time to time. Take building a high mound as example, if the last basket of earth is not added to it, the mound will never be completed. If you can notice this, we will have a stable and prosperous country for generations."

This idiom means failing to succeed for lack of a final effort.

姑息养奸

从前，永州这地方有一个好讲忌讳的人。因为他的生肖属鼠，就把老鼠看得像神仙一样。

他家里从来不养猫和狗，也不准别人捕捉老鼠。于是，附近的老鼠成群结队地来到他的家中。他家中的各种器具全被老鼠咬坏，家中的一日三餐，也是吃老鼠嘴边剩下的东西。白天，成群的老鼠在屋中东窜西跑，见了人也丝毫不害怕；到了晚上，老鼠们更是互相斗殴，吱吱怪叫，弄得盆器倾侧，使人无法入睡。然而，这位属鼠的主人对老鼠情有独钟，丝毫不放在心上。后来，他搬走了，另外搬来一户人家。老鼠们以为新主人和旧主人一样，照旧活动。新主人看到这种情况，惊奇地说：“想不到前屋主姑息养奸，把这些丑类纵容到如此猖獗的地步。”于是，他借来了几只猫，又让家人堵洞灌水。几天之中，打死的老鼠堆得像小山丘一样。

该成语比喻对坏人不惩治教育，一味迁就。

To Tolerate Evil Is to Abet It

Once upon a time, there was a person in Yongzhou who believed in taboo. He treated mouse as God because he was born in the year of mouse.

He never kept dogs or cats in his house, and no one was allowed to catch mice. So the mice nearby flocked to his house. All kinds of utensils were gnawed by mice, and his three meals a day were what was left behind by the mice. During the day, groups of mice ran around the house without fear. In the evening, the mice even fought with each other, making strange noises, tilting the basin and making people unable to sleep. However, the owner of the house didn't care at all. Later, he moved away. The mice thought that the new owner and the old owner were the same, so they acted as wildly as before. Seeing this, the new owner was surprised and said, "I can't believe that the former owner tolerated and connived at these ugly things to such an extent." So he borrowed cats and asked his family to plug the holes and fill them up with water. Within a few days, the mice were wiped out entirely.

The idiom means tolerating evil instead of punishing the evildoers.

G

贾人渡河

从前，济水的南面有个商人，渡河时从船上落下了水，停留在水中的浮草上，在那里求救。有一个渔夫用船去救他，还没有靠近，商人就急忙嚎叫道：“我是济水一带的大富翁，你如果能救了我，我给你一百两金子。”渔夫把他救上岸后，商人却只给了他十两金子。渔夫说：“当初你答应给我一百两金子，可现在只给十两，这岂不是不讲信用吗？”商人勃然大怒道：“你一个打鱼的，一天的收入该有多少？你突然间得到十两金子，还不满足吗？”渔夫失望地走了。

后来有一天，这商人乘船顺吕梁湖而下，船触礁沉没，他再一次落水。正好原先救过他的那个渔夫也在那里。有人问渔夫：“你为什么不去救他呢？”渔夫说：“他就是那个答应给我一百两金子而不兑现承诺的人。”渔夫撑船上岸，远远地观看那位商人在水中挣扎，商人很快就沉入水底淹死了。

该成语通常用来比喻那些说话、做事不讲信用的人。

A Merchant Crossing a River

Once upon a time, there was a merchant in the south of Jishui River who fell into water from the boat when crossing the river. He stayed on the floating grass in the water and asked for help. A fisherman rescued him, but before he came near, the merchant howled hastily, "I am a rich man in Jishui River area. If you can save me, I will give you 100 taels of gold." After the fisherman saved him ashore, however, the merchant only gave him 10 taels of gold. The fisherman said, "In the beginning, you promised to give me 100 taels of gold, but now you only give me 10 taels of gold. Is this your way to keep your word?" The merchant flew into a rage, "How much do you earn one day as a fisherman? You got 10 taels of gold by luck and you are still unsatisfied." The fisherman left with disappointment.

Later, the merchant took a boat down Lyuliang Lake. The boat hit rocks and sank. He fell into the water again. The fisherman who had saved him was also there. Someone asked the fisherman, "Why don't you go and save him?" "The fisherman said, "He is the one who promised to give me a 100 taels of gold for saving his life but did not keep his promise." The fisherman punted ashore and watched the businessman struggling in the water from a distance. The businessman soon sank into the lake and drowned.

The idiom is used to describe those who can't keep his word and never keep a promise.

G

瓜田李下

袁韦修是南北朝时期北齐人，他少年老成，性格沉稳，很有见识，18 岁为官，后来又升为博陵太守。他政绩突出，很有声望，成为远近知名的人物。袁韦修做官能清白自守，不收贿赂，人们送了他一个雅号“清郎”。

有一次袁韦修到外地考察地方官吏，路经兖州。他的老朋友邢邵正在兖州做刺史，邢邵拿出一匹白绸送他作为纪念。袁韦修谢绝说：“我这次路过这里，与往常不同呀，瓜田李下，古人是最谨慎的呀！你难道忘了古人说的走过瓜地不要弯腰提鞋子，走到李树下不要伸手整帽子吗？这是为了躲避嫌疑啊！我领受你的心意了。东西不能收，不能留下话柄呀！”

该成语指容易涉嫌的场合，要低调行事，避免嫌疑。

Don’t Do Anything to Arouse Suspicion

In the Northern and Southern Dynasties (AD 439–589), there was a man named Yuan Weixiu in the State of Northern Qi. He was a knowledgeable youth with warm disposition. He became an official at the age of 18 and later became the Prefecture of Boling. In addition to his outstanding achievements, he was innocent and upright, so people prized him an elegant name “Uncorrupted Official”.

Once, Yuan Weixiu went to other places to inspect local officials and passed Yanzhou. His old friend Xing Shao was the Governor of Yanzhou and offered him a roll of white silk as gift. Yuan Weixiu declined with thanks and said, “I’m on a business trip and it is different from casual visiting. Ancient wise men said that don’t bend to pull on your shoes in a melon patch and don’t reach to adjust your hat under a plum tree, which tells us that don’t do anything to arouse suspicion. I can feel your passion for our friendship, but I can’t accept your gift in order not to leave a subject for ridicule.”

The idiom means that people should be as low-key as possible in suspicious surroundings.

含沙射影

传说水里面有一种奇怪的动物，名叫蜮。它头上有角，背上有甲，没有眼睛，长了三只脚，有翅膀能飞，嘴里有一个像弩一样的东西。有的说它平时隐蔽水中，在暗中偷袭人类。如果听见人的脚步声，它就用嘴含着细沙朝人射来，人或者人的影子要是被射中了，就会生病。

唐朝的大诗人白居易，听了这个故事还写了一首诗，诗中说：

含沙射人影，
虽病人不知。

“含沙射影”这个成语用来比喻在暗地里对人进行诽谤、中伤。

Spitting Sand on a Shadow

Legend has it that there was once a strange animal named Yu in the water. It had horns, a shell, wings and three legs, but no eyes. There was a catapult in its mouth. If Yu heard the steps of a person, it would shoot sand from its mouth. If even the shadow was hit, the person would fall ill.

Bai Juyi, a great poet of the Tang Dynasty, heard this story and wrote a poem:

Shooting at people's shadow by blowing out sand,

And those who were shot at would never know it.

This idiom indicates vilifying others by insinuation.

好好先生

东汉有位士人司马徽善于识别人才，但由于当时社会斗争相当复杂，他自己却经常装糊涂，从来不说别人的短处，不管是好是歹，他总是回答“好”。日子久了，他也就成为“好好先生”。有一天，他在路上碰到一位熟人。那人问他近来身体是否安好。司马徽回答说：“好”。又有一天，他的一位朋友前来拜访，伤心地谈起了自己的儿子死了。不料，司马徽听了竟说：“太好。”他的妻子等朋友走后责备他说：“人家以为你是有德行的人，所以直言相告。哪里有听别人说儿子死了，反而说好的？”司马徽回答说：“好啊，你的话也是太好。”妻子听了，哭笑不得。

该成语形容一味包容、对原则问题漠不关心，并且从不愿冒犯别人的人。

Mr. Goody-goody

In the Three Kingdoms Period (AD 190–280), there was a scholar named Sima Hui, who was good at identifying talents. But because of the complexity of the society at that time, he often pretended to be confused and never talked about people's shortcomings. Whether good or bad, he always answered "good". After a long time, he became a "Mr. Goody-goody". One day, he met an acquaintance on the road and the man asked him if he was well recently. Sima Hui replied, "Good". Another day, a friend of his came to visit and talked sadly about the death of his son. Unexpectedly, Sima Hui said: "Good". After his friends left, his wife scolded him and said, "People think you are a man of virtue, so they tell you the truth that his son died. How can you say 'good' to him? Sima Hui replied, "Well, your words are good." Hearing this, his wife didn't know whether to cry or laugh.

The idiom describes benign and accommodating person who is indifferent to matter of principle and tries never to offend anyone.

好逸恶劳

东汉和帝时的太医郭玉，医术很高明，常常手到病除。郭玉为人仁义厚道，他为穷苦百姓治病，总是尽心尽力，药到病除；为达官贵人治病，却常常不能见效。和帝认为郭玉是存心不给富人好好治病，就责问他。

郭玉说："为人扎针治病，要靠感觉，靠意会。人的皮肤肌肉经络那么细嫩、精密，一定要全神贯注，不能有丝毫分心。那些尊贵的人居高临下地接待我，使我心有疑惧。因此为他们治病有四难：他们总是自作主张，自以为是而不听从我的指挥，这是第一难；态度不谦和，是第二难；筋骨不够强壮，难以用药，是第三难；好逸恶劳，是第四难。扎针的深浅，有一定的要求，全靠用心去把握，去体会。可是我又是担心害怕，又是谨慎小心，哪里能专心致志、全神贯注地为他们治病呢？这就是我给达官贵人治病常常治不好的原因啊！"和帝听了郭玉这番话，就没怪罪他。

该成语释义为贪图安逸、厌恶劳动。

Seek After Comfort and Abominate Labor

Guo Yu was a great imperial physician in the Eastern Han Dynasty (AD 25–220) during Emperor He's reign. With wonderful medical skills and a kind heart, Guo Yu treated the poor with all his efforts, and their illness departed immediately. But when he treated the dignitaries, his treatment was not so effective. The Emperor thought that he was deliberately not treating the dignitaries well and questioned him.

Guo Yu said, "I depend on feelings and communication when treating people with acupuncture. People's skin and muscles are so delicate and precise that I must be absorbed without any distraction. The dignitaries always gave me a condescending reception, which made me suspicious and frightened. Therefore, there are four difficulties in curing their diseases: first, they always make their own decisions, considering themselves always right and do not follow my instructions; second, they are not courteous; third, their physical conditions are not good enough to take varied medicine; last, they are indolent. There are certain requirements for the depth of pricking the acupuncture points, which depends on my personal feelings and experience. However, being both worried and frightened, how can I concentrate on treating them? After hearing Guo Yu's remarks, the Emperor did not blame him.

The idiom means coveting coziness and hating labor.

合浦珠还

东汉时，合浦郡沿海盛产珍珠。那里产的珍珠又圆又大，色泽纯正，一直誉满海内外，人们称它为“合浦珠”。当地百姓都以采珠为生，以此向邻郡交趾换取粮食。

采珠的收益很高，一些官吏就乘机贪赃枉法，巧立名目盘剥珠民。为了捞到更多的油水，他们不顾珠蚌的生长规律，一味地叫珠民去捕捞。结果，珠蚌逐渐迁移到邻近的交趾郡内，在合浦能捕捞到的越来越少了。合浦沿海的渔民向来靠采珠为生，很少有人种植稻米。采珠多，收入高，买粮食花些钱不在乎。如今产珠少，收入大量减少，渔民们连买粮食的钱都没有，不少人因此而饿死。

Recovery of Pearl Mussel in Hepu

During the Eastern Han Dynasty (AD 25–220), the coast in Hepu County was rich in pearls. The round and big pearls with beautiful color had been well-known at home and abroad. People called them "Hepu Pearls". The local people all made a living by collecting pearls and exchanged for food with the neighboring Jiaozhi County.

The profit from pearl collection was very high, so some officials took the opportunity to abuse the law and exploit local people under various pretexts. In order to get more money, they ignored the natural growth of the pearl mussel and ordered the local people to collect pearl without intervals. As a result, the pearl mussels gradually migrated to the neighboring Jiaozhi County, and fewer and fewer could be found in Hepu. The local people in Hepu who lived along the coast used to make a living by collecting pearls, and few people cultivated rice. The pearl collecting once brought high income, and the local didn't care about spending money on food and daily necessities. Later the production of pearls became low and their income also greatly decreased. The local people even didn't have enough money to buy food, some of whom were starved to death.

汉顺帝刘保继位后，派了一个名叫孟尝的人当合浦太守。孟尝到任后，很快找出了当地渔民没有饭吃的原因；下令革除弊端，废除盘剥的非法规定，并不准渔民滥捕乱采，以便保护珠蚌的资源。不到一年，珠蚌又繁衍起来，合浦又成了盛产珍珠的地方。

该成语比喻东西失而复得或人去而复回。

When Emperor Liu Bao of Han Dynasty succeeded to the throne, he appointed Meng Chang to be the prefect of Hepu. After Meng Chang took office, he soon found out the reason why the local people had no food. He ordered to get rid of the malpractice and abolish the illegal regulations of exploitation. Indiscriminate collecting of pearls was also banned in order to protect the multiplicity of pearl mussels. Within less than a year, pearl mussel resources recovered, and Hepu resumed a place rich in pearls.

The idiom means regaining what is lost.

河东狮吼

苏东坡因不满宰相王安石的某些变法措施，被贬到黄州。在黄州，他认识了一位名叫陈慥的人，两人很谈得来。陈慥很好客，朋友来了，必定热忱招待，有时还要喊几个歌女作陪。

可是陈慥的妻子柳氏却很凶悍，嫉妒心很强。她丈夫喊来歌女和客人一起听歌吟诗的时候，她就在隔壁房间用棍杖使劲敲打墙壁，并大声叫嚷，闹得大家不欢而散。陈慥很怕她，处处赔小心，就怕惹得她发火，使自己下不了台。

苏东坡给陈慥写了首打油诗："龙丘居士亦可怜，谈空说有夜不眠；忽闻河东狮子吼，拄杖落手心茫然。"

该成语比喻妻子妒悍，用来嘲笑丈夫怕老婆。

Lioness's Roar
—A Shrew Scolding Her Husband

Su Dongpo was demoted to Huangzhou because he was dissatisfied with some political reform measures of Prime Minister Wang Anshi. In Huangzhou, he met a man named Chen Zao and they got along well with each other. Chen Zao was very hospitable and when friends came, he would give a warm welcome. Sometimes sing-song girls would be invited to accompany them.

However, his wife, the Liu, was very jealous and fierce, not permitting him to get in touch with other women. When the sing-song girls came, she beat the wall with a stick and shouted loudly in the next room, which resulted in an early end of the gathering. Chen Zao was very afraid of her and tried hard to compensate her.

Poet Su Dongpo made up a poem for him: "Scholar Chen Zao is very pitiable, talking and not sleeping in the night. Suddenly, in the east to the river a lion gnarled and then the walking-stick fell from his hand. He was at a loss what to do." Hedong was the hometown of Chen Zao's wife, and the lion in the poem was referring to her.

The idiom is used to describe the phenomenon that the wife is strict to her husband and the husband is afraid of his wife.

H

侯门似海

唐代时，有一位叫崔郊的秀才，他的姑母家里有一位端庄美丽、天赋歌喉的使唤丫头。崔郊很爱她，她也很敬慕崔郊。崔郊的姑母不知这一情况。由于家境贫困，姑母后来将这位婢女卖到了大官的府第中。

崔郊非常想念她。但高官的府第门禁森严，普通人怎么进得去？从此，崔郊一直没见着这位心上人。有一年的清明节，崔郊偶然遇见了她，她已是官家的人了，不敢和崔郊打招呼，崔郊也不敢上前问询。两人四目相对，竟如咫尺天涯。崔郊心里很难过，但又无法向人诉说，便写了一首诗《赠去婢》："公子王孙逐后尘，绿珠垂泪滴罗巾，侯门一入深如海，从此萧郎是路人。"

后人用“侯门似海”形容显贵之家门禁森严，普通人无法进入。

The Noble Mansion Resembling the Deep Sea

In the Tang Dynasty (AD 960–1279), there was a scholar named Cui Jiao and a dignified and beautiful maid who was good at singing in his aunt's family. Cui Jiao loved her very much and the maid admired Cui Jiao in return. Cui Jiao's aunt did not know about it and sold the maid to a noble mansion due to poor family circumstances.

Cui Jiao missed her very much, but it was impossible for ordinary people to get into the high-ranking noble mansion which was intensively guarded. Since then, Cui Jiao had never seen the maid until Tomb-sweeping Day. Cui Jiao met her by chance, but she was a servant of a noble family, so neither Cui Jiao nor she dared to greet each other. They only looked at each other with exuding tenderness and love. At that time, Cui Jiao was weighted down with anxiety and he could not help writing a poem: "Young noble are living in the same way, tear drops wet her clothes. Once getting into the gate of a noble house that is as deep as the sea, the former love becomes a stranger."

The idiom is used to describe that the mansions of the nobility are inaccessible to the common people.

后来居上

汉武帝时，朝中有个大臣叫汲黯，为人正直，敢说敢为，批评别人的缺点不留情面，甚至对皇帝也时有顶撞。

有一次，汉武帝说要实行儒家的仁义之政，为老百姓办好事。没等皇帝把话说完，汲黯就说："陛下内心里那么贪婪多欲，表面上却要装得实行仁政，这是何苦呢？"一句话把皇帝噎了回去。武帝回到宫里以后，对身边的人说，汲黯这个人也未免太粗太直了。

从此以后，汲黯的官职再也没有提升。他当主爵都尉的时候，公孙弘、张汤都还是不起眼的小官，后来，他们一个劲儿往上升，公孙弘当上了丞相，张汤做上了御史大夫，可他汲黯还蹲在原地没动窝。有一天，汲黯对武帝说，陛下使用群臣，跟码劈柴一样，是"后来者居上"啊！汉武帝当然听得出这是发牢骚。于是，转脸对臣下们说："人真是不能不学习啊！你们听汲黯说话，越来越离谱了！"

该成语用来称赞后来的胜过先前的。

Catching Up from Behind

During the reign of Emperor Wu of the Han Dynasty (202 BC –AD 220), there was a minister named Ji An. He was upright and dared to make sharp comment on others. He criticized other people's shortcomings viciously and even sometimes contradicted the Emperor.

The Emperor once mentioned that he would carry out the policy of benevolence for the sake of common people. Before the Emperor had finished speaking, Ji An said, "Your Majesty, greed is in your heart, so what's the point to pretend to be benevolent." The Emperor was speechless. After returning to the palace, the Emperor said to the people around him that Ji An was too rude and straightforward.

For this reason, Ji An was never promoted again. When he ranked ninth among the senior officials, both Gongsun Hong and Zhang Tang were just low-ranking officials of little importance. Later on, they were promoted continuously while Ji An's post remained the same. One day, Ji An said to the Emperor, "Your Majesty, when you promote officials, you put the later comers first like piling wood. After Ji An went away, the Emperor said, "Reading and learning are so important. Hearing what Ji An has said, I feel that now he has less scholarship than before and has gone beyond what is proper."

This idiom is used to praise the later who becomes the first.

H

后起之秀

东晋时，王忱在少年时代就显露出才气，很受亲友的推崇。他的舅父范宁，是当时朝中有名的大臣，对王忱也很器重，有著名文士拜访，他总让王忱到场接待。

有一次，王忱去看望舅舅，遇到了比他早出名的张玄。舅舅要他俩交谈交谈。张玄早就听说王忱志趣不凡，很想与他谈谈。他年龄比王忱要大，自然希望王忱先给自己打招呼，就端正地坐着等候。不料，王忱见张玄这等模样，看不上眼，也默默坐着，一言不发。张玄见他这样，自己又放不下架子，对坐了一会，怏怏不乐地离去。

事后，范宁责备王忱说："张玄是吴中的优秀人才，你为什么不好好与他谈谈？"王忱傲慢地回答说："他要是真心想和我来往，完全可以来找我谈谈嘛。"范宁听了这话，倒反而称赞起外甥来了："你这样风流俊逸，真是后来的优秀人才。"王忱笑着回答说："没有您这样的舅舅，哪来我这样的外甥？"

该成语喻义从后辈中成长起来的优秀人才。

A Promising Youngster

In the Eastern Jin Dynasty (AD 317–420), Wang Chen showed great talent when he was young and was very popular with relatives and friends. His uncle Fan Ning, a famous minister in court, also valued Wang Chen very much. He always brought him along when he met famous scholars.

Once, Wang Chen went to visit his uncle and met Zhang Xuan, a famous person at that time. His uncle introduced Wang Chen to Zhang Xuan. Zhang Xuan had long heard of Wang Chen's extraordinary talent and would like to talk with him. Thinking that he was older than Wang Chen, Zhang Xuan sat upright and waited for a greeting first. But when Wang Chen felt Zhang Xuan's arrogance, he showed indifference. When Zhang Xuan found that they had nothing in common, he stood up to leave with a bad mood.

Fan Ning blamed Wang Chen and said, "Zhang Xuan is an outstanding talent in Wuzhong. Why not have a talk with him?" Wang Chen replied haughtily, "If he really wanted to get in touch with me, why didn't he come to talk to me." Hearing the wise reply, Fan Ning praised his nephew instead, "You are such an elegant and outstanding person and you deserve the title of a promising youngster." Wang Chen answered with a smile, "Like uncle, like nephew."

This idiom refers to outstanding young people.

哄堂大笑

宋朝的时候，有个姓冯的人和一个姓和的人在一起工作。姓和的是个急性子，姓冯的是个慢性子。

一天，姓冯的穿了一双新靴子，姓和的见了后说：我俩的靴子一模一样，你买靴子用了多少钱？姓冯的慢慢地抬起左脚说：“九百钱”。姓和的一听：“什么，九百钱？我这一双花了一千八百钱呢！”他马上质问身旁的仆人说：“原来你背着我贪污钱了！看我回去好收拾你！”这时，姓冯的又慢慢地抬起右脚说：“这一只也花了九百钱。”在场的人听他这么一说，立即哄堂大笑起来。

这个成语形容满屋子的人都笑了起来。

Explode with Laughter

In the Song Dynasty (AD 960–1279), Mr. Feng with a slow temper worked with Mr. He with a short temper.

One day, Mr. Feng wore a new pair of boots. When Mr. IIe saw thcm, he said, "Our boots are exactly the same. How much did you pay for them?" Mr. Feng slowly raised his left foot and said, "900." Hearing this, Mr. He said, "What, 900? But mine cost 1800!" He immediately questioned the servant beside him and said, "So you've embezzled money behind my back! I'll punish you afterward! "At that time, Mr. Feng slowly raised his right foot and said, "This one also costs 900." All the people present burst into laughter.

This idiom means the whole room rocking with laughter.

囫囵吞枣

古时候有个老先生，他教了很多学生。一天课余时间，学生们拿出新鲜的梨子和大枣吃了起来。这时，先生家里来了一位客人。这位客人是个医生，他看到学生们都在不停地吃着梨子和大枣，就劝他们说：“虽然梨子有益于牙齿，但吃多了却会伤脾；大枣是有益于脾，可是吃多了就会损坏牙齿。”

听了这位客人的话，一个愚钝的学生想了很久才说：“那我吃梨的时候光嚼不咽下去，这样就不能伤我的脾了；吃枣就整个儿吞下去而不嚼，也就伤不了我的牙齿了。”客人说：“唉，真没办法，你整个儿一个囫囵吞枣呀！”

该成语比喻对事物不加分析思考。

Swallow a Date Whole

In ancient times there was an old scholar who had many students. One day after school, the students took out fresh pears and dates to eat. At this time, a guest who was a doctor came to visit the scholar. Seeing that the students were eating pears and dates, he said, "Eating too many pears is good to teeth but harmful to the spleen. But eating raw date excessively, on the contrary, is good to the spleen but harmful to teeth."

A silly student thought for a long time and said, "I chew pears and don't swallow them, so my spleen won't be hurt. I swallow the dates without chewing them, so my teeth won't be hurt." The doctor said, "You are swallowing a date whole."

The idiom is used to describe that someone reads without understanding.

狐假虎威

一天，楚宣王问他的大臣：“我听说北方诸国非常害怕咱们国家的大臣昭奚恤，不知他到底怎么样？”大臣们没有回答。

一位名叫江乙的大臣讲了个故事，说：“有只老虎到处找各种野兽作为自己的美味佳肴，有一天，它抓到了一只狐狸。狐狸说：‘你不敢吃我。天帝派我管理天下的野兽，今天你要是吃了我，就是违背了天帝的命令。你要是认为我说的话不可靠，我可以走在前面，你跟在我后面，咱们来看看野兽们见了我之后有没有胆敢不逃走的！’老虎认为它说得有道理，于是就和它一起往前走，野兽们见到它们后都逃走了。老虎不知道野兽们其实害怕的是自己，还以为它们真的害怕狐狸。”

讲完故事，江乙说：“现在大王的兵权都在昭奚恤手上，北方的人民所怕的，实际不过是大王的兵权罢了。”

该成语比喻倚仗别人的威势来欺压人。

The Fox Borrowing the Tiger's Terror

One day, the King Xuan of the State of Chu asked his ministers, "I heard that the northern realms are very afraid of General Zhao Xixu. Do you know?" The ministers kept silence.

A minister named Jiang Yi then told a story: "A tiger looked everywhere for all kinds of wild animals as delicacies. One day, it caught a fox. The fox said, 'You dare not to eat me. I'm appointed by the God to manage the wild animals in the world. If you eat me today, you are against the God's order. If you don't think what I say is reliable, you may follow me and see how other beasts treat me. I'm sure that the wild animals will disappear after seeing me!' The tiger hesitated to believe the fox and he decided to walk along with it. The wild animals all fled at the sight of them. The tiger did not know who they were actually afraid of, and thought that they were really afraid of the fox. "

At the end of the story, Jiang Yi added the finishing touch, "Now Zhao Xixu is in charge of the troops. What the people of the north are afraid of is actually your troops."

This idiom refers to relying on the power of others to bully people.

虎口余生

宋朝年间，浙江湖州西山下住着一个名叫朱泰的年轻人。一个寒冷的冬天早晨，朱泰拿起斧子，准备上山砍柴卖钱。朱泰砍了半天，觉得有些累了，便在一块石头上坐下来。才休息了一会儿，忽听背后传来一阵令人心惊胆战的吼叫，只见一头猛虎从一片矮树丛中蹿出来，向他扑来。那猛虎张开血盆大口，朱泰见已没有退路，举起斧子死拼，猛虎却一口咬住了他的大腿。

朱泰大叫一声："娘啊，儿不能服侍您了！"然后闭着眼睛等死。过了很长一段时间，朱泰挣扎着爬起来，发现自己的大腿上鲜血还在流，而那只猛虎已经不见了。朱泰忽然瞥见那把斧子掉在一边，上面沾满了虎血！原来，那猛虎咬住朱泰的一瞬间，朱泰感到一阵剧痛，手一扬，那把斧子落下来正好砸在猛虎的头上，猛虎就慌忙逃走了。朱泰回到家，把这件事对母亲说了，母亲流着泪说："孩子，你真是虎口余生啊！"

该成语形容侥幸渡过难关，得以生存。

Escape from a Tiger's Jaws

During the Song Dynasty (AD 960–1279), a young man named Zhu Tai lived under the Western Hills of Huzhou, Zhejiang Province. On a cold winter morning, Zhu Tai picked up an axe and prepared to go up the mountain to cut firewood. Then he would sell it to support his family. After working for half a day, Zhu Tai felt tired and sat down on a stone. After a short rest, he suddenly heard a terrifying roar behind. A tiger snarled and sprang on him. There was no way out and Zhu Tai held up his axe to fight when the tiger bit his thigh.

He cried, "It doesn't matter if I would die, but I can't take care of my poor mother." After a long period of time, Zhu Tai struggled to get up and found that blood was still flowing out of his thigh, while the tiger disappeared. Zhu Tai suddenly caught a glimpse of the axe falling to one side covered with tiger blood! It turned out that the moment the tiger bit Zhu Tai, Zhu Tai felt a sharp pain and he hit the tiger's head with the axe in hand. Zhu Tai came home and told his mother about what happened. Her mother cried and said, "Son, you have escaped from the tiger's mouth today!"

This idiom describes a man that survived from a difficult situation by luck.

H

画饼充饥

三国时期，有一个人叫卢毓，在魏国做官，由于他为魏文帝曹丕出了许多好主意，因此受到朝廷器重，升为侍中、中书郎。

有一次，魏文帝对卢毓说："国家能不能得到有才能的人，关键就在你了。选拔人才，不要取那些有名声的，名声不过是在地上画一个饼，不能吃的。"

卢毓回答说："名声不是衡量人才的标准，但是，可以发现常士。一般人才敬慕教化，仰慕善美，然后有名气，他们是不应受到排斥的。我以为主要的是对他们进行考核，看他们是否真有才学。现在废除了考试法，全靠名誉提升或降职，所以真伪难辨，虚实混淆。"

魏文帝采纳了卢毓的意见，下令制定考试法。

该成语比喻用空想来安慰自己。

Drawing Cakes to Allay Hunger

During the Three Kingdoms Period (AD 190–280), there was a man named Lu Yu who worked as an official in the State of Wei. Because he offered many good ideas for Cao Pi, the King of Wei, he was highly valued by the court and was promoted to the position of minister of the court and then the head of the secretariat.

Once, the King said to Lu Yu, "You are the key to whether our state can get talented people. When selecting talents, don't choose those who are famous, for fame is nothing more than drawing a cake on the ground which you can't eat."

Lu Yu replied, "Fame is not a measure of talents, but a way to find ordinary talents. Those who has fame because of their high accomplishments and good behavior deserves our respect. In addition, I think it is necessary to examine whether they are really talented. Now the examination law has been abolished, and it depends entirely on one's reputation for promotion or demotion. As a result, it is difficult to tell the truth from the false. "

The King took Lu Yu's advice and ordered the enactment of examination law.

This idiom refers to comforting oneself with fantasy.

H

画龙点睛

南北朝时期，有个画家叫张僧繇。有一次，他奉命到金陵的安乐寺，在墙壁上面画了四条龙，可是都没有画出眼睛。看画的人觉得很奇怪，问他为什么不画出眼睛。他说："眼睛是龙的关键，要是画上眼睛，龙就会飞走了。"大家都认为很荒诞。张僧繇只好拿起笔来，刚给两条龙点上眼睛，立刻电闪雷鸣，两条龙乘云腾空而去，墙上只剩下两条没有画眼睛的龙。

"画龙点睛"这个成语用来比喻讲话或写文章时，在关键地方加一两句重要的话，使内容更加生动有力。

Bringing the Painted Dragon to Life by Putting in the Pupils of Its Eyes

In the Southern and Northern Dynasties Period (AD 439–589), there was a painter called Zhang Zengyou. Once he went to Anle Temple in Nanjing and painted on the wall four dragons as request, but gave nonc of them eyes. The onlookers felt that this was odd, and asked why all dragons did not have eyes. He answered, "Eyes are crucial for dragons. With the eyes added, the dragons would fly away." Nobody believed this, so Zhang Zengyou had no choice but to take up his brush and add pupils to two of the dragons. No sooner had he finished than the two dragons flew into the sky amid a thunderstorm. The two without eyes were still left on the wall.

This idiom is used to indicate that an artistic work seems extremely lifelike if a wonderful stroke is added at a critical place.

画蛇添足

战国时代有个楚国人，在祭祖仪式结束后，赏给来帮忙的门客一卮酒。门客们互相商量说："几个人一起喝肯定不够。我们都来画蛇，谁先画好谁就喝这酒。"

一个人先把蛇画好了，他左手拿起酒准备喝，右手继续画，说："我能够给蛇添上脚！"没等他画完，另一个人画好了，夺过他的酒说："蛇本来是没有脚的，你怎么能给它添上脚呢？"于是就把酒一饮而尽。

那个给蛇画脚的人最终没有喝到酒。

该成语告诉我们不要耍小聪明或不要做徒劳无功的事。

Drawing a Snake and Adding Feet to It

In the Warring States Period (AD 960–1279), a man of the State of Chu gave his retainers a beaker of liquor when the sacrificial rite was over. Obviously a beaker of liquor was not enough to go around. So the retainers started a discussion among themselves and one of them suggested, "Since there is no enough liquor for all of us, why not draw a snake to decide who has the priority to enjoy it? The one who finishes the drawing first will sample it. OK?"

One retainer finished his drawing quickly enough and grabbed the beaker with his left hand, while his right hand continued to draw. Seeing the others were still busy drawing, he said euphorically: "See, I can add feet to it." At this moment, another man finished his drawing and snatched the beaker, and alleged: "Snakes have no feet at all. How can you add feet to it?" With this he gulped down the liquor.

The man who added feet to the snake lost the chance to drink the liquor.

This idiom means "Don't gilt the lily" or "Don't carry coal to Newcastle".

H

讳疾忌医

战国时期，名医扁鹊去见蔡桓公。对桓公说：“你生病了，现在病还在皮肤的纹理之间，若不赶快医治，病情将会加重！”桓公听了笑着说：“我没有病。”

十天以后，扁鹊又去见桓公，说：“您的病已经发展到肌肉里，如果不治，还会加重。”桓公不理睬他。

再过了十天，扁鹊又去见桓公，说：“您的病已经转到肠胃里去了，再不从速医治，就会更加严重了。”桓公仍旧不理睬他。

又过了十天，扁鹊去见桓公时，对他望了一望，回身就走。桓公觉得很奇怪，于是派使者去问扁鹊。扁鹊对使者说：“病在皮肤的纹理间是烫熨的力量所能达到的；病在肌肤是针灸可以治疗的；在肠胃是汤药可以治愈的；病若是到了骨髓里，那是司命所掌管的事了，我也没有办法了。而今病已在骨髓，我再也没有办法了。

五天以后，桓公浑身疼痛，赶忙派人去请扁鹊，扁鹊却早已经逃到秦国了。桓公不久就病死了。

该成语指隐晦自己的错误和缺点，怕别人指出来。

Hiding Sickness for Fear of Treatment

In the Warring States Period (457–221 BC), the famous doctor Bian Que visited the King of the State of Qi. He said, “Your Majesty, you are already beginning to suffer from disease, but the disease is only at the skin level. Please take some measures, or it would get worse.” The King laughed and said, “I’m quite well.”

Ten days later, Bian Que visited the King again and said, “Your disease has developed to the muscles. If you ignore it, the disease will get worse.” The King turned his back upon what Bian Que said.

Another ten days passed, Bian Que visited the King and said, “Your disease has moved into your stomach. If you don’t take immediate treatment, it will be very dangerous.” The King turned his back upon his words again.

Another ten days later when Bian Que visited the King, he said nothing and went away. The King was surprised and sent a servant to ask why. Que answered, “At first, the illness was only at skin-deep. Then it developed to the muscles, even the internal organs. But I still could cure it through acupuncture and herbal medicine. However, when the illness has penetrated into his bones, I can do nothing to handle it.” Five days later, the King felt the pain from the head to foot and sent a servant for Bian Que. But Bian Que had escaped to the State of Qin. Soon after that, the King passed away.

The idiom means concealing one’s shortcomings for fear of criticism.

J

鸡鸣狗盗

战国时候，孟尝君出使秦国。秦昭王将他留下当相国，孟尝君不敢得罪秦昭王，只好留下来。不久，大臣们劝秦王说："留下孟尝君对秦国是不利的，他出身王族，怎么会真心为秦国办事呢？"秦昭王便改变了主意，把孟尝君软禁起来，打算杀掉他。

孟尝君派人去求见秦昭王的宠妃请求帮助。妃子答应了，条件是拿孟尝君那一件天下无双的狐白裘做报酬。这可叫孟尝君为难了，因为刚到秦国，他便把这件狐白裘献给了秦昭王。就在这时候，有一个门客说："我能把狐白裘找来！"说完就走了。原来这个门客最善于装狗偷东西。他摸清情况，借着月光，轻易地钻进贮藏室把狐裘偷出来，献给秦王宠妃。宠妃见到狐白裘高兴极了，想方设法说服秦昭王释放了孟尝君。

Crow Like a Cock and Snatch Like a Dog

During the Warring States Period (457–221 BC), Lord Mengchang was sent on a diplomatic mission to the State of Qin. The King Zhao of the State of Qin asked Lord Mengchang to stay and assumed him the post of the Changcellor of State, so Lord Mengchang stayed unwillingly. Soon a minister said to the King, "As Lord Mengchang is a relative of the King of Qin, he would never serve us wholeheartedly and will do harm to our state." As a result, the King Zhao of Qin didn't appoint Lord Mengchang as the prime minister and even put him under house arrest and intended to kill him.

Lord Mengchang sent a subordinate to visit King Zhao's favorite concubine for help. The royal concubine promised to help them provided that they could give her a white fox-fur robe Lord Mengchang possessed. Unfortunately, Lord Mengchang had given the only white fox-fur robe to King Zhao. At that moment, one of his men was good at disguising into a dog to steal things. So he disguised himself into a dog and stole the white fox-fur robe from the palace. After receiving the robe, the royal concubine successfully persuaded the King to release Lord Mengchang.

孟尝君获得自由后马上驱车离开秦国。不一会儿，秦昭王后悔放掉了孟尝君，马上派人去追。孟尝君星夜兼程，半夜走到了函谷关。当时关防法令规定，鸡鸣后才可以放来往客人出关。孟尝君害怕追兵赶来，这时门客中有个地位低下的人能够模仿鸡叫，他一叫，许多鸡一起叫了起来，于是孟尝君交验出关凭证，才出了关。孟尝君靠着鸡鸣狗盗之士逃回了齐国。

该成语指微不足道的本领和偷偷摸摸的行为。

He immediately led his subordinates to leave. After a while, the King changed his mind and ordered to capture Lord Mengchang back. Lord Mengchang travelled day and night and arrived at Hangu Pass at midnight. According to the law, the gate would not be opened until cock crows. Lord Mengchang was very anxious about the chasing troops. A subordinate recommended himself for being able to imitate cock crow. So he began to crow like a cock and all the cocks near the pass began to crow. Then Lord Mengchang showed his identification and went through the boundary areas. Lord Mengchang's escape was relied on the ability of his subordinates to crow like a cock and snatch like a dog.

The idiom indicates disgrace and improper behaviors.

J

惊弓之鸟

更赢是战国时魏国有名的射箭能手。有一天，更赢跟魏王到郊外打猎。一只大雁从远处慢慢地飞来，边飞边鸣。更赢仔细看了看，指着大雁对魏王说：“大王，我不用箭，只要拉一下弓，这只大雁就能掉下来。”

国王不相信。更赢便对准天上飞来的一只雁射去，果真那只雁听到拉弦的声音就掉了下来。国王感到很奇怪。更赢说：“那是一只受过伤的雁。它一听到我拉开弓弦的声响，就惊慌得支持不住，自然要掉下来了。”魏王更加奇怪了，问：“你怎么知道的？”

更赢说：“它飞得慢，叫得很悲惨。飞得慢，因为它受过箭伤，伤口没有愈合，还在作痛；叫得悲惨，因为它离开同伴，孤单失群，得不到帮助。它一听到弦响，心里很害怕，就拼命往高处飞。它一使劲，伤口又裂开了，就掉下来了。”

该成语比喻经过惊吓的人碰到一点动静就非常害怕。

Birds Startled by the Mere Twang of a Bowstring

In the Warring States Period (457–221 BC), there was a military officer in the State of Wei named Geng Lei who was good at shooting arrows. One day he accompanied the King of the State of Wei on hunting. A wild goose came into their sight and he said to the King: "I can shoot down birds by simply plucking my bowstring."

When the King expressed doubt, Geng Lei pointed his bow at a wild goose flying in the sky, twanged the bowstring, and the goose fell to the ground. The King was surprised and said, "How skillful you are!" Geng Lei said, "This goose has been hurt in the past. Hearing the twang of the bowstring, it fell down." The King continued, "How could you know about these details?"

Geng Lei answered, "The wild goose flied slowly with wretched call, which indicates that it was injured before and has been away from the flock. It was frightened because of the twang of the bowstring and wanted to fly higher, and then its wound would crack and it would fall down."

This idiom means that if one has been frightened in the past, one will be timid in a similar situation.

J

精卫填海

炎帝有个女儿，名叫精卫，性格开朗活泼，喜欢打抱不平。一天，她走出小村，找小朋友玩耍，看到一个大孩子把小孩子当马骑。精卫走过去，指着大孩子怒斥道："你这个人太不知羞耻，欺负小孩子算什么本事？"

大孩子见精卫是个小姑娘，走到精卫面前说："我是海龙王的儿子，你是什么人？竟敢来管我！"精卫说："龙王的儿子有什么了不起，我还是炎帝的女儿呢！"龙王的儿子说着动手就打精卫，见打不过，只好灰溜溜地返回大海。

过了些天，精卫到海中游泳，刚巧被龙王的儿子发现了。他搅动海水，掀起狂风恶浪，精卫来不及挣扎，就被淹死了。精卫死后，变成一只红爪白嘴的小鸟，她用嘴衔来石头与树枝投向大海，立志要把大海填平。

该成语比喻不怕艰难困苦，不达目的誓不罢休的坚强意志。

Jingwei Fills Up the Sea

Emperor Yan in remote antiquity had a daughter named Jingwei, who was outgoing and always spoke up for the oppressed. One day, she walked out of the small village and looked for mates. She saw an elderly child riding on a little boy's back. Jingwei walked over and thundered, "Shame on you!Are you going to show off your power by bullying the young? "

Seeing that Jingwei was a little girl, the elder child approached Jingwei and said, "I am the son of the Dragon King. Who are you and how dare you to shout at me!" Jingwei said, "What's the big deal about the son of the Dragon King? I am the daughter of Emperor Yan! The son of the Dragon King tried to hit Jingwei but suffered a great deal. He felt depressed and returned to the sea.

Some days later, Jingwei went swimming in the sea and was discovered by the son of the Dragon King. He stirred up the sea and set off fierce winds and waves. Jingwei was drowned before she could struggle. After Jingwei died, she became a bird with red claws and a white beak. Every day she would pick up twigs and pebbles and drop them into the sea with a will to fill up the sea.

This idiom describes an indomitable will to achieve one's goal regardless of all difficulties.

J

井底之蛙

一口废井里住着一只青蛙。有一天，青蛙在井边碰上了一只从海里来的大龟。

青蛙就对海龟夸口说："你看，我住在这里多快乐！有时高兴了，就在井栏边跳跃一阵；疲倦了，就回到井里，在砖洞边睡一会儿。或者只留出头和嘴巴，安安静静地把全身泡在水里；或者在软绵绵的泥浆里散步，也很舒适。看看那些虾和蝌蚪，谁也比不上我。而且，我是这个井的主人，在这井里极自由自在，你为什么不常到井里来游赏呢！"

那海龟听了青蛙的话，倒真想进去看看。但它的左脚还没有整个伸进去，右脚就已经被绊住了。它连忙后退了两步，把大海的情形告诉青蛙说："你看过海吗？海的广大，哪止千里；海的深度，哪止千来丈。古时候，十年有九年大水，海里的水，涨不了多少；后来，八年里有七年大旱，海里的水，也不见得浅了多少。可见大海是不受旱涝影响的。住在那样的大海里，才是真的快乐呢！"井蛙听了海龟的一番话，吃惊地呆在那里，再没有话可说了。

该成语比喻见识狭窄的人。

A Frog in a Well

A frog lived in an abandoned well met a big turtle from the sea one day.

The frog said, "I am so happy to live in my well. I can jump at the edge of well for a while at ease; when tired, I can go back to the well and sleep by the brick cave; I can leave only the head and mouth above water and soak my body in the water as I wish; or walk in the soft mud to enjoy the comfort. Looking at those shrimps and tadpoles, I'm sure no one can match me. Welcome to my well! "

The turtle really wanted to go inside and have a look. However, when his left foot had not yet fully stepped into the well, his right foot got blocked. He stepped back and told the frog about the sea. "Have you ever seen the sea? The vast sea is boundless. It is so deep that no one can measure. In ancient times, there were nine floods within ten years, while the water in the sea did not increase much. Later, there were seven droughts within eight years, while the water in the sea did not become shallower. It can be seen that the sea is not affected by drought and flood. The greatest happiness lies in living in the sea." After listening to the turtle's words, the frog stayed there in surprise and had nothing more to say.

This idiom refers to people with very limited horizon.

K

开门揖盗

三国时代，江东的孙策遭了暗算，重伤而死。他的弟弟孙权这时才 15 岁，天天啼哭，无法处理朝政。臣下们劝说没用，都很着急。谋士张昭对孙权说："现在天下大乱，豺狼满道，如果你只顾悲啼，不理政事……这好比大开着房门，拱着手把强盗请来，必将自取其祸。"孙权觉得张昭说的对，马上换了正装，开始理事，视察军队，安定了军心、民心。

"开门揖盗"的意思是开门请强盗进来，比喻引进坏人，招来祸患。

Open the Door to Robbers

During the Three Kingdoms Period (AD 190–280), Sun Ce of Jiangdong fell to a dark scheme and died of serious injuries. His 15-year-old younger brother Sun Quan was crying every day and unable to deal with the official affairs. The ministers were all very anxious because their persuasion was ignored. Counselor Zhang Zhao said to Sun Quan, "In the world of chaos, the cruel and the wicked are in power. If you immerse yourself in depression and ignore the political affairs, it is like opening the door widely and inviting bandits with your open arms, which will lead into disaster." Sun Quan felt that he was right and immediately wore his uniform to handle the political affairs. Through army inspection and varied well-being policies, the state became stabilized and united.

The idiom means inviting disaster by letting in evil-doers.

刻舟求剑

战国时，楚国有个人坐船渡江。船到江心，他一不小心，把随身携带的一把宝剑掉落江中。他赶紧去抓，已经来不及了。船上的人对此感到非常惋惜，但那楚人似乎胸有成竹，马上掏出一把小刀，在船舷上刻上一个记号，并向大家说："这是我宝剑落水的地方，所以我要刻上一个记号。"大家都不理解他为什么这样做，也不再去问他。

船靠岸后那人立即在船上刻记号的地方下水，去捞取掉落的宝剑。捞了半天，不见宝剑的影子。他觉得很奇怪，自言自语说："我的宝剑不就是在这里掉下去吗？我还在这里刻了记号呢，怎么会找不到的呢？"至此，船上的人纷纷大笑起来，说："船一直在行进，而你的宝剑却沉入了水底不动，你怎么找得到你的剑呢？"

该成语指做事不知进退，墨守成规，不懂得随着客观情况的变化来处理事情。

Notching the Boat to Retrieve the Sword

In the Warring States Period (457–221 BC), a man in the State of Chu dropped a sword into the water by accident when he was crossing a river in a boat. People on the boat all regretted his loss. The man then made a mark on the side of the boat at the spot where the sword had fallen overboard and said, “This is the place where I dropped it.” People on the boat were all puzzled and did not inquiry anymore.

When the boat reached the shore, he jumped from the marked spot into the water to look for his sword but in vain. He said to himself, “This is exactly the place where I dropped my sword and the mark here is absolutely right, but why?” People on the boat all laughed at him and said, “The boat is moving, but your sword stayed still at the bottom of the river. It’s impossible for you to retrieve it.”

This idiom satirizes those who stick to rules instead of taking into consideration of changed circumstances.

K

空中楼阁

从前有个富翁，有一次他到另一个富翁的家里，看见一座三层的楼房，富丽堂皇，宽敞明朗，十分羡慕，心里想："我的钱财并不比他少，为什么以前没想到造一座这样的楼呢？"他立刻唤来木匠，问道："你能不能照着那家的样子造一座漂亮的楼？"木匠回答说："没问题。"

于是木匠照着他的吩咐，挖土动工。第一层刚盖好，准备盖第二层的时候，富翁就问木匠："你这是打算造什么？"木匠回答道："造三层的楼呀！"富翁又说："我不要下面二层，你先给我造第三层。"木匠答道："没这样的事！哪有不造最下一层楼而造第二层楼的？不造第二层楼又怎么谈得上造第三层楼呢？"说完摇摇头拿上他的工具就走了。

该成语比喻虚幻的事物或脱离实际的空想，不合实际的计划。

Castles in the Air

Once upon a time there was a rich man. He went to another rich man's house and saw a three-story building, magnificent, spacious and clear. He was very envious and thought: "I had no less money than him. Why haven't I thought of building such a building before?" So he asked a carpenter to build a three-story building. The carpenter replied, "No problcm."

Upon request, the carpenter started. As soon as the first floor was finished, the rich man asked the carpenter, "What are you going to build?" The carpenter replied, "A three-story building." The rich man said to the architect, "I want only the third story; not the first and second stories." The architect asked, "But without the first and second stories, how can I build the third story?" Shaking his head, he packed up his things and left.

This idiom indicates an unrealistic or impractical plan or fantasy.

滥竽充数

南郭先生是齐国人，齐国当时在位的君王是齐宣王，宣王非常喜欢听一种古代的簧乐器竽吹奏出来的声音，而且他喜欢听合奏，打算组织三百人的乐团。南郭先生听说宣王要用丰富的口粮供养一大批吹竽的人，于是就去央求宣王也让他加入，从此南郭先生成为三百名吹竽手之一。每当宣王要听竽合奏的时候，南郭先生就在乐团里头装模作样一番，反正人多他不吹出声音，也没有人知道，因为他装的还挺有模有样的，就这样相安无事地过了好几年。

后来宣王去世，他的儿子涢王继位，涢王不喜欢听合奏，喜欢听独奏。南郭先生本来就不会吹竽，如果要他在君王面前独奏，肯定会露出马脚，所以在轮到他之前，他就逃之夭夭了。

该成语比喻无本领的冒充有本领，次货冒充好货。

Pass Oneself Off as a Member of the Ensemble

Mr. Nanguo was a man from the State of Qi, in the Warring States Period (457–221 BC). The King Xuan of the State of Qi was very fond of listening to yu, an ancient wind instrument, and especially enjoyed the orchestras. So he selected 300 players and ordered them to play yu together for him.

Mr. Nanguo heard that the King would treat the players munificently, so he volunteered to join the band after pleading with the King. Mr. Nanguo, who couldn't play the instrument, passed himself off as one of the musicians. In this way, he pretended to be an excellent player for years.

After King Xuan passed away, his son King Min succeeded to the throne. King Min also loved yu but he preferred solo performance. Mr Nanguo was bound to betray himself, so slipped away from the orchestra before his turn.

This idiom is used to describe those who have no actual skills but pretend to be experts.

L

狼狈为奸

狼和狈是两种经常一起偷吃猪、羊的野兽。它们唯一不同的是：狼的两条前腿长，两条后腿短；而狈却是两条前腿短，两条后腿长。

有一回，一只狼和一只狈共同来到一个羊圈外，看到羊圈中的羊又多又肥，就想偷吃。但是羊圈的墙和门，都很高，狼和狈都不能爬去。于是，它们就想了一个办法。狈先蹲下身来，狼爬到狈的身上。然后，狈用前腿抓住羊圈的门，慢慢伸直身子。狈伸直身子后，狼将腿抓住羊圈的门，慢慢伸直身子，把两只长长的前腿伸进羊圈，把羊圈中的羊偷了出来。

该成语用来形容那些相互勾结干坏事的人。

A Wolf Working Hand in Glove with a Jackal

Wolves and jackals often worked together to prey on domestic animals such as pig and goat. They were quite similar but wolves had long forelegs and short latter legs, while jackals had short forelegs and long rear legs.

Once they came to a sheepfold the walls of which were firmly built and too high for them to get over. Then they had an idea: The wolf stood on the neck of the jackal, and the jackal stood up on its latter legs. In this way the wolf reached the sheep and stole them out of the sheepfold.

This idiom is used to describe doing evil things in collusion with others.

L

老马识途

春秋时代，齐桓公应燕国的要求，出兵攻打入侵燕国的山戎，相国管仲和大夫隰朋随同前往。齐军是春天出征的，到凯旋时已是冬天，草木变了样。大军在崇山峻岭的一个山谷里转来转去，最后迷了路，再也找不到归路。时间一长，军队的给养发生困难，情况非常危急。

管仲思索了好久，对齐桓公说：“大王，我认为老马有认路的本领，可以利用它在前面领路，带引大军出山谷。” 齐桓公同意试试看。管仲立即挑出几匹老马，解开缰绳，让它们在大军的最前面自由行走。大军就紧跟着它们东走西走，最后终于走出山谷，找到了回齐国的大路。

该成语比喻有经验的人办事效果好。

An Old Horse Knows the Way

In the Spring-Autumn Period (770–476 BC), Duke Huan of Qi led an army to attack minority tribes that invaded the State of Yan from the north, with Guan Zhong and Xi Peng as entourage. They went in spring when green grass covered the ground. But when they came back, it was winter. The troops lost their way in a valley and were moving to and fro. As time went by, the provision of the army became inadequate, making the situation very critical.

While everybody was worrying, Guan Zhong, the Duke's chief minister, suggested, "An old horse may know the way." Upon permission, he ordered several old horses to lead the army. Finally, they moved out of the valley and found the way back to the State of Qi.

This idiom means that a man of long experience knows the ropes.

L

梁上君子

东汉时期有一个叫陈寔的人，总是以平和的心对待事物。当时年成不好，民众没有收成，有小偷夜间进入陈寔家里，躲在房梁上。陈寔发现了，就起来整顿衣服，让子孙聚拢过来，正色训诫他们说："人不可以不自己努力。不善良的人不一定本性是坏的，坏习惯往往由不注重品性修养而致。梁上君子就是这样的人！"小偷大惊，从房梁跳到地上，跪拜在地，诚恳认罪。

该成语特指偷东西的人。

A Gentleman on the Beam

In the Eastern Han Dynasty (AD 25–220), there was a broad-minded man called Chen Shi. One year, people suffered a lot from poor harvest. One night, a thief slipped into his room and hid on the beam. Chen Shi, noticing the thief, called up all his family and said, "One must have a desire to make progress. Evildoers are not born evil. But if one gets used to doing evil things, one will form bad behavior and be hard to make a change. The gentleman on the beam is such a man." The thief on the beam was very frightened, so he jumped down from the beam and gave Chen Shi a grand kowtow to beg forgiveness.

This idiom is used to refer to a thief.

量体裁衣

南齐时期，有个官员叫张融，后来官至司徒长史。张融很有学问，手段高明，点子颇多，又对齐高帝萧道成忠心耿耿。公元 479 年，萧道成建立齐朝，定都建康（今南京）。高帝认为张融是举世无双的能人，一再给他加官晋级，并常常给予特殊的恩宠。

有一次高帝手诏张融，同时把自己穿过的一件衣服送给张融。手诏上写着：现在送给你一件旧衣，是我自己穿过的，已经叫人按照你的体格重新裁剪了，送给你穿应该很合适。张融得到手诏和衣服后，心里乐滋滋的，不知如何是好。在当时，皇帝把自己的衣服赠给臣子，是一种不同寻常的赏赐，足见张融当时是何等受宠。

该成语比喻按照实际情况办事。

Cut the Clothes According to the Figure

In the Southern Qi (AD 479–502) period, there was an official named Zhang Rong who was later promoted to a high post. He was not only a wise and well-connected official, but also loyal to the Emperor of Qi. In the year 479, the Emperor of Qi established the Qi Dynasty in Jiankang, the present Nanjing. The Emperor highly valued Zhang Rong's ability and offered him chances of promotion.

The Emperor once issued imperial edict and gave Zhang Rong an article of clothing. He said, "I give an article of old clothing to you today. It is mine and I had it cut and it fits you now." Zhang Rong was delighted beyond measure. At that time, receiving the Emperor's clothes as gifts was an exceptional reward, showing the trust and favor from the Emperor.

The idiom means acting according to actual conditions.

L

临渴掘井

春秋时期，鲁昭公亲近小人，不听品格高尚之人的规劝，结果被赶出国家，逃到了齐国，这才明白自己原来的所作所为是错误的。齐景公觉得昭公已知道悔过，认为若让他回去，应该能成为一个贤良的国君。

齐国大夫晏子却认为：掉在水里的人，一定要等到掉进水里以后，才会想起应该防备失足；犹如面临灾难的人，才急着铸造兵器；吃东西塞住咽喉的人，才急着去挖井取水。虽然这时候用最快的速度，但是已经来不及了。”

该成语比喻平时对各种事情不做准备，临时需要时才忙着采取措施去应付。

Start Digging a Well When Thirsty

In the Spring-Autumn Period (770–476 BC), Duke Zhao of the State of Lu was on intimate terms with people of evil intentions and ignored the suggestions offered by the noble-minded people. In the end, he was exiled and fled to the State of Qi. He admitted his mistakes to Duke Jing of Qi and Duke Jing advised him to go back to Lu, as he might become a wise ruler, since he recognized his faults.

But Yanzi, an official of Qi said, "It is too late to take precautions when one has fallen into the water, to make weapons when one is endangered, and to dig a well when one is choked in eating and needs water desperately. Though fast, it is too late."

This idiom warns against not being prepared, but seeking help at the last moment.

临危不惧

春秋时期，孔子乘学生颜回驾驶的马车周游各国。他们来到匡地，当地人把孔子误认为是他们所憎恨之人，便纠集军队围攻他们。

他的学生子路被冲散了，隔了好久才奋力冲进包围圈，起初他担心孔子的安危，现在见他正在谈笑风生，子路问老师："何故？"孔子曰："怕什么？在水中来去，不怕蛟龙，是渔夫之勇；在野处来去，不怕虎豹，是猎人之勇；能掌握自己命运，认识当前局势，临大难而不惧怕者，圣人之勇也！"

该成语表示遇到危难的时候，一点也不怕。

Facing Danger Fearlessly

In the Spring-Autumn Period (770–476 BC), Confucius traveled around the states by carriage driven by his disciple Yanhui. When they came to the place of Kuang, they were surrounded by the local people for Confucius resembling a man the local people hated.

Confucius and his disciple Zilu were kept apart from each other. At last Zilu made a break through because he worried his teacher's safety. When Zilu came to Confucius, he found his teacher was very calm. Zilu was puzzled and asked Confucius for the reason. Confucius said, "What are you afraid of? Swimming in the river, the fisherman is brave enough to show no fear of the dragon. Walking in the wild, the hunter is brave enough to show no fear of the tigers and leopards. Being able to control one's own fate and seeing through the situation at present, this is the braveness of a saint!"

The idiom means retaining one's usual composure in the face of danger.

M

马革裹尸

马援是东汉的开国元勋，他平定了边境的动乱，威震南方，被封为伏波将军。

马援回到京城洛阳，大家都来向他祝贺，其中有个名叫孟翼的官员说了许多恭维的话，表示皇上肯定有封赏，从此高官厚禄之类。马援对孟翼说：“如今，匈奴和乌桓还在北方不断侵扰，我打算向朝廷请求当个先锋，做一个有志的男儿。男儿应该战死在边疆荒野的战场上，只用马的皮革裹着尸体就行了，怎么能和那些懦夫一般，享受荣华富贵呢？”孟翼听了由衷地佩服。一个月后，马援又奔赴北方前线。63 岁时马援病死在军中。

“马革裹尸”形容视死如归的决心。

Die on the Battlefield

Ma Yuan was the founding general of the Eastern Han Dynasty (AD 25–220). He put down the rebellion on the border, and had a great impact on the south, so he was honored as General Fubo.

When Ma Yuan returned to the capital city Luoyang, everyone came to congratulate him. One of the officials named Meng Yi said many flattering words, saying that the Emperor must had prepared a huge reward and would guarantee him high position and massive gains. Ma Yuan said to Meng Yi, "At present, the minorities of Huns and Wu Huan are still harassing in the north. I will volunteer to be a pioneer and be a man full of ambitions. A real man should die on the battlefield and be wrapped in a horsehide after death. How can I enjoy the splendor and wealth like those cowards?" Meng Yi admired him sincerely. A month later, Ma Yuan went to the northern front again. At the age of 63, Ma Yuan died of illness and laid down his life on the battlefield.

The idiom describes the determination to fight without the fear of death.

买椟还珠

春秋时代，楚国有一个商人，专门卖珠宝的。有一次他到齐国去兜售珠宝，为了珠宝畅销起见，特地用名贵的木料，造成许多小盒子，把盒子雕刻装饰得非常精致美观，使盒子会发出一种香味，然后把珠宝装在盒子里面。

有一个郑国人，看见装宝珠的盒子既精致又美观，问明了价钱后，就买了一个。可是没走几步他又回来了，说："先生，您将一颗珍珠忘放在盒子里了，我特意回来还珠子的。"于是郑人将珍珠交还给了楚人。

该成语比喻没有眼光、取舍不当的人。

Keeping the Glittering Casket and Returning the Pearls

In the Spring-Autumn Period (770–476 BC), there was a merchant in the State of Chu who specialized in selling jewelry. Once he went to Qi State to sell jewelry for business. To make his jewelry popular, he made many small boxes from precious wood. The boxes were carved and decorated beautifully so that the boxes would give off a delicate fragrance. Then the jewelry was put into the boxes.

There was a man from the State of Zheng who saw the exquisite and beautiful boxes. After asking the price, he bought one. But he came back after a few steps later and said, “Sir, it seems that you left a pearl in the box and here you are.”

This idiom refers to people who make a wrong choice and lack sound judgment.

满城风雨

潘大临是宋代黄州的一位诗人，他写过不少好诗。有一年重阳节快到了，他的一位好友写信来问他："你最近有新的作品吗？"潘大临回信说："关于秋天的景色，每一件都能够写出好诗来。昨天我靠在床上休息，听到窗外风吹打着树林的声音，我便起来在墙壁上写道：'满城风雨近重阳'。可是这时收租金的人却突然来了，这让我完全失去了兴致而无法再写下去了。因此我现在只有这一句寄给你了。"

该成语比喻消息一经传出，就引起轰动，到处议论纷纷。

The Talk of the Town

In the Song Dynasty (AD 960–1279), there was a renowned poet named Pan Dalin who lived in Huangzhou. As the Double Ninth Festival was approaching, one of his friends wrote a letter asking whether he had newly composed poems. Pan Dalin replied, "Everything in the charming autumn is inspiring enough for me to write poems. Yesterday, when I was having a rest, watching the trees sway in the autumn wind and rain, inspired by the scene, I wrote a beautiful line: 'The Double Ninth Festival is approaching with wind and rain sweeping across the town.' Just at this moment, the rent collector came to demand payment and my inspiration vanished. So this is the only line that I can share with you."

Later the first line written by Pan Dalin became an idiom which means the stir and wide discussion caused by the spread of news.

盲人摸象

从前，有四个盲人很想知道大象是什么样子，可他们看不见，只好用手摸。

胖盲人先摸到了大象的牙齿。他就说："我知道了，大象就像一个又大、又粗、又光滑的大萝卜。"高个子盲人摸到的是大象的耳朵。"不对，不对，大象明明是一把大蒲扇嘛！"他大叫起来。"你们净瞎说，大象只是根大柱子。"原来矮个子盲人摸到了大象的腿。而那位年老的盲人呢，却嘟囔："唉，大象哪有那么大，它只不过是一根草绳。"原来他摸到的是大象的尾巴。四个盲人争吵不休，都说自己摸到的才是大象真正的样子。

该成语比喻片面观察事物的人，不了解事物的整体。

Blind Men Sizing Up an Elephant

Once upon a time, there were four blind men who wished to know what an elephant looked like, but what they could do was nothing but touching it with their hands.

The fat blind man felt the elephant's tusks and said, "An elephant is like a big, thick and smooth turnip." The tall blind man touched the elephant's ears and shouted, "No, no, the elephant is obviously a big fan!" "You're talking drivel. It is like a big column," said the short blind man when he put his arms around one of the elephant's legs. But the aged blind man who held the tail said, "An elephant is merely a rope." They then fell to arguing with each other, saying that what they felt was what the elephant really looked like.

This idiom is used to satirize those who know only part of a thing rather than the entirety or essence.

M

毛遂自荐

战国时，秦国出兵攻打赵国，包围了赵都邯郸，情况十分危急，于是赵王派平原君前往楚国，请求援救。平原君打算在其门下食客中挑选出二十个文武人才一同前往，但只挑选出十九个，剩下的都不符合条件。这时，有一个名叫毛遂的人，主动向平原君自我推荐，请求加入前往楚国的行列。

到了楚国，平原君和楚王会谈，从早上到中午，都还没有结果。毛遂于是持剑走到楚王面前，极力说明赵、楚联合抗秦的利害关系。楚王终于被说服，答应赵国愿意出兵援救。于是两国当场歃血为盟，誓守联合抗秦的盟约。

该成语比喻自告奋勇，自我推荐。

Mao Sui Volunteering for Service

During the Warring States Period (AD 960–1279), the State of Qin sent troops to attack the State of Zhao. When Handan, the capital of Zhao was besieged by the Qin's troops, the King of the State Zhao sent Lord Pingyuan to the State of Chu for help. He planned to select a team of 20 capable men to go with him, but only 19 were selected and the rest did not meet the requirements. At this time, a man named Mao Sui voluntarily recommended himself to Lord Pingyuan to join in the team.

Upon their arrival in the State of Chu, Lord Pingyuan and the King of the State of Chu engaged in negotiations from the morning till noon, but no agreement was reached. When the negotiations were stalled because of the King of Chu's hesitation, Mao Sui approached him, brandishing a sword. Mao Sui explained the gains and losses of their alliance against the State of Qin in an agitated tone. At last, the King of Chu agreed to help the State of Zhao and they swore an oath of alliance.

This idiom means recommending oneself.

门庭若市

战国时代，大臣邹忌劝谏齐威王说："现在齐国地方千里，城池众多，大王接触的人也多，所受的蒙蔽也一定更多。大王如能开诚布公地征求意见，一定对国家有益。"

齐威王听了，觉得很有道理，立刻下令说"无论是谁，能当面指出我过失的，给上赏；上奏章规劝我的，给中赏；在朝廷或街市中议论我的过失，并传到我耳中的，给下赏！"命令一下，群臣前去进谏的，一时川流不息，朝廷门口每天像市场一样热闹。

该成语用来形容来往人多、热闹非凡的景象。

A Courtyard as Crowded as a Fair Market

In the Warring States Period (457–221 BC), the minister Zou Ji proposed to the King Wei of the State of Qi, “Now the State of Qi occupies one thousand li and has many cities. Your Majesty, you have so many concubines and the subordinates dote on you very much. Who isn’t afraid of you? So you are hoodwinked very much. If you can gather opinions widely on ruling the state, our state will prosper.”

Therefore, the King Wei of Qi issued an order: “Regardless of whether a man is a minister or an official, anyone who points out my faults in person will get the first prize; anyone who advises me in a memorial will be rewarded the second prize; anyone who criticizes me in public will get the third prize.” When people learned about this, they flocked to the palace to present their opinions. The area in front of the palace was very like a market.

The idiom describes a very busy scene.

M

孟母三迁

孟子是战国时期的大学问家，他有一个很伟大的母亲。孟子的母亲，世人称为孟母。孟子小时候，居住的地方离墓地很近，孟子学了些祭拜之类的事，玩起办理丧事的游戏。他的母亲说：“这个地方不适合孩子居住。”于是将家搬到集市旁，孟子学了些做买卖和屠杀的事。母亲又想：“这个地方还是不适合孩子居住。”又将家搬到学宫旁边。孟子学会了在朝廷上鞠躬行礼及进退的礼节。孟母说：“这才是孩子居住的地方。”就在这里定居下来了。

该成语用来表示人应该要接近好的人、事、物，才能学习到好的习惯。

Three Moves by Mencius's Mother

In the Warring States Period (457–221 BC), there was a famous scholar named Mencius who had a great mother. When Mencius was young, they lived near a graveyard. Mencius often imitated the funeral ceremony and built tombs. His mother thought that was very disadvantageous to Mencius. So she moved to a place near a market. Because there were many businessmen, Mencius was imperceptibly influenced by what he saw and heard and learned how to do business and how to slaughter livestock in a short time. His mother was very disappointed again and moved their house to a place near a school. Mencius began to learn how to read books and the etiquettes among officials. Mencius's mother was very satisfied and said, "This is the very place I'm looking for." So they settled down.

The idiom means that a man's future is in connection with his surroundings.

名落孙山

在我国宋朝的时候，有一个名叫孙山的才子，他不但为人幽默，而且很善于说笑话。

有一次，他和一个同乡的儿子一同到京城，去参加举人的考试。放榜的时候，孙山的名字虽然被列在榜文的倒数第一名，但仍然是榜上有名，而和他一起去的那位同乡的儿子，却没有考上。

不久，孙山先回到家里，同乡便来问他儿子有没有考取。孙山既不好意思直说，又不便隐瞒，便笑了笑说："榜上的最后一名是我孙山，而令郎的名字却还在我孙山的后面。"

该成语比喻考试没有通过或选拔没有被录取。

Come After Sun Shan

In the Song Dynasty (AD 960–1279), there was a scholar named Sun Shan. He was humorous and always told jokes.

One year he went to take the imperial examination with his neighbor's son. When the result came out, he was at the bottom of the list of successful candidates. Though he ranked the last, he was included in the list. But his neighbor's son was not in the list.

Back to his hometown, one of his neighbors asked him whether the neighbor's son had also passed. Sun Shan felt embarrassed to tell the truth directly, so he said with a smile, "Sun Shan was the last on the list. Your son came after Sun Shan."

The idiom is used to indicate failing in an examination or competition.

磨杵成针

唐朝著名大诗人李白小时候不喜欢念书。一天，李白又没有去上学，走着走着，不知不觉到了城外。

在一个破茅屋门口，坐着一个满头白发的老婆婆，正在磨一根棍子般粗的铁杵。李白走过去问“老婆婆，您在做什么？”老婆婆抬起头，对李白笑了笑说，“我要把这根铁杵磨成一根绣花针。”接着又低下头继续磨着。李白又问：“可是，铁杵这么粗，什么时候能磨成细细的绣花针呢？”老婆婆说：“只要我下的功夫比别人深，没有做不到的事情。”

老婆婆的一番话，令李白很惭愧，于是回去之后，再没有逃过学。每天的学习也特别用功，终于成了名垂千古的诗仙。

该成语比喻只要有恒心，再难的事也能做成。

Grind an Iron Pestle into a Needle

Li Bai, a famous poet in Tang Dynasty (AD 618–907), did not like studying when he was a child. One day, Li Bai skipped class again. Walking along the street, he went outside the city.

At the door of a shabby hut sat an old woman with white hair, grinding an iron pestle as thick as a stick. Li Bai walked over and asked, "Granny, what are you doing?" The old woman smiled and said, "I'm going to grind this iron pestle into an embroidery needle." Then she lowered her head to continue grinding. Li Bai continued to ask, "What a thick iron pestle! When can you grind it into a fine embroidery needle?" "The old woman said, "As long as I persist to the end, I can do it."

After having heard those words, Li Bai was very ashamed of what he had done. Since then, he had never skipped class after he went back. He studied very hard every day and finally became a famous poet through the ages.

The idiom means that any task can be accomplished as long as one persists to the end.

N

南辕北辙

魏王想攻打赵国，季梁劝他说：“我在大路上遇到一个赶着车向北走的人，告诉我说：‘我要去楚国。’我问他：‘你要去的楚国在南面，为什么要向北呢？’他说：‘我的马好。’我说：‘您的马虽然好，但这不是去楚国的路啊！’他又说：‘我的路费很充足。’我说：‘你的路费虽然多，但这不是去楚国的路啊！’他又说：‘给我驾车的人本领很高。’他不知道方向错了，赶路的条件越好，离楚国的距离就会越远。”

季梁接着说：“现在大王动不动就想称霸诸侯，办什么事都想取得天下的信任，依仗自己国家强大、军队精锐，而去攻打邯郸，想扩展地盘抬高声威，岂不知您这样的行动越多，距离统一天下为王的目标就越远，这正像要去楚国却向北走的行为一样啊！”

该成语比喻行动和目的正好相反。

Try to Go South by Driving the Chariot North

In the Warring States Period (457–221 BC), the King of the State of Wei intended to send troops to the State of Zhao. Ji Liang tried to persuade him through a story: "Once I met a man whose carriage was heading north, and the man told me, 'I want to go to the State of Chu.' I asked him, 'Why are you heading north if you want to go to the State of Chu in the south?' The man answered, 'I prepared enough money for the journey.' I replied, "But this is the wrong way." He continued, 'my driver is highly skilled at driving a carriage.' The man didn't consider the direction first. The better his conditions were, the further he was away from his destination."

"Your Majesty", Ji Liang said, "If you want to proclaim hegemony and obtain the trust of other states, it's not correct to depend on the power of the nation and the strength of the army. If you invade Handan to expand the territory, the more you do, the further will you be away from becoming the king of trust. It's just like going to the State of Chu in the south by driving north."

The idiom means acting in a way that defeats one's purpose.

怒发冲冠

战国时代，赵惠文王得到一块稀世的璧玉，称为和氏璧。秦昭王知道后，便企图据为己有。于是他假意写信给赵王，表示愿用 15 座城来换这块璧。赵王怕有诈，不想把和氏璧送去，但又怕秦王派兵来犯。赵王召见蔺相如，并派他带了和氏璧出使秦国。

蔺相如把和氏璧献给秦王，秦王接过璧后，非常高兴，看了又看，根本没有交付城池的意思。蔺相如见秦王如此轻蔑无礼，便上前道："这璧上还有点小的毛病，请让我指给大王看。"

蔺相如把璧拿到手后，极度愤怒，头发直竖，顶起帽子，激昂地说："赵王和大臣们商量后，都认为秦国想骗取和氏璧，因而本不打算把璧送给秦国。今天我到这里，发现果真如此，所以我把璧取了回来。大王如要威逼我，我情愿把自己的头与璧一起在柱子上撞个粉碎！"在这种情况下，秦王只得道歉，并答应五天后受璧。蔺相如预料秦王不会交城，私下让人把璧送归赵国。

该成语形容人愤怒到了极点。

So Angry that One's Hair Raises One's Hat

During the Warring States Period (457–221 BC), the King Huiwen of the State of Zhao received a rare piece of jade called Heshi Jade. After King Zhao of the State of Qin knew about it, he tried to take it for himself. So he wrote to the King of Zhao and offered to exchange 15 cities for this piece of jade. The King of Zhao thought that the King of Qin might cheat and did not want to offer Heshi Jade, but he was afraid that the State of Zhao would be in danger if he refused. So the King of Zhao sent Lin Xiangru to the State of Qin with the Heshi Jade.

Lin Xiangru presented the jade to the King of Qin. The King was very happy after taking over the jade and looked at it over again and again, showing no intention to exchange the city for the jade. Seeing that the King of Qin was so contemptuous and disrespectful, Lin Xiangru stepped forward and said, "Your Majesty, there is a flaw in this jade and please let me show you."

When Lin Xiangru took the jade, he was so angry that his hair raised his hat. He said excitedly, "After discussing with the ministers, the King of Zhao considered that Qin wanted to gain the jade by cheating, so he did not intend to give the jade to you. I come here today and find out the truth, so I took it back. Your Majesty, if you force me, I would rather smash my head and the jade together against the pillar!" In this case, the King of Qin had to apologize and promised to receive the jade five days later. Lin Xiangru anticipated that the King of Qin would never hand over the city, so he arranged privately and got the jade intact back to the State of Zhao.

The idiom means being extremely angry.

P

披荆斩棘

冯异是东汉初期一位著名的军事将领，是皇帝刘秀手下的一员大将，立下不少战功，成为东汉的开国功臣之一。公元30年，冯异到京城洛阳朝拜光武帝。光武帝隆重地接待了他，并向文武百官介绍说："他是我当年起兵时的主将，为我劈开了道路上丛生的荆棘，扫除了重重障碍，平定了关中广大地区，是个有功之臣啊！"由于冯异谦虚好学，所以深得人们敬仰。

该成语比喻在清除前进道路上的障碍，克服困难。

Break Through Brambles and Thorns

Feng Yi was a famous military general who served Liu Xiu, the Emperor of the Eastern Han Dynasty (AD 25–220). He made many achievements and helped the Emperor attain the throne, becoming one of the founding heroes. In AD 30, Feng Yi went to Luoyang, the capital city, to pay respect to the Emperor Guangwu. The Emperor received him ceremoniously and introduced him to civil and military officials, "Feng Yi helped me to gain power. He was the commanding general when I dispatched the army. I succeeded because he broke through the thistles and thorns on the way and stabilized vast area of Guanzhong Region." Because Feng Yi was modest and knowledgeable, he was deeply respected by people.

This idiom refers to blazing a way through all manners of obstacles.

P

破釜沉舟

秦朝末年，楚霸王项羽率领部队与秦军作战。部队渡过漳河以后，项羽命令士兵把所有的船只都毁掉沉到河底，把行军的饭锅全部打碎，每人只发给三天的粮食。项羽这样做的目的，是向大家表明只能胜利前进、不能失败后退的决心。

楚军士兵见主帅的决心这么大，就谁也不打算再活着回去。在项羽亲自指挥下，他们以一当十，以十当百，拼死拼活地向秦军冲杀过去，经过连续冲锋，把秦军打得大败。秦军的几个主将，有的被杀，有的当了俘虏，有的投了降。这一仗终于打垮了秦军，又过了两年，秦朝就灭亡了。

该成语比喻下定最后的决心，不顾一切干到底。

Break the Cauldrons and Sink the Boats

During the late years of the Qin Dynasty (221–207 BC), Xiang Yu led a rebellion. After crossing the Zhanghe River, Xiang Yu ordered his men to sink all their boats and break their cooking pots. Each soldier was allocated three days' rations. Xiang Yu warned them that there was no way to retreat and the only way to survive was to advancc and fight.

The soldiers of the Chu army saw that the commander in chief was so determined that no one intended to return alive. Under Xiang Yu's personal command, they pit one against ten in killing the soldiers of Qin. After several fierce battles, some of Qin's chief commanders were killed, some became prisoners and some surrendered. The defeat led to the downfall of Qin Dynasty two years later.

This idiom is used to indicate one's firm determination to achieve the goal at any cost.

Q

杞人忧天

春秋时代的杞国，有一个喜欢胡思乱想的人。有一天，他竟然想到：假如有一天，天塌了下来，那该怎么办呢？我们岂不是无路可逃了吗？

从此以后，他几乎每天为这个问题发愁。朋友都很替他担心，都跑来劝他说：“你何必为这件事自寻烦恼呢？天空怎么会塌下来呢？再说即使真的塌下来，那也不是你一个人忧虑发愁就可以解决的啊，想开点吧！”

可是，无论人家怎么说，他都不相信，仍然时常为这个不必要的问题担忧。

该成语讽刺那些为一些不切实际的事情而忧愁的人。

A Man of Qi Who Feared That the Sky Might Fall

In the Spring-Autumn Period (770–476 BC), there was a man in the State of Qi who was worrying all the time that one day in the future the sky would fall. "What if the sky falls? Where can I find a shelter at that time?"

From then on, he worried about that all day long. His friends were all worried about him and told him, "Why do you bother yourself about this? The sky will never fall. Even if the sky does fall down, it's not something you can solve by worrying alone. Just relax."

He didn't believe in others and still suffered a lot from his fears that were groundless.

The idiom satirizes those who has groundless fears.

Q

千里鹅毛

唐朝有一个地方官，偶然得到了一只稀有的天鹅，便派一位名叫缅伯高的心腹拿去向皇帝进贡。缅伯高抱着天鹅，走到潘阳湖边时，忽然觉得应该停下来给天鹅洗个澡，就小心翼翼地将天鹅放入水中。

不料，天鹅却振翅飞走了，只掉下一根鹅毛。缅伯高没有办法，只好拿着这根鹅毛面见皇帝。他害怕皇帝处罚自己，就编了一首顺口溜，大意是这样的："我来向您朝贡，经过了万水千山，可到了潘阳湖时天鹅飞走了；我悲痛欲绝，今天上复天子，请您饶了缅伯高。再说，千里送鹅毛，礼轻情意重。"皇帝听后，饶了缅伯高。

该成语比喻情深义重的微小礼品。

A Goose Feather Brought from Afar

In the Tang Dynasty (AD 618–907), a local magistrate captured a rare swan. He appointed a person named Mian Bogao to present the swan to the emperor. Mian Bogao held the swan with his arms with special care to make sure that nothing would go wrong. When he arrived at Panyang Lake, he stopped for a rest and put the swan in the water for a bath.

To his surprise, the swan flew away and left a feather. It was impossible for Mian Bogao to catch the swan, so he brought the swan feather to present to the emperor. He was so afraid of being punished that he wrote doggerel: "I meant to bring a swan to present to the Tang court despite of the long journey of towering mountains. On the bank of Panyang Lake the swan flew away and I fell to the ground with depression. I've reported to you the Emperor of Tang. Please show the mercy upon Mian Bogao. Small as my gift is, the sincerity contained is heavy. From thousands of miles afar I've brought you a swan feather. " After having heard the doggerel, the emperor forgave Mian Bogao.

The idiom indicates a small gift sent from afar which conveys sincere heart.

Q

黔驴技穷

从前贵州一带没有毛驴，有人从北方运来一头毛驴放到山脚下吃草。山上的老虎发现了这个怪物，开始只是远远地望着，然后慢慢地靠近毛驴，驴子大叫一声，老虎吓了一跳，以为驴子要吃掉自己。时间一长，老虎觉得驴子并没有什么恶意，逐渐走近去戏弄它，触犯它。最后发现毛驴只能用蹄踢，再也没有别的本事。于是立即扑过去，一口把它咬死吃掉了。

该成语比喻有限的一点本领也已经用完了。

A Guizhou Donkey with Exhausted Tricks

In ancient times there were no donkey in Guizhou Province. Somebody brought a donkey from somewhere and left it at the foot of a mountain. When the donkey was grazing, a tiger saw it and was very afraid of it, thinking that it might be a kind of monster. The tiger kept a distance from the donkey and observed it, then got near. The donkey brayed at the sight of the tiger, and the tiger was frightened and ran away. It thought the donkey might eat itself but after several attempts, the tiger found out that the donkey had no special tricks. With more days passing by, the tiger found out that when the donkey was angry, it kicked with its hoofs and nothing more. Then the tiger jumped on the donkey and ate it.

The idiom is used to indicate that one looks impressive but lack of real tricks.

人面桃花

相传，唐朝诗人崔护进京应试，于清明节游长安城南，见一村舍为桃花环绕。崔护因口渴敲门讨水，有一美丽的少女开门送水，两人一见钟情，相对而视，脉脉含情。

A Charming Face Among Peach Blossoms

This idiom originates from a beautiful romantic story that happened in the Tang Dynasty (AD 618–907).

One year, Cui Hu, a poet of Tang, went to Chang'an, the capital of China at that time, to take the imperial examination. On tomb-sweeping day, he went out to the southern suburb of the city to relax himself, where he saw a cottage surrounded by peach blossoms. He was thirsty after a long walk, so he knocked at the door of the cottage to ask for some water. A beautiful girl came to answer the door, and her face was as beautiful as the peach blossoms in the early spring, making Cui fall in love with her at the first sight. It seemed that the girl was also impressed by Cui, for she looked into Cui's eyes for some time before she blushed and left.

第二年清明，崔护重游旧地，桃花依然盛开，而门却锁着。崔护不胜惆怅，提笔写《题都城南庄》诗在门上，“去年今日此门中，人面桃花相映红。人面不知何处去，桃花依旧笑春风。”那少女外出回来，看到门上的诗，后悔外出，相思成病，绝食而死。过了几天，崔护又来敲门，出来一位老人说：“我女儿读了门上的诗，抱病而死，尸体还放在屋内。”崔护跑进屋内，跪在少女的尸体面前大声哭叫“我崔护来了！”那少女竟活过来了，两人遂结为百年之好。

后人取诗中“人面桃花”指所爱慕而不能相见的女子，也用于无缘再见的伤感情景。

This unexpected encounter made Cui fall into love-sickness. On the next tomb-sweeping day, Cui couldn't wait to come to the cottage again, expecting to meet his beloved girl again. However, it was a pity that despite the same peach blossoms, the door was locked, and the girl was nowhere to be found. Feeling disappointed, Cui then wrote a poem on the door, which reads like this:

In this cottage on this day last year, a pink face unveiled,
In beauty with the pink peach blossoms side by side.
I do not know today where the pink face has gone,
In vernal wind still smile pink peach blossoms full-blown.

The girl, when coming back, saw the poem, and knew at once who wrote it. She was so regretful that she went out on such a special day, then fell ill and died.

Days later, Cui came back again, and was informed by an old man that his beloved girl had already been dead, which made Cui burst into tears. He then went inside the cottage and cried beside her dead body, saying heart-breakingly, "I'm Cui Hu, the one who wrote the poem. I'm back, but why did you leave?" To everyone's surprise, the girl came back to her life. Cui was so glad to see the girl live and vivid again that they two got married soon.

From then on, people in China use the phrase to describe the beloved girl whom a man can not meet, or the melancholy scene in which people have no chance to meet each other again.

日暮途穷

春秋末期，楚平王的太子建有两个老师，一个是伍奢，一个是费无忌。费无忌得到荒淫无道的楚平王的宠爱，可是他又怕太子登位后会对他不利，于是便诬告太子及伍奢。没想到平王竟然相信，盛怒之下下令将太子及伍奢处死。

On One's Last Legs

During the late Spring-Autumn Period (770–221 BC), Prince Jian, the crown prince of Chu, had two preceptors, respectively Wu She and Fei Wuji. King Ping, the ruler of Chu, was notorious for his lechery and arrogance. There were always political infighting and intrigue among the officials. Prince Jian and Wu She fell victims to such competitions since Fei Wuji spoke ill of them in front of the king for fear that they might go against Fei once Prince Jian ascended the throne. Sadly, Fei's lies worked. King Ping was easily taken in by the fake stories and became so irritated that he issued an instruction to put Prince Jian and Wu She to death.

心狠的费无忌还不愿罢休，他想到伍奢有两个儿子，于是他又派人杀害了伍奢的大儿子伍尚，只有伍奢的小儿子伍员逃过了一劫。平王听信费无忌的谎言，认为伍员是叛徒，因此下令追捕伍员。伍员为了逃命，一夜之间头发胡子全白了。后来他逃到了吴国，帮助吴王，建议派兵攻打楚国，经过五次战争，终于打到楚国都城，这时平王已死，伍员为了报杀父兄之仇，便挖出平王的尸体，亲自鞭尸。伍员的老朋友知道之后便责备他。伤心的伍员对他说："我像一个走路的人，此时天色已晚，但是路却很远，所以会做些违背常理的事。"

To eliminate the source of the trouble, Fei also sent killers to get Wu Shang and Wu Yuan, the two sons of Wu She. Fortunately, Wu Yuan, the second son of Wu She, narrowly escaped in the ruthless murder and went away, which was framed by Fei as defection. King Ping believed Fei's words once again and issued an order to kill Wu Yuan, who, out of great anxiety, turned a gray-haired man overnight. Wu Yuan succeeded in taking refuge in the state of Wu. Under Wu Yuan's help, the King of Wu finally defeated the troop of Chu, creating a good opportunity for Wu Yuan to revenge himself on King Ping, then a dead man already. Wu Yuan exhumed King Ping's dead body for public flogging, which was thought by his old friends as an inhuman deed. To respond to his friends, Wu Yuan gave the following explanation, "I'm just like a person who is still far from his destination when the darkness is drawing. That is to say, I am on my last legs, having no choice but to do something that may be contrary to ethics or morality."

R

如火如荼

春秋时代末期，吴国国王夫差连续征服了越国、鲁国和齐国，雄心勃勃，又继续向西北进军，打算一鼓作气征服晋国。

可正在这个时候，越王勾践抄了吴王的后路。他带领军队一直打到吴国的国都苏州，又派人马占据淮河，把吴王的退路切断了。

这消息给吴王夫差当头泼了一盆冷水，他非常震惊，立即召集文臣武将商量对策。大家说，现在退回去会两头挨打；如果能打败晋国，就等于在诸侯国中当定了霸主，再回去收拾越王勾践也不算晚。大主意已经拿定，当务之急是尽快征服晋国。考虑再三，决定出奇制胜。

Like a Raging Fire

During the late Spring-Autumn Period (770–221 BC), Fu Chai, the ruler of the State of Wu, defeated the states of Yue, Lu and Chi consecutively. These military victories encouraged Fu Chai's ambition so greatly that he planned to conquer the State of Jin.

However, Gou Jian, ruler of the State of Wu, attacked Fu Chai in the rear when Fu Chai's troop were on their way to Jin. Gou Jian's troop took Soochow, the capital of Wu, and took control of Huaihe River, making it impossible for Fu Chai's troop to retreat.

Fu Chai, taken aback by the unexpected attack, summoned all his think tank to find solutions to deal with the crisis. A consensus was finally reached: it is by no means a wise choice to retreat for it will make their troop assaulted by both the Jin army and the Yue army. The right way is to defeat Jin first, and then Fu Chai will become the hegemon, making it a piece of cake to deal with Gou Jian. With this consensus in mind, Fu Chai determined to launch a sudden attack against Jin, so as to defeat Jin as soon as possible.

一天傍晚，吴王下达了命令。全军将士吃得饱饱的，马也喂足了草料。从全军中挑出三万精兵强将。每一万人摆成一个方阵，共摆三个方阵。每个方阵横竖都是一百人。每一行排头的都是军官。每十行，也就是一千人，由一个大夫负责。每个方阵由一名将军率领。中间的方阵白盔白甲、白衣服、白旗帜、白弓箭，由吴王自己掌握，称为中军；左边的方阵，红盔红甲、红衣服、红旗帜、红弓箭；右边的方阵则一水儿黑色。吴军半夜出发，黎明时分到达离晋军仅有一里路的地方。天色刚刚显出亮色，吴军鼓声大作，欢呼之声震天动地。晋军从梦中醒来，一看吴军那三个方阵和声威气势，简直都惊呆了：那白色方阵，望之如荼——像开满白花的茅草地；那红色方阵，望之如火——像熊熊燃烧的火焰；而那黑色的方阵，简直就像深不可测的大海。被这骇人的场面完全震住的晋军，很快就被打败了。

从那时起，人们便用“如火如荼”来形容某一事件或活动旺盛热烈的势头。

One day, before the nightfall came, Fu Chai gave out the order to attack Jin. Officers and soldiers, as well as war horses, all went out to battle on full stomachs. 30,000 soldiers were selected as crack troops and were evenly divided into three phalanxes, 10,000 soldiers in one phalanx. In each phalanx, 100 soldiers were lined up in every direction, the one at the top of each line being officer. Every ten lines were led by a senior officer, while every phalanx was led by a general. The phalanx in the middle, called middle troop, was led by Fu Chai himself. Soldiers in the middle troop all wore white suits of amour, and carried white flags and white bows and arrows. Soldiers in the phalanx on the left all wore red suits of amour, and carried red flags and red bows and arrows. The phalanx on the right was all black, as splendid as the other two phalanxes. They set out at midnight and were just a stone's throw away from the army of Jin at dawn. Jin's army were still in their sleep when Wu soldiers beat drums and shouted, making Jin soldiers awake to find the three phalanxes in their full tides. They mistook the white phalanx for field with flowering rush, the red phalanx a sea of raging fire. Totally shocked from the horrendous scenery, Jin soldiers were defeated in a short time.

Since then, people use the phrase "like a raging fire" to refer to tremendous momentum of certain events.

R

如鱼得水

三国时期，刘备曾长期依附于宗亲刘表。可是刘备是个胸怀大志的人，他并不想长久地寄人篱下，只做别人的客将。正好这个时候徐庶向他推荐诸葛亮是个难得的人才，徐庶劝刘备一定要网罗诸葛亮。

为了请诸葛亮协助自己获得天下，刘备曾经三次亲自到他住地隆中的茅庐拜访他，诸葛亮看到刘备非常诚恳，最后才同意与刘备见面。刘备向他请教许多治理国家的方法，诸葛亮仔细分析了当时的情势，建议刘备先占据荆州，这样才能有机会和曹操、孙权鼎足而立，互相抗衡。

刘备很欣赏诸葛亮的见解，而且和诸葛亮的感情逐渐加深，刘备甚至高兴地对结拜兄弟关羽及张飞两人说:“我得到诸葛亮的辅助，就好像鱼得了水一样。”

从此，该成语便用于形容找到了志同道合的伙伴或身处于理想的环境中。

To Feel Just Like a Fish in Water

In the Three Kingdoms Period (AD 220–280), Liu Bei had clung to Liu Biao, his clan relative, for a long time. However, Liu Bei had his ambition, dreaming to build up his own army and get rid of being others' guest commander. Xu Shu recommended Zhuge Liang to him as a rare talent, of which Liu Bei approved without any doubt.

In order to get Zhuge Liang's assistance, Liu Bei went to the thatched cottage in Long Zhong where Zhuge Liang lived for three times. Zhuge Liang was then touched by Liu Bei's sincerity and they met each other finally, exchanging ideas on how to govern a state. Zhuge Liang suggested Liu Bei to take Jingzhou as his base area, and to develop a state to confront the two other states, respectively led by Cao Cao and Sun Quan.

Liu Bei trusted Zhuge Liang and their respects to each other became deeper day by day. One day, Liu Bei even told Guan Yu and Zhang Fei, his two sworn brothers, "With Zhuge Liang's assistance, I felt just like a fish in water."

From then on, this phrase is used to signify finding a boon companion or an ideal situation.

R

入木三分

王羲之是中国古代一位杰出的书法家，在历史上享有很高的评价，被后人称为“书圣”。

有一天，他把字写在木板上，拿给刻字的人照着雕刻。这个人先用刀削木板，却发现笔迹竟然透进木板里有三分深度，他惊讶地说道：“这写字的手可真有力呀！”这件事情可是轰动了整个京城，“入木三分”也就成了人人皆知的成语了。

于是，后来的人便根据这段故事的情节，直接用“入木三分”来形容人们写文章，或者是说话的内容非常深刻。

以后只要说故事的人，把故事的情节说得生动逼真，我们也可以夸赞他说故事说得“入木三分”。

Written in a Forceful Hand

Wang Xizhi, an outstanding calligrapher in ancient China, enjoys a high reputation and is honored as "Sage of Calligraphy".

One day, with an ink brush in hand, Wang wrote some Chinese words on a piece of wood, so as to make an engraver inscribe the words. The engraver, when cutting the wood, found the ink of the handwriting had penetrated into the wood for almost a centimeter. The engraver then exclaimed, "These words are written in a forceful hand!" This caused a sensation in whole capital.

Since then, the phrase "written in a forceful hand" became a popularly accepted idiom in China to refer to sharp ideas and insightful views.

In addition, when a story is told in a very vivid way, this idiom is also used as a compliment to the story-teller, which means he has made the story almost a real one.

R

如坐针毡

西晋时候有个叫杜锡的人，学识渊博，性格非常耿直，在做了太子中舍人以后，多次规劝晋惠帝的儿子愍怀太子。愍怀太子不仅不听劝告，反而对杜锡心怀怨恨，便故意在杜锡坐的毡垫中放了一些针。杜锡没有发觉，屁股被扎得鲜血直流。第二天，太子故意问杜锡：“你昨天出了什么事？”杜锡难以开口，只好说：“昨天喝醉了，不知道干了些什么。”太子说：“你喜欢责备别人，为什么自己也做错了事呢？”杜锡不敢回答，又不能走，哭笑不得。

后来，人们用“如坐针毡”这个成语，来形容人们心神不定、坐立不安的样子。

On Pins and Needles

In the Western Jin Dynasty (AD 265–316), there was a man of deep learning named Du Xi, who was candid and upright. When working in the cabinet as a minister, he had chance to be by the side of Prince Min Huai, the crown prince of Emperor Huidi. Min Huai was a man with no attempts to make progress, and had an irritable disposition. As a minister, Du Xi regarded it as his obligation to help the prince to mend his ways, criticizing him everyday.

However, Min Huai was not a wise man who would take advice with a receptive mind. Instead, he was unhappy about Du Xi's advice and was thinking of teaching Du a lesson.

One day, he secretly sent someone to fill the cushion that Du Xi usually sat on with needles. Du Xi didn't notice the needles, and was stuck so badly that he even bled.

On the following day, Min Huai asked Du, "I heard you were injured. What happened?" Feeling embarrassed to tell the truth, Du answered, "Actually I knew nothing because I was quite drunk yesterday." Min Huai then laughed, saying, "How come you also do wrong things?" This made Du very embarrassed.

Nowadays, people use the phrase "on pins and needles" to describe people who feel anxious and preoccupied.

塞翁失马

靠近北方边境一带居住的人中有一个精通术数的人。

有一天，他们家的马无缘无故跑到了胡人的住地。人们都前来安慰他。那个老人说："这怎么就不能是一件好事呢？"过了几个月，那匹马带着胡人的良马回来了。人们都前来祝贺他们一家。那个老人说："这怎么就不能是一件坏事呢？"

他家中有很多好马，他的儿子喜欢骑马，结果从马上掉下来摔得大腿骨折。人们都前来安慰他们一家。那个老人说："这怎么就不能是一件好事呢？"过了一年，胡人大举入侵边境一带，壮年男子都拿起弓箭去作战。靠近边境一带的人，绝大部分都死了。唯独这个人的儿子因为腿瘸的缘故免于征战，父子得以保全生命。

现在人们用"塞翁失马"这个成语来安慰遭受不幸的人。它表明：不幸有时也会成为好运，而好运有时也会变成不幸。

A Blessing in Disguise

In ancient time, among border residents in northern China, there was an old man skillful at astrology.

One day, one of his horses ran off to the territory of the barbarians. His neighbors came to console him, for which he replied, "This might turn out to be a good thing." Months later, his horse came back to him with a steed of the barbarians'. IIis neighbors then came again to congratulate him, for which the old man replied, "This might turn out to be a misfortune."

His prediction was once again proved to be correct. One day, his son, when riding a horse, dropped from the horse back and broke his legs. This time, neighbors came again to comfort him, for which, just like before, the old man replied in an unexpected way, "This might eventually turn out to be a blessing in disguise."

A year later, when the barbarians invaded the border, young border residents, except the old man's son, were recruited to fight against the barbarians, and most of them were killed in the war. Due to the broken legs, the son's life was spared.

Nowadays people use the phrase "a blessing in disguise" as a comfort to people suffering misfortune, which implies: bad luck may turn out to be good luck, while good luck may turn out to bring disaster.

三顾茅庐

东汉末年，诸葛亮居住在隆中的茅庐里。

谋士徐庶向刘备推荐说：诸葛亮是个奇才。刘备为了请诸葛亮帮助自己打天下，就同关羽、张飞一起去请他出山。可是诸葛亮不在家，刘备只好留下姓名，怏怏不乐地回去。隔了几天，刘备打听到诸葛亮回来了，又带着关羽、张飞冒着风雪前去。哪知诸葛亮又出门了，刘备他们又空走一趟。

刘备第三次去隆中，终于见到了诸葛亮。在交谈中，诸葛亮对天下形势做了非常精辟的分析，刘备十分叹服。

刘备三顾茅庐，使诸葛亮非常感动，答应出山相助。刘备尊诸葛亮为军师，对关羽、张飞说："我之有孔明，犹鱼之有水也！"

诸葛亮初出茅庐，就帮刘备打了不少胜仗，为刘备奠定了蜀汉的国基。

"三顾茅庐"成语由此而来。

Three Visits to the Cottage

In the late Eastern Han Dynasty (AD 25–220), Zhuge Liang lived in a thatched cottage in Longzhong as a recluse.

Xu Shu, an adviser to Liu Bei, recommended Zhuge Liang as a rare talent, of which Liu Bei approved without any doubt. In order to get Zhuge Liang's assistance, Liu Bei went to Zhuge's cottage in company with Guan Yu and Zhang Fei, his two sworn brothers. Unfortunately Zhuge Liang was not at home, so Liu Bei had to present his visiting card to Zhuge's servant and went back. Later, in a snowy and windy day, Liu, still in company with Guan and Zhang, visited the thatched cottage the second time. It was hard for Liu to accept that Zhuge was not at home once again.

It is the third visit when Liu Bei finally met Zhuge Liang in person. Liu admired Zhuge's ideas on how to confront other military forces in China at that time, as well as insights about how to run a state.

Liu Bei's three visits to the cottage, which showed his sincerity, made Zhuge Liang greatly moved. He complied with Liu's request and became his prime minister. With the help of Zhuge, Liu enlarged his territory and later established his own state—the Sate of Shu. Liu was grateful for Zhuge's help. One day, Liu even told Guan Yu and Zhang Fei, "With Zhuge Liang's assistance, I felt just like a fish in water."

Now the phrase "three visits to the cottage" used a lot to refer to refer to people's thirst for talents.

S

三人成虎

战国时代，魏王为了与赵国签订盟约，不得不去赵国首都——邯郸——当人质，这在当时是很常见的。魏国大臣庞恭陪伴魏国太子到邯郸做人质。

在临行前，庞恭对魏王说："要是现在有个人跑来说，热闹的街上出现了一只老虎，大王您相不相信？""不信！"魏王立刻答道。"如果同时有两个人跑来说，热闹的街上有一只大老虎，您相信吗？"庞恭又问。"我会怀疑。"魏王回答道。"那么要是三个人异口同声地说街上有只老虎时，您会相信吗？"庞恭接着问。魏王想了一会儿回答："我会相信。"

A Repeated Slander Makes Others Believe

In the Warring States Period (475–221 BC), the King of Wei, in order to sign a treaty of alliance with the State of Zhao, had to send the crown prince to Handan, the capital of Zhao, as a hostage, which was a usual practice between states at that time. Pang Gong, a minister of Wei, was to company the crown prince.

For fear that the King of Wei would doubt his loyalty, Pang, before leaving, asked the King a strange question, "if someone tell you there is a tiger on the street, would you believe it?"

"Of course I will not believe it!" the King answered without hesitate.

"Then if another man comes to tell you there is a tiger on the street, would you believe it?" Pang Gong asked again.

"In that case, I may think twice about it." the King seemed not so sure this time.

"Then if a third man comes to tell you about the tiger on the street, would you still not believe it?" Pang Gong repeated the question again.

For this, the King thought for a while and answered, "I think I will believe it."

于是庞恭就劝诫魏王："街市上不会有老虎，这是很明显的事。可是经过三个人一说，好像真的有了老虎。现在我要随太子去邯郸，邯郸可比街市远得多！一定会有更多的人在背后进谗言。希望大王明察此事。"魏王道："一切我自己知道。"可是，庞恭走前就有人诽谤他。随着谗言渐多，魏王忘记了"三人成虎"的故事，开始怀疑庞恭。庞恭从邯郸归来后，魏王果然没有再召见他了。

这个故事便是"三人成虎"的由来，比喻说的人多了，就能使人们把谣言当成事实。

"But you know there will be no tiger in the street. However, three whispers will make others believe it is a truth. It means a repeated slander makes others believe. Now I am to go to Handan with the crown prince and Handan is far further from your majesty than the street. I believe there will be more whispers about my going to Handan. I do hope your majesty will bc pcrceptive."

Hearing this, the King replied, "I know what you mean. Don't worry! Off you go!"

However, when Pang went to Handan, and after the King had heard enough rumors about Pang, the King forgot the three whispers story at once and began to suspect Pang. When Pang returned from Handan, the King didn't even summon him to the palace.

From the story comes the idiom "a repeated slander makes others believe." It suggests that gossips can be believed by repeat.

丧家之犬

春秋时期，孔子带领他的学生到各诸侯国讲学，因孔子是保守派，与当时诸侯争霸不合拍，常常受到冷遇。

一天，孔子和他的一行弟子又来到郑国。不料，在都城的东门外，孔子和他的弟子们走散了，只好孤零零地站在城门下等候。他的弟子子贡焦急地到处寻找孔子。有个郑国人问他找谁，他急切地说："喔，我在找我的老师，不知你见到过他吗？"那郑国人回答说："东门口有个老头儿，非常古怪。他那没精打采的样子，活像一条居丧人家的狗，不知他是不是你的老师？"子贡赶紧来到东门，找到了孔子，如实地将那郑国人的话说了。孔子听后很坦然地笑着说："外形、相貌，是细枝末节。不过说我像条无家可归的狗，确实是这样！确实是这样啊！"

To Feel Lost like a Stray Dog

In the Spring-Autumn Period (770–221 BC), Confucius and his disciples travelled to different states to deliver speeches about political issues and ritual principles. However, due to the fact Confucius' ideas were regarded as conservative by most rulers, Confucius seldom met courteous reception.

One day, Confucius' group arrived at the State of Zheng. Unfortunately, Confucius strayed away from his disciples and had no choice but to wait for his disciples lonely at the east gate of Zheng's capital.

Zi Gong, a disciple of Confucius, went everywhere in hurry to look for his teacher. A local resident inquired what made him seem so anxious. Zi Gong then answered, "I am looking for my teacher—an old man. Did you see an old man?"

The resident thought for a second and said, "I noticed there was a weird old man at the east gate, looking just like a stray dog. Do you mean him?"

Hearing the resident's words, Zi Gong rushed to the east gate in no time, only to find his teacher still waiting there alone.

Feeling so glad to find his teacher, Zi Gong told Confucius what the local resident said about him, for which Confucius replied, laughing, "although appearance is not an important thing for me, I do feel like a stray dog when I am waiting at the east gate."

杀鸡儆猴

有个耍猴戏的，新买了一只受过训练的猴子。这猴子可机灵了，他一听到鼓声就会跳舞，一听到锣声就会翻筋斗，可是就不听新主人的指挥。耍猴戏的使劲打鼓，使劲敲锣，猴子眨眨眼睛，一动也不动，只装作没听见。耍猴戏的想了个法子，他抓了一只公鸡来，对着公鸡又打鼓，又敲锣。公鸡怎么会演戏呢，它听到鼓声锣声早吓呆了，蹲在地上动也不敢动。耍猴戏的拿起一把刀，一刀把公鸡宰了。这一下可把猴子吓坏了。耍猴戏的一打鼓，它就连忙跳舞，一敲锣，他就连忙翻跟斗，一点儿也不敢含糊。“杀鸡儆猴”就是从这个故事来的。

后来，人们用“杀鸡儆猴”这个成语来指通过惩罚一个不相干的人，来威胁另一个人。

To Kill the Chicken to Frighten the Monkey

In ancient China, monkey tricks used to be a traditional performance. One man bought a well-trained but mischievous monkey, which would do everything except following its master's instructions. The monkey could dance and somersault to the accompaniment of gongs and drums, but when the master gave instructions by beating drums and sounding gongs, the monkey would do nothing but pretending that it had not heard anything.

To frighten the monkey, the man got a chicken, and began beating drums and sounding gongs. The chicken, thrilled by the sound, kept its body unmoved on the ground. The man then killed the motionless chicken, which greatly frightened the monkey.

In order not to be killed like the chicken, the monkey became very obedient thereafter, beginning to dance and somersault once its master gave instructions.

Since then, the phrase "to kill the chicken to frighten the monkey" became an idiom used metaphorically to mean frightening someone by punishing others.

S

赏罚分明

魏惠王问卜皮说："人们对我有什么批评？"

卜皮坦率地回答说："我听人们说您很慈惠。"

惠王听了人们的颂扬，大喜道："那么我的功绩将会怎样？"

卜皮断然回答说："您的功绩将会以国家的灭亡告终。"

惠王并没有因卜皮的话而大动肝火，反而继续问道："慈与惠，不是美德吗？为什么却会导致国家的灭亡？"

卜皮解释说："慈是怜悯，惠是施予。慈的话，您就连犯罪的恶人都不处罚。惠的话，即使无功的人，您也会奖。如果犯罪的人不被处罚，无功的人又获奖赏，不用说，国家会走向灭亡之路了。"

后来，人们习惯用"赏罚分明"一词，来形容处理事情明明白白。

To Put the Saddle on the Right Horse

In the Warring States Period (475–221 BC), King Hui of Wei, once asked Bo Pi, one of his ministers, "What remarks have the people made about me?"

"I've heard people saying that you are a merciful and generous lord." Bo Pi answered frankly.

Taking it as a high remark to him by the people, King Hui couldn't control his rejoicing at what Bo Pi said, and kept asking, "So where will this lead me? How far will my achievement go?"

"This will lead to our country's destruction!" Bo Pi still answered in a frank and blunt way.

Bo Pi's answer didn't make King Hui fly into rage. Instead, he asked Bo again, "But why? In my mind, mercy and generosity are virtues rather than misdeeds. Why will they lead to our country's destruction?"

"Mercy means sympathy, and generosity means giving freely," Bo Pi explained. "These are indeed virtues, but virtues sometimes go to extremes, because being merciful, you'll pardon those who do wrong, and being generous you'll reward even those who do not deserve it. When the offenders of the law get off scot-free and the undeserved get rewards, it goes without saying that the state is heading toward destruction."

Nowadays, people use the phrase "to put the saddle on the right horse" to emphasize the importance of handling things in a clear and fair way.

S

甚嚣尘上

春秋时期，晋、楚两国经常发生战争。晋国袭击郑国，郑国向楚国求援，楚王亲率大军援郑。

双方在郑地鄢陵相遇。楚王求胜心切，虽然遇上了当时军事上普遍忌讳的晦日（阴历月终），仍命令部队抢占有利地形，准备进攻。楚王亲自登上侦察车，察看晋军动静，太宰伯州犁跟在后面。

只见晋军营内一阵烟尘弥漫开来，楚王说："看，那边喧嚣得厉害，尘土飞扬起来了！"伯州犁答道："晋军正在塞井平灶！说明快开战了。"楚王下令说："好，打吧！"

两军交锋，楚、郑两国阵容不严密，而晋军在晋厉公的率领下，攻击勇猛。这一仗，从清晨一直打到星星出来才收场。最后以楚军彻底失败而告终。

现在，"甚嚣尘上"这个成语被用来形容消息普遍流传、议论纷纷，也用来指敌方狂妄叫嚣。

Making a Great Clamor

In the Spring-Autumn Period (770–221 BC), the State of Jin maintained a hostile relationship with the State of Chu. As a result, when the State of Zheng was attacked by Jin, the king of Zheng sought for help from Chu and the king of Chu led his army in person to aid Zheng.

The battle took place at Yanling of Zheng. It was well-accepted in ancient China that battles should not take place at the end of each synoptic month. However, the King of Chu was so eager to win the battle that he chose to turn a blind eye to the unfavorable date. He got on the scout carriage to view the enemy army, with Bo Zhouli, one of his ministers, on his rear.

After watching for a while, the King of Chu said, "it is quite noisy over there. I can see they are making a great clamor. A cloud of dust has been stirred up. What are they doing there?" For this, Bo answer, "They are filling up wells and destroying their hearth, which means they are ready to fight." "Then let's fight!" the King ordered.

However, the army of Chu was obviously not as well prepared as their enemies. Although the war lasted from daybreak till the evening, it ended up with Chu being defeated.

This idiom is now used to mean wide-spread news and rumors. It sometimes also means the arrogant clamor of the enemy.

S

世外桃源

东晋文学家陶渊明在《桃花源记》中记载：一个渔夫只身划船进入一个山洞，发现一座桃源，这里的居民男耕女织，大人小孩均参加劳动，没有赋税和徭役，人们的关系十分淳朴亲切，到处是一片安乐祥和的气氛，与外面的世界隔绝。

人们用“世外桃源”一词，代指与现实社会隔绝、生活安乐的理想境界，后也指环境幽静、生活安逸的地方。

A Land of Idyllic Beauty

Tao Yuanming, a very famous writer in the Eastern Jin Dynasty, ever portrayed in *Peach Blossom Spring*, one of his master pieces, a land of idyllic beauty. He depicted the land in this way: a fisherman, in an unexpected way, rowed into cave, which led to a land of peach blossoms. Residents there all had their own business to do, men plowing and women weaving, adults working and children learning. There was no taxation and corvee. People were maintaining a simple and intimate relationship, making the land an isolated but peaceful and safe place.

Nowadays, people use the phrase "a land of idyllic beauty" to refer to an ideal place which was away from the messy reality. It also means a place of serenity and comfort.

S

势如破竹

三国末年，蜀国灭亡，晋武帝司马炎夺取魏国政权以后，准备出兵攻打东吴，实现统一全国的愿望。他召集文武大臣们商量灭吴大计。多数人认为，吴国还有一定实力，一举消灭它恐怕不易，不如有了足够的准备再说。

大将杜预不同意多数人的看法，写了一道奏章给晋武帝。杜预认为，必须趁目前吴国衰弱灭掉它，不然等它有了实力就很难打败它了。司马炎看了杜预的奏章，找自己最信任的大臣张华征求意见。张华非常同意杜预的分析，也劝司马炎快快攻打吴国，以免留下后患。于是司马炎就下了决心，任命杜预做征南大将军。公元 279 年，晋武帝司马炎调动了二十多万兵马，攻打吴国。在沅江、湘江以南的吴军听到风声吓破了胆，纷纷打开城门投降。司马炎下令让杜预从小路向吴国国都建业进发。此时，有人担心长江水势暴涨，不如暂收兵等到冬天进攻更有利。杜预坚决反对退兵，他说："现在趁士气高涨，斗志正旺，取得一个又一个胜利，势如破竹（像用快刀劈竹子一样，劈过几节后竹子就迎刃破裂），一举攻击吴国不会再费多大力气了！"晋朝大军在杜预的率领下，直冲向吴都建业，不久就攻占建业灭了吴国。

如今，人们用此成语比喻作战或工作节节胜利，毫无阻碍。

Like Splitting a Bamboo

In the late Three Kingdoms Period (AD 220–280), the sate of Shu was ruined. Sima Yan, the emperor of Jin, after usurping Wei, wished to conquer Wu, the last state of this period. He summoned all his officials to discuss on the plan. Most officials believed it was not a good timing to conquer Wu, because enough preparation should be made before setting out the army.

Du Yu, a general of Jin, believed just the opposite and sent in a memorial to the emperor. In the memorial, Du stated that Wu was now in a recovering stage, so a war should be started against it before its full recovery. The emperor showed the memorial to Zhang Hua, his most trusted official. Zhang agreed with Du totally, making the king make up his mind to attack Wu in no time. In A.D. 279, the king assembled 200 thousand soldiers to attack Wu. The Wu armies on the south of Yuan River and Xiang River all surrendered out of great fear. The king then ordered Du Yu to set out through shortcuts for Jianye, the capital of Wu. For fear of the rising tide of the Yangtze River, someone suggested holding back the attack until the coming winter. Du Yu was strongly against this idea, saying, "thanks to the victories we have just made against Wu, our soldiers are all in high morale. It is the best opportunity to conquer Wu. This is just like splitting a bamboo with a sharp knife. With some bamboo joints split apart, we can then split the entire bamboo without too much effort, because it will split naturally."

What Du had predicted was later proved to be quite true. By continuing their attacks against Wu, the army of Jin conquered Wu in a short time.

Nowadays, people use the phrase "like splitting a bamboo" as a metaphor for successive victories at work or in wars.

手不释卷

三国时期吴国大将吕蒙未受太多教育，孙权鼓励他学习史书与兵法。吕蒙总是推说军队事多没有时间学习，

孙权说："时间嘛，要自己去挤出来。从前汉光武帝在行军作战的紧张关头，手里还总是拿着一本书不肯放下来呢！为什么你就没有时间呢？"

停了停，孙权又说："我并不是要你去研究学问，而只是要你翻阅一些古书，从中得到一些启发罢了。"

吕蒙问："可我不知道应该去读哪些书？"

孙权听了，微笑着说："你可以先读些《孙子》《六韬》等兵法书，再读些《左传》《史记》等历史书，这些书对于以后带兵打仗很有好处。"

吕蒙听了孙权的话，回去便开始读书学习，从此手不释卷，并坚持不懈。最后做了吴国的主将，有勇有谋，屡建奇功。

Being a Diligent Reader

In the Three Kingdoms Period (AD 220–280), there was a general in the State of Wu named Lyu Meng. Although he was a general in the army, Lyu had not been well educated. Sun Quan, his lord, encouraged him to do some reading, especially about history and military. However, Lyu always said he was just too busy to read.

One day, Sun encouraged Lyu to do some reading again, and Lyu once again said he had no time. Sun then continued, "Time is just like the water in the sponge. You twist it, then you get it. Emperor Guangwu, a busy man as he was, always read even when he was on a march. Are you busier than him?"

Seeing Lyu had no reply, Sun kept saying, "I don't mean to make you choose study as your career. I only want you to be a diligent reader, because a diligent reader can have inspiration through reading."

"This sounds a good idea, but what books am I going to read?" Lv asked.

For this, Sun Quan replied, laughing, "*The Art of War*, as well as *Six Strategies* can be the first choice, for they are books on the art of war. After reading them, you can also choose history books like *the Spring and Autumn Annals* or *Shih Chi*. You will find them useful."

From then on, Lyu Meng became a diligent reader, making himself a courageous and intelligent general in the Sate of Wu.

守株待兔

春秋时代，宋国有个农夫，一天在耕田的时候，忽然跑来一只兔子，恰巧碰在树桩上，脖子折断死了。农夫把兔子拾回家去，美美地吃了一顿兔肉。晚上他想："我何必辛辛苦苦地种地呢？每天在树下捡一只兔子就够我吃的了。"他从此不再耕作，每天坐在树下等待兔子的到来。

"守株待兔"这个成语，常用来讽刺那些不想经过努力、存在侥幸心理、希望得到意外收获的人。

To Wait for a Careless Hare

In the Spring-Autumn Period (770–221 BC), a farmer in the State of Song was working in the filed, when suddenly a hare ran into his field, and unluckily got killed itself by bumping into a tree stump.

The farmer was glad to take the dead hare back home to cook a delicious meal for himself. At night, lying in the bed with a full stomach, he entertained a wild hope, "if only I can get dead hare everyday! Then I don't have to work in the field anymore."

From then on, he forgot his farm work. Instead, he did nothing but wait beside the stump for another careless hare day by day.

Now in China, people use the phrase "to wait for a careless hare" to satirize daydreamers who are like the hare-waiting farmer.

熟能生巧

陈尧咨擅长射箭，当时世上没有人能和他相比，他也凭着这一点自夸。

他曾在自家的园圃里射箭，观者无不叫绝。有个卖油的老翁也放下挑着的担子，站在一旁，不在意地斜着眼看他，久久地不离去。老翁见到陈尧咨射出的箭十支能中八九支，他也只不过微微地点点头赞许这情况。

陈尧咨看到了，跑过来问道："你也会射箭吗？我射箭的本领难道不精湛吗？"老翁说："没有什么别的奥秘，只不过是熟能生巧罢了。"陈尧咨听后愤愤地说："你怎么敢轻视我射箭的技术！"老翁说："凭着我倒油的经验就可知道这个道理。"于是老翁取过一个葫芦立放在地上，用铜钱盖在它的口上，慢慢地用勺子把油倒进葫芦，油从铜钱的孔中注进去，却不沾湿铜钱。老人说："我这点手艺也没有什么别的奥秘，只是熟能生巧罢了。"陈尧咨见此，面带微笑地冲着老人点头。

Practice Makes Perfect

Chen Yaozi, an official in the Song Dynasty (AD 960–1279), was skilled in the art of archery. It was said that no man in Song was better at archery than him, of which he felt very proud.

One day he was practicing archery in his garden, attracting a crowd of people to watch. He was so skilled that everyone in the crowd watched with amazement. However, an old oil peddler, who laid down his burden watching, looked sideways at Chen's performance, seeming not amazed at all. Although Chen seldom missed any shots, the old man was still not amazed, occasionally giving slight nod of approval.

Chen then came close to the old man, saying, "Don't you think I'm a good archer? Are you better at this than me?"

"Not bad, but I will never call it amazing, because practice makes perfect. With enough practice, everyone can be like you." for that, the old man answered.

Hearing the old man's words, Chen said resentfully, "How dare you make light of my archery skill!"

"Because I practice everyday. Not for archery, of course, but pouring the oil." The old man answered calmly.

The old man then laid a bottle gourd on the ground, and sealed its spout with a copper cash. There was a hole in the middle of the copper cash, through which the old man poured oil into the bottle gourd. After the gourd was filled with oil, Chen was amazed to find the copper cash without any oil at all. The old man said, "That's why I said practice makes perfect."

Chen then looked at the old man with smile and nodded his head.

蜀犬吠日

唐朝时期著名的文学家柳宗元，曾经讲过一个“蜀犬吠日”的故事。在西南地区的蜀地气候多雨多雾，有时阴雨连绵、雾气蒙蒙长达数月，一年四季很难看见太阳，结果那里的狗一见到太阳出来，都感到很惊奇，就大声狂叫起来。

“蜀犬吠日”这个成语后用来比喻少见多怪，对本来很平常的事情，由于见识短浅而感到奇怪。

Uncalled-for Excitement Out of Sheer Ignorance

In Tang Dynasty (AD 618–907), Liu Zongyuan, a well-known scholar, ever wrote a story about “uncalled-for excitement out of sheer ignorance”. In his story, the “uncalled excitement” came from dogs in Shu, a region in southwest China. In Shu, you could hardly see the sunshine since it was cloudy and foggy most of the year on account of its landform. When a sunny day came, dogs in Shu would bark furiously out of great excitement.

This idiom is used to indicate being surprised at something normal, due to one’s ignorance.

S

束之高阁

庾翼是东晋人，他从小就有过人的才智和远大的志向，作战中屡立奇功，被封为都亭侯，官至征西将军。

与他同时代的殷浩也很有才能，而且长于高谈阔论。殷浩20岁的时候就出了名，后来做了扬州刺史，不久又调任建武将军，都督扬、豫、徐、兖、青五州的军事，但是在讨伐许昌和洛阳敌人的战役中，却屡打败仗，被革了职。

后来有人向庾翼建议，让殷浩重新出来做官，庾翼对此不以为然。他认为殷浩是一个徒有虚名的清谈家，只会高谈阔论，而没有真才实干，于是带着鄙夷的神情说:“他像无用之物一样，只好把他捆起来放到高楼上去，等到天下太平后，再来考虑任用他。”“束之高阁”这个成语由此而来。

从此，“束之高阁”指丢在一旁不予理睬。

To Be Put in the Attic

In the East Jin Dynasty (AD 317–420), Yu Yi, due to his innate quick wit and lofty ambition, as well as the meritorious military service he had done in battles, was made the Marquis of Duting, and the General of West Expedition.

Yin Hao, another talent in Yu Yi's time, got his fame in metaphysics when he was still a young man of 20 years age. Yin was appointed the mayor of Yangzhou and later was promoted to the post of General Jianwu, a post supervising the military affairs of five cities, respectively Yangzhou, Yuzhou, Yanzhou, Xuzhou and Qingzhou. However, Yin's official career came to an end after he lost battles against Luoyang and Xuchang.

One day, someone recommended that Yin serve as a member of Yu's think tank, for which Yu refused without too much thinking. In Yu's mind, Yin was just a man who enjoyed undeserved reputation, because he believed Yin to be impractical. With a look of contempt, he said, "A person like Yin is just like a white elephant. We just can't take the risk to rely on such kind of persons in the battlefields. Instead, they shall be tied up in and put in the attic until the country come to its peace and prosperity."

Since then, this idiom "to be put in the attic" is used to refer to putting something away without using it.

水落石出

苏轼是宋朝著名的诗人。他除了写诗歌之外，也喜欢喝酒和外出游玩。在大自然的怀抱中，他呼吸新鲜的空气，放松自己疲劳的身心。

一天，苏轼又和一群友人来到赤壁下的长江岸边，登上小舟，泛舟游玩。这时，只听见东流的江水发出潺潺的声响，在这样寂静的夜晚，显得特别清脆。一座座高大的山峰屹立在两岸，显得格外陡峭。那时正值冬季，江水下落，江水之下的很多石头都露了出来。这壮观美丽的景观让苏轼兴致大发，他当即作赋一首，其中的一句便是“山高月小，水落石出”。

“水落石出”，本来是指冬天的一种风景，但后人把这“水落石出”四字，用作真相最终被发现的意思。

When the Water Subsides, the Rocks Emerge

This phrase is a sentence excerpted from a masterpiece written by Su Shi, one of the most outstanding poets of Song Dynasty (AD 960–1279). Many poets in China had great fun in drinking with friends and enjoying the beauties of nature, for which Su Shi was not an exception. In touring the scenic spots, Su relaxed himself both physically and mentally by breathing the fresh air, as well as smelling the aroma of plants.

One day, Su Shi and his friends were boating in the Yangtze River in the area named Red Cliff. It was such a serene moonlit evening that the sound of trickling water sounded much louder than in daytime. Looking above, Su Shi could see high peaks stand towering stoically like giants, looking very precipitous. It was in mid-winter, and the river was not in its full tide with rocks in the river bed emerging. All these pictures inspired Su Shi so much that a poem jumped into his mind, one sentence of which was "compared with the giant peak, the full moon seems small. When the water subsides, the rocks emerge."

This phrase, originally used by Su Shi to describe the winter scenery, was later used by Chinese people to mean that all secrets may eventually come to light.

四面楚歌

秦朝末年，项羽和刘邦原来约定以鸿沟东西边作为界线，互不侵犯。后来刘邦听从张良和陈平的规劝，觉得应该趁项羽衰弱的时候消灭他，于是，便把项羽紧紧围在垓下这个地方。

这时，项羽手下的兵士已经很少，粮食又没有了。夜里听见四面围住他的军队都唱起楚地的民歌，不禁非常吃惊地说：“刘邦已经得到了楚地了吗？为什么他的部队里面楚人这么多呢？”说着，心里已丧失了斗志，便从床上爬起来，在营帐里面喝酒，并和他最宠爱的妃子虞姬一同唱歌。唱完，直掉眼泪，在一旁的人也非常难过，都觉得抬不起头来。虞姬自刎于项羽的马前，项羽英雄末路，带了仅剩兵卒至乌江，最终自刎于江边。

“四面楚歌”这个成语比喻四面受到敌人的攻击，处于孤立危急的困境。

Besieged on All Sides

At the end of Qin Dynasty (221–207 BC), Chu and Han, two military powers at that time respectively led by Xiang Yu and Liu Bang, ever signed a non-aggression agreement, promising never to cross Honggou, a canal dividing the two powers on its two sides. With the decline of Xiang Yu's power, Liu Bang's ambition was growing. He soon followed Zhang Liang and Chen Ping's advice of eliminating Xiang Yu's troop, and besieged Xiang Yu's troop at a place called Gaixia.

With fewer and fewer soldiers and limited provisions, Xiang Yu was in a desperate situation. In such a critical period, one evening, Xiang Yu felt very surprised to hear the surrounding troops singing folk songs of Chu. This made Xiang Yu feel more desperate, because he thought the soldiers singing Chu folk songs were Chu soldiers drafted into the Han army, which might mean that Han army had occupied the whole of Chu. In great despair, Xiang Yu drank a lot, aiming to drown his sorrows in wine. His beloved concubine Yu didn't leave him but sing and dance with him. Everyone on site knew this was a farewell ceremony, so they all choked in sobs, great sorrows in heart. To show her true love to Xiang Yu, Consort Yu killed herself before Xiang Yu who began his final battle toward Liu Bang. Xiang Yu got through the close siege and fled to Wujiang River. Feeling ashamed to go back home, he killed himself beside the river.

This idiom is used metaphorically to mean being in a helpless and critical situation, surrounded by the enemy on all sides.

T

昙花一现

相传昙花原是天上一个小花仙，后来凡心私动，喜欢上一个叫作韦陀的小神，玉帝得知后大怒，把昙花变做一朵小花，让她在每天里只有一个时辰的花期。

昙花非常痴情，她算好韦陀每天晚饭后下山挑水的时间，并选择此时盛开，只希望能借此见心上人一面。于是，就有了“昙花一现，只为韦陀”的传说，也因此昙花也叫作韦陀花。

后来，人们用“昙花一现”来比喻事物或人物出现不久就消失了。

A Flash in the Pan

According to Chinese mythology, night bloom was originally a flower fairy living in Heaven. She fell in love with a demigod named Veda, for which Jade Emperor, the supreme deity of Taoism, felt very angry. The emperor turned the fairy in love into a tiny flower, which can only blossom at night, and its blossom can only last for a brief period.

However, the fairy didn't feel regretful. Instead, she chose to blossom when everyday Veda carried water down the mountain, in order to see her beloved everyday. People then took "night bloom blossoms for her beloved Veda" as a beautiful legend. From then on, night blooms were also called Veda blooms by people.

According to the legend, a phrase "a flash in the pan" was made, which is used mainly to describe things which disappear shortly after they come into being, just like the blossom of night blooms.

T

谈虎色变

很久很久以前，在一个僻静的小山村里住着一个农夫。有一天，他在山上砍柴时碰到了老虎，凶猛的老虎想吃掉他，农夫被老虎狠狠地咬了一口，但是却很幸运地逃脱了，捡回了一条命。

随着日子一天天地过去，农夫的伤口渐渐地愈合了，但是他还是会偶尔想到那段可怕的经历。一天，同村的一个人正在给大家讲老虎伤人的故事，讲得有声有色，周围的人都听得津津有味。农夫恰好路过，刚好听到了。他的脸色顿时变得苍白，身体不停地颤抖。这是因为他有被咬的亲身感受，所以才会有很强烈的反应。

后来，“谈虎色变”就用来比喻一提到可怕的事就情绪紧张起来，连脸色都变了。

To Turn Pale at the Mention of a Tiger

Once upon a time, there lived a farmer in a small and tranquil village. One day, out of bad luck, he was injured by a hungry tiger when he went to the mountains to chop wood. Fortunately, though a narrow escape, he succeeded in escaping from the mouth of the tiger.

With time elapsing, his physical wounds were healing day by day. However, his mental injury didn't get healed due to the terrible memory lingering in his mind. One day, another resident in the village was sharing a story about tigers with a crowd of local residents, when the farmer happened to pass by. Unlike the other residents who showed great interest and easiness in listening to the tiger-story, the farmer, when hearing the word "tiger", began to tremble with his face turning pale at once. Small wonder it was because he was the only one in the village who had ever fallen into victim of tigers in person.

Afterwards, "to turn pale at the mention of a tiger" is used to refer that somebody becomes extremely frightened when he is informed of something bad that he suffered before.

贪小失大

战国时期，蜀国国君生性贪婪，秦惠王听说后想讨伐他。但是通往蜀地的山路深涧十分险峻，军队没有路可以通往蜀国。于是秦军雕凿石牛，把许多贵重的东西放在牛的后面，用来送给蜀国。

蜀国国君贪图宝物，就劈开山路填平谷地，派了五个大力士来迎接石牛。秦惠王率领军队紧随其后，蜀国从而灭亡，蜀国国君也因此而被天下人耻笑。

人们多用此成语来比喻只谋求眼前的好处而不顾长远的利益。

Penny-wise and Pound Foolish

In the Warring States Period (475–221 BC), King Hui of Qin intended to conquer the State of Shu. Hearing that the Lord of Shu was likened to a buzzard by the people in his state, King Hui developed an idea, aiming to conquer Shu with minimal loss. At that timc, although Shu was not as powerful as Qin, it was hard to conquer due to its geographical advantage of steep mountain roads.

King Hui's idea was to carve stones into cow statues, and to put jewellery and treasures at the back of the cow statues as presents for the Lord of Shu.

The Lord of Shu, well-known as a man who was penny-wise and pound foolish, couldn't wait to take the "gifts" from King Hui, for which he built a road in the mountains directly leading to his state, and sent five men of unusual strength to help transport the cow statues. What he didn't know was that an army was at the back of the cow statues too. It was the army of King Hui, following the five men of unusual strength, and waiting for an opportunity to attack Shu.

The result, beyond doubt, was that Shu was conquered by the army from Qin. The Lord of Shu, therefore, was forever remembered as a penny-wise but pound foolish man.

From then on, the phrase is used a lot to describe someone like the Lord of Shu.

T

坦腹东床

东晋时期，书法家王羲之年轻时很有才华。太尉郗鉴很器重他，想把女儿嫁给他，于是派人向王羲之伯父王导求亲。

王导让来人到东边厢房里去看王家子弟。门生回去后，对郗鉴说："王家子弟个个不错，可是一听到有信使来，都显得拘谨不自然，只有一个人坐在东床上，袒腹而食，若无其事。"郗鉴说："这正是我要选的佳婿。"一打听，原来正是王羲之。郗鉴就把女儿嫁给了他。

后来，"坦腹东床"一词，就成了合格女婿、如意郎君的代名词，多为中国父母使用。

A Worthy Son-in-law

In Eastern Jin Dynasty (AD 317–420), there was a gifted calligrapher named Wang Xizhi, who was thought highly of by Chi Jian, the Great Commandant. Chi appreciated Xizhi's talent so much that he even developed an idea to marry his daughter to Xizhi. One day, he sent a man to seek a marriage alliance from Wang Dao, Xizhi's father.

Wang Dao then led the man to the east wing-room, where all his sons were. The man then went back to Chi Jian, reporting, "All boys of the Wang family are good-looking and graceful, but when they saw me, they were all too formal and unnatural, except one."

"What about that one?" Chi Jian asked eagerly.

"He was sitting idly on the east seat, eating something with his breast and abdomen exposed, as if I were not there."

"He must be Wang Xizhi, and that is what I want my son-in-law to be!" Chi exclaimed in great excitement.

It was proved later that the boy was indeed Wang Xizhi, so Chi Jian made his wish fulfilled to marry his daughter to Xizhi.

From then on, the phrase "a worthy son-in-law" is used a lot by Chinese parents.

螳臂当车

春秋时，齐国的国君齐庄公，有一次坐着车出去打猎，忽见路旁有一只小小的虫子，伸出两条臂膀似的前腿，想阻挡前进中的车轮。

庄公问驾车的人："这是一只什么虫子？"驾车的人答道："这是一只螳螂，它见车子来了，不知赶快退避，却还要来阻挡，真是不自量力！"庄公笑道："好一个出色的勇士，我们别伤害它吧！"说着，就叫驾车的人车子靠边，让开它，从路旁走过去。

这件事情很快就传开了。人们都说庄公敬爱勇士，便有好多勇敢的武士纷纷来投奔他。

但是，"螳臂当车"作为一句成语，却并不用来比喻出色的勇士，而是用来比喻自不量力的可笑人物。

A Mantis Raising Its Forelegs

In the Spring-Autumn Period (770–221 BC), the King of Qi, on his chariot to go for a hunting, saw a small insect on the road with its arm-liked forelegs raised, as if trying to block the way.

The King asked his carter what kind of insect it was, for which the carter answered, "it is a mantis. So stupid is it that instead of trying to avoid the coming chariot, it tries to block the way. How presumptuous it is!"

"I don't think so. I think it is a brave warrior. Let it go!" the King answered, laughing.

Under the King's order, the carter then changed another lane and spared the mantis' life.

Later, the story spread very fast, and the King was believed to be a wise king who adored warriors. As a result, countless brave warriors came to the State of Qi, making Qi a powerful state.

However, in China, for thousands of years, the phrase "a mantis raising its forelegs" was not used to refer to brave warriors. Instead, it is a metaphor for men who overestimate themselves.

天花乱坠

魏晋南北朝时佛教盛行，全国有寺庙 3 万多所，僧尼 200 多万人。

南朝的梁武帝带头求神拜佛，在全国大建寺庙。他曾经三次舍身同泰寺，他还聘请古印度僧人波罗末到中国讲经。波罗末翻译了不少印度佛经，并培养了许多中国弟子。有了经书，讲经的风气更加兴盛。为了教化民众，佛教徒编了许许多多讲经的传说。其中一则是：云光法师讲经，感动了上天，天上的鲜花纷纷坠落。

后来，佛教在中国分成许多宗派，影响最大的是“禅宗”。宋真宗时，道原和尚编了一本《景德传灯录》，记载了禅宗师徒的故事。书中讲到对佛意要真正领会，反对“讲得天花乱坠”。

从此，“天花乱坠”就有了贬义，形容人说话巧妙动听，但虚妄、空洞、不着边际。

As If It Were Raining Flowers

The Wei, Jin and Northern-Southern Dynasties were a time in Chinese history when Buddhism flourished. It was calculated that there were altogether more than 30,000 temples and 2 million monks and nuns all over the country.

Emperor Wu of the Liang Dynasty was a firm believer to Buddhism. With his support, numerous temples were built all over the country. He ever invited a monk named Paramartha from Ancient India to explain the sutra, and even gave up the throne and became a monk in the Temple of Tongtai for three times. Paramartha translated a lot of Buddhist scriptures into Chinese and had many disciples in China. With the translated scriptures, Buddhism had more and more believers in China. To enlarge Buddhism's influence, some Buddhists made up legends about sermon, one of which is about Master Yunguang: Yunguang ever explained the sutra so profoundly and subtly that the God of Flowers was moved and sent divine flowers down to the earth. Soon the land was covered with flowers.

However, with the further development of Buddhism, different Buddhism sects were made in China, of which Zen had the biggest influence. In Song Dynasty, a monk named Dao Yuan wrote a book about Buddhist history. In the book, he took a negative view toward the legend of Master Yunguang. From his perspective, when explaining the sutra, a monk should fully understand the Buddhist texts, instead of explaining it in a way "as if it were raining flowers".

From then on, the phrase "as if it were raining flowers" had a negative connotation, which was similar to the meaning of the phrase "to talk one's head off".

T

天涯海角

唐朝文学家韩愈从小失去父母，由兄长韩会一家养大，他勤奋学习终于考取了进士，直到 40 岁才正式被任命为校书郎，虽是不起眼的小官，但他也终于定居长安。为了回报韩会一家的养育之恩，他想接嫂子及侄儿十二郎来长安居住，可惜他们中途去世，这让他十分悲伤。韩愈作《祭十二郎文》倾诉他们骨肉相隔天涯海角的痛苦之情。这篇祭文，一字一泪，令人读来心酸。祭文中有“一在天之涯，一在地之角”的句子。后人便把“天涯海角”，用来比喻极其遥远的地方。

All the Corners of the Earth

In the Tang Dynasty (AD 618–907), Han Yu, a well-known scholar in China, lost his parents at an early age, and was raised by Han Hui, his elder brother. Although Han Yu was a very diligent learner, he passed the imperial examination very late and didn't get his official post until at the age of 40, being appointed as a collator in the cabinet. Though an inferior official, Han Yu finally settled down in Chang'an, the capital of Tang. To pay back the upbringing of Han Hui's family, Han Yu invited them to come to Chang'an to live with him. It is a pity that all the family died on the way to Chang'an, which made Han Yu fall into great sadness.

Han Yu then wrote an essay entitled *an Elegiac Address to the Twelfth Nephew*, which expresses his grief in eternally losing his beloved family, especially his most beloved nephew. When reading this essay, readers can imagine how Han Yu shed tears when writing it. There is a sentence excerpted from the essay, which reads, "It is heartbreaking that we two are separated into different corners of the world, one in this end, the other in the other end."

From then on, this phrase "all the corners of the world" was used to refer to remote places.

天衣无缝

古时候有个叫郭翰的先生，他能诗善画，性格诙谐，喜欢开玩笑。

盛夏的一个夜晚，他在树下乘凉，但见长天如碧，白云舒卷，明月高挂，清风徐来，满院飘香。这时，一位长得异常美丽的仙女含笑站在郭翰面前。他仔细地观察那个女子，发现她身上穿的衣服连一条缝都没有，感到非常奇怪，便问那个女子。女子回答说："天衣本来就用不着针线缝合的呀！"

"天衣无缝"这个成语用来比喻处理事情十分周密，不露一点痕迹，也比喻诗文写得很精辟，找不出一点毛病。

A Seamless Heavenly Robe

In ancient China, there was a man called Guo Han. Guo had superior abilities in writing and painting and was born with a humorous personality.

One mid-summer evening, Guo was sitting cozily under a tree. It was a serene and bright night, with a blue sky, a full moon, swirling clouds, cool breezes, and fresh floral fragrance. He was enjoying himself when a lady with extraordinary beauty came before him. He observed the lady closely, and was surprised to find that she was dressed in a seamless robe. He asked why the lady's robe was seamless, for which the lady answered, "it's nothing to be surprised at, because it is a heavenly robe, and all heavenly robes are not sown with thread and needle."

Nowadays, this idiom is used metaphorically to indicate the flawless handling of things. It can also be used to indicate perfectly written poems or other literary articles.

同舟共济

春秋时期，吴国和越国经常互相打仗。两国的人民也都将对方视为仇人。

有一次，两国的人恰巧共同坐一艘船渡河。船刚开的时候，他们在船上互相瞪着对方，一副要打架的样子。但是船开到河中央的时候，突然遇到了大风雨，眼见船就要翻了。为了保住性命，他们顾不得彼此的仇恨，纷纷互相救助，并且合力稳定船身，才逃过这一劫，安全到达河的对岸。

现在，这个成语就用来形容人们齐心协力，共同渡过难关。

Crossing a River in the Same Boat

In the Spring-Autumn Period (770–221 BC), Wu and Yue, two states at that time, when settling disputes between them, often resorted to arms. Frequent wars even made their people hold a hostile attitude toward each other.

One day, a man from Wu met another man from Yue in a boat crossing a river. They were hostile against each other at first, glaring at each other, looking as if to fight. Things changed when a storm came. It was such a big storm that the boat almost tipped over. At this crucial moment, they worked in full cooperation and with unity of purpose, which made them go ashore in safety.

Nowadays, "crossing a river in the same boat" means gathering together to overcome difficulties.

T

投鼠忌器

《汉书》中有这么个故事：有个富人，很喜欢古董并收藏了很多。其中有一件稀有的玉盂，工艺精湛，具有很高的历史价值，深受这个富人的喜爱。

一天晚上，一只老鼠跳进了这个玉盂，想去吃里边的一些剩菜，正巧被这个富人看到了。他非常恼火，盛怒之下，拿了块石头砸向老鼠。当然，老鼠是被砸死了，可是那个珍贵的玉盂也被打破了。这件事使富人非常难过，他深深后悔自己的鲁莽带来的不可挽回的损失。

人们从这个故事中总结到：目光短浅、做事不计后果的人，极有可能遭遇祸事。

如今，人们常用“投鼠忌器”一词，来劝人在做事时先考虑后果。

Sparing the Rat to Save the Jar

In *The History of the Han Dynasty*, a biographical history book in China, there is a story telling of a rich man, who was keen on collecting antiques. One of his favorite antiques was a rare jar made of jade, exquisitely crafted and of historical value.

One evening, he saw a rat eating leftover dishes in the jade jar and was infuriated by the scene. In a fit of rage, he cast a piece of stone to the rat in the jar. The stone hit the jar precisely, which, of course, killed the rat, but, at the same time, broke the jar into pieces. He then felt very regretful for his rash behavior. However, no matter how regretful he felt, he had already permanently lost his favorite jar.

We can realize from the story that any one, who cares for the present and overlooks consequences is apt to bring disasters upon himself.

Nowadays, the phrase "sparing the rat to save the jar" is used a lot as a warning for people to take unbearable consequence into consideration when they are doing things.

T

偷天换日

战国时期魏国公子信陵君想设法解救被秦国围攻的赵国。本来魏王已经派出一支军队，但因为害怕秦国的报复，所以把军队停留在边境上，不进也不退。

信陵君门下有一位食客叫侯嬴，献了一计，建议信陵君偷盗魏王兵符，率领边境这支部队前去救赵。于是信陵君就去拜托魏王爱妾如姬帮忙。信陵君对如姬曾有报父仇之恩，如姬很快就答应了。于是就有了“如姬窃符”的情节。明代《如姬窃符》中有两句：“偷天换日，强似携云握雨。”意思是说：“为了报恩，我来魏王寝宫盗符，用偷天换日的手段，要胜过用博取魏王的恩爱来取得。”

后用“偷天换日”比喻骗局之大与技巧之妙。

In an Underhand Attempt

In the Warring States Period (475–221 BC), Lord Xinling, determined to rescue the State of Zhao from the siege of Qin. The King of Wei, although having already sent an army to save Zhao, was hesitant at the last moment for fear of Qin's future revenge, and ordered thc army to be stationed near the border.

Lord Xinling then summoned all his subordinates to discuss how to save Zhao, for which one of his subordinates named Hou Ying offered an advice. Hou suggested Xinling to steal the commander's seal of Wei, and then use the seal to order the army near the border to rescue Zhao. He then referred to Ru Ji for help, a concubine of the King of Wei. Xinling ever helped Ru Ji to revenge on her father's murderer, so Ru Ji consented without hesitance. She went to the King's chamber and stole the seal in secret, which was recorded in biographies as "Ru Ji's taking the seal in secret". In Ming Dynasty, a writer ever wrote a play about this historical event, in which Ru Ji said: "an underhand attempt is better than the King's favor", which means "to get the King's seal, stealing it in secret is more effective than winning the King's love and consent."

From then on, the phrase "in an underhand attempt" was used to refer to a great swindle with cunning tricks.

T

图穷匕见

战国末期秦国非常强大，它想吞并其他国家，统一天下。公元前 228 年，秦国的军队占领了其中一个国家。接着又准备入侵燕国。燕国的太子丹就派了一名叫荆轲的勇士前往秦国刺杀秦王。

为了获得秦王的信任，荆轲带上了一张地图，上面画着燕国最富饶的地方，准备献给秦王。他在这张地图里藏了一把非常锋利的匕首。他来到秦国，见到秦王，恭敬地将地图献上，然后，慢慢打开地图给秦王看。当地图完全打开时，他抽出那把藏着的匕首，刺向秦王。但秦王躲开了，跑到了一根大柱子后。秦王的卫士们立刻跑来围住他，马上就把他给杀了。燕国太子刺杀秦王的计划失败了。后来，燕国也被秦国给吞并了。

后来，人们用这个成语来比喻事情发展到最后，真相或本意就露出来了。

When the Map Is Unrolled, the Dagger Is Revealed

In the end of the Warring States Period (475–221 BC), the Sate of Qin, the most powerful state in that period, wanted to annex the other states and unite China. After annexing a state in 228 BC., Qin was preparing to conquer the State of Yan. The Crown Prince of Yan, in order to protect his people and country, sent a warrior named Jing Ke to assassinate the King of Qin.

To get the trust of the King of Qin, Jing Ke carried a map of the most fertile parts of Yan with him as a gift for the King. Hidden inside the rolled map was a sharp dagger. When Jing entered Qin's palace, he presented the map to the king with respect and slowly unrolled it. When the map was completely unrolled, the hidden dagger appeared. Jing Ke then grabbed it and stabbed at the King. But the King dodged the dagger and hid himself behind a pillar. Jing Ke had never gotten the chance to kill the King as he was soon killed by the palace guards. The plan has failed. Later, Qin wiped off Yan.

The idiom refers to the real intention or reality which is revealed in the end.

兔死狗烹

范蠡和文仲是春秋时期越国的两个大官。越王勾践不听范蠡劝告，盲目进攻邻国吴国，结果被吴国打败，他自己也被吴王抓去做苦力。范蠡说服勾践忍受耻辱，假装服从，等待机会再报仇。文仲也多次到吴国拜访，并且帮助勾践恢复信心。几年以后，吴王把勾践放回越国。在范蠡和文仲的相助下，越国很快就恢复了以前的强大，最后把吴国给灭了。

因为范蠡和文仲为越国做出了巨大的贡献，越王赏给他们很多财宝，还把国土的一半分给范蠡。但范蠡很了解勾践这个人，所以他决定谢绝这些赏赐，找个地方隐居起来。他还写信给文仲，告诉他："当天上的鸟儿被射完了，弓箭也就没用了。当所有的兔子被抓完了，猎狗也将被杀了吃掉。我劝你还是早点离开勾践，免得惹来灾祸。"文仲看完信后，接受了范蠡的劝告，他假装生病，不再参加朝中会议。但太迟了，勾践听信了别人对他的谣言，逼他自杀了。

后来，人们用"兔死狗烹"来比喻事情成功以后，把出过大力的人杀掉。

Hounds Killed for Food Once All the Hares Are Bagged

Fan Li and Wen Zhong were two high-ranking officials of the State of Wu in the Spring-Autumn Period (770–476 BC). Despite Fan's sincere and well-intentioned advice for not attacking the State of Wu, Gou Jian, the King of Yue, still launched an unprepared war toward Wu, which ended up with Yue's being fatally defeated, as well as Gou Jian's being caught alive as a slave to the King of Wu. Fan Li persuaded him to endure humiliation, pretend to surrender and wait for an opportunity to avenge. Wen Zhong also visited Wu for several times, with the secret purpose of helping Gou Jian to regain his confidence. With their encouragement and help, Gou Jian succeeded in making the King of Wu believe his allegiance, and was set free years later. Still with the help of Fan and Wen, the State of Yue rapidly rehabilitated and later annexed the Wu.

To reward Fan's and Wen's great contribution to Yue, Gou Jian declared to give them large sum of money. He also promised to give Fan half of the state. But Fan rejected and decided to live in seclusion for knowing Gou too well. He also wrote a letter to Wen, saying, "when all the flying birds have been shot down, the good bow is put away; when all the hares have been bagged, the hounds are killed for food. I suggest you to withdraw in order to avoid disaster."

Having read the letter, Wen Zhong chose to accept Fan's advice and asked for leave from attending the imperial court meetings by feigning illness. It was a pity that it was already too late for him to withdraw. Days later, he was forced to kill himself.

Nowadays, people use the phrase to mean trusted aides are eliminated when they have outlived their usefulness.

土崩瓦解

商纣王是商朝的末代君主，相传是一个暴虐无道的昏君。他贪恋酒色、荒淫无度，整日花天酒地，寻欢作乐，不理朝政；他听信谗言，重用奸臣，残害忠良，戮杀无辜；他强征暴敛，动用巨资，强迫百姓为自己修建宫苑；他惨无人道，制造种种酷刑，以观看人受刑后的痛苦为乐。在他暗无天日的统治下，百姓们怨声载道，苦不堪言。

虽说商朝的疆土辽阔广袤，士兵不下数万，但打起仗来，因为兵士不愿意为纣王战死，所以“倒矢而射”把兵器扔在一边。商朝军队士气如此低落，商朝的政权自然是岌岌可危了。

所以，当周武王左手擎着用黄金作装饰的大钺，右手持着用牦牛尾装饰的白色旌旗、坐着战车，势不可挡地杀来时，所到之处，无不披靡。纣王军队的溃败、商纣王政权的垮台，就如瓦片碎裂、泥土倒塌，迅速而无法挽救。

中国人后来用“土崩瓦解”形容不可抵挡的崩塌或事物的分离。

To Collapse Like a House of Cards

Legend has it that King Zhou, the last king of Shang Dynasty, was a tyrant, who indulged himself in luxury and excessive physical pleasure and ignored the affairs of the state. He believed one-side story and were biased toward the treacherous court officials, persecuting upright and faithful officers, as well as killing innocent people. He also spent money lavishly on palace construction and punishment instrument making, which tortured countless innocent people to death. It is no exaggeration to say that under his reign, people were leading a dog's life, and complaints were heard everywhere.

Although Shang had a vast territory and a huge quantity of military forces, soldiers were disloyal to the King. Therefore, when wars broke out, no soldier would die for the King. Instead, most of them chose to drop the weapons and worked as guides for the enemy force. With such a force of low morale, the kingdom was definitely on the hazard.

It was not hard to expect that when King Wu of Zhou led his force in a chariot to attack Shang, with a battle-axe decorated with pure gold in his left hand, and a banner ornamented with yak tail in his right hand, the army of Shang couldn't make any resistance. The regime of Shang then collapsed in a short time, just like the collapse of a house of cards.

People in China then use the phrase to refer to the irresistible collapse or split of things.

外强中干

秦国和晋国之间发生了战争，晋惠公要使用郑国赠送的马来驾车。大臣庆郑劝告惠公说：“自古以来，打仗时都要用本国的好马，因为它土生土长，熟悉道路，听从使唤。用外国的马，不好驾驭，一遇到意外，就会乱踢乱叫。而且这种马外表看起来好像很强壮，实际上并没有什么能耐，怎么能作战呢？”但是惠公没有听从庆郑的劝说。战斗打响后，晋国的车马便乱跑一气，很快陷入泥泞，进退不得。结果被秦军打得大败，晋惠公也被秦军活捉了。

Outwardly Strong but Inwardly Weak

In the Spring-Autumn Period (770–221 BC), a war ever broke out between Qin and Jin, two powerful states at that time. To make his force armed to teeth, Duke Hui of Jin decided to take horses presented by the State of Zheng as battle steeds, because these horses were of strong physiques. However, an official named Qing Zheng suggested him not to, saying, "It is a tradition that in wars, local horses should be taken as war steeds, because local horses are familiar with the terrain, and are easy to ride. As for horses from other states, they are unacquainted with the local terrain and are hard to manage when accidents happen. Besides, these horses from Zheng are outwardly strong but inwardly weak. How can they be used as war steeds?"

Unfortunately for Jin, Duke Hui didn't accept Qing Zheng's advice, which was proved to be wise suggestion when the Zheng horses were running everywhere in fright, leading to Jin's being defeated in a short time. It is worth mentioning that even Duke Hui, who turned a deaf ear to Qing Zheng's suggestion, was captured alive by Qin.

完璧归赵

在战国时代，楚国有一件叫和氏璧的宝玉，为赵惠文王所得。秦昭王听说后，表示愿意用 15 城换取和氏璧。赵惠文王召见蔺相如，蔺相如表示愿带和氏璧去秦国，如果赵国得到秦国的城邑，就将和氏璧留在秦国，反之，一定完璧归赵。

蔺相如到秦国后，将和氏璧献上，秦昭王大喜，却全无将城邑给赵之意。蔺相如诓说玉上有一小疵点，要指给秦昭王看，拿回了宝玉。

To Return the Jade Intact to the State of Zhao

In the Warring States Period (475–221 BC), there was a priceless gem named the Jade of the He Family in the State of Chu, which was gotten by King Huiwen, the King of Zhao. The jade was so priceless that King Zhao the king of another more powerful state named Qin, also wanted to get the jade from the King of Zhao, promising to exchange it with 15 cities.

It posed a thorny issue for the King of Zhao since he knew the King of Qin so well as a greedy and unfaithful man, who might get the jade without giving any city. He then summoned Lin Xiangru, a famous diplomat at that time, for advice. Lin suggested that he take the jade to Qin for the exchange. If the King of Qin kept the promise of giving 15 cities to the State of Zhao, he would give the jade to the King of Qin for exchange. Otherwise, he promised to bring the jade intact back to the Sate of Zhao.

When arriving at Qin, and presenting the jade to the King of Qin, Lin noticed that the King of Qin was totally absorbed in appreciating the jade, without showing any attempt to give 15 cities. Feeling angry and humiliated, Lin determined to cheat the King of Qin saying, "I have to tell you, Your Majesty, there are some tiny flaws in the jade. Let me show you!" Not knowing Lin was cheating him, the King of Qin returned the jade to Lin.

拿回宝玉后，蔺相如说："赵王担心秦国自恃强大，得和氏璧而不给城邑，经过我劝说方才答应。不料大王礼仪简慢，毫无交割城邑的诚意，现在若大王一定要抢走宝玉，我宁可将脑袋与宝玉一起在柱子上撞碎。"秦昭王无奈，只得答应划出 15 个城邑给赵。

蔺相如估计秦昭王不过是假意应付，便提出要秦昭王斋戒 5 日，再郑重其事地交换。秦昭王只好应允。

蔺相如拿着那块宝玉到了公馆里，就叫一个手下人打扮成一个买卖人的样儿，把那块宝玉包着，藏在身上，偷偷地从小道回到赵国去了。至于秦王会把他怎么样，他一点也没有考虑。

后来秦王发觉这件事，后悔已经来不及了，想发兵攻打赵国吧，又怕赵国在军事上做了准备。最后秦王只好放蔺相如回到赵国去。

这件事情在历史上叫作"完璧归赵"。直到今天，人们谈起这段故事来，还对蔺相如的英勇行为翘大拇指哩。

With the jade in hand, Lin ran to one of the pillars in the palace, shouting, "before my coming here, the King of Zhao told me his doubt about your promise, for which I assure him that I do believe you will keep your promise. However, I now see you have no intention to keep the promise, so I will pump my head to the pillar rashly with the jade in hand, in case you urged me to give you the jade." For fear of the ruin of the jade, the King of Qin once again promised to give 15 cities to Zhao.

Being quite clear in mind that the King of Qin was making another empty promise, Lin then required that a ceremony was needed for the exchange of the jade, and before the ceremony, the King of Qin had to fast for 5 days to show his sincerity.

In that night, Lin instructed one of his soldiers, in shabby clothes, to send the jade back to the State Zhao secretly. Lin stayed in the State Qin for 5 other days himself, never thinking about himself.

Five days later, when the King of Qin knew the jade had already been in Zhao, felt extremely angry, swearing to conquer Zhao at once. However, after thinking twice, the King of Qin gave up his idea to attack Zhao, for fear that Zhao might be already well-prepared. Without any alternative, he let Lin go back to Zhao.

Since then, the story "to return the jade intact back to the State of Zhao" became popular in China. Till now, people in China are still talking about Lin Xiangru's braveness.

玩火自焚

春秋时期，卫国的王子州吁杀死了他的哥哥卫桓公，成为卫国的国君。州吁是个暴君，他压迫百姓，到处侵略别的国家。他想利用战争来分散百姓的注意力，减少人们对他的不满，巩固他的专政统治。

鲁国的君王知道州吁篡夺了王位，还想吞并其他国家，就问他手下的一名官员："你认为州吁的目的能达到吗？"那位官员说道："州吁到处打仗，给人民来了灾难。人民不会支持他。他这个人又反复无常，身边没有什么亲信。他不可能实现自己的野心。而且，战争就像火。无休止地打仗，最后，火会烧到自己身上。"

果然，不到一年，卫国人民就在陈国的帮助下推翻了州吁的统治，并处死了他。

后来，人们用这个成语来比喻干害人的勾当，最后受害的还是自己。

Whoever Plays with Fire Gets Burned

In the Spring-Autumn Period (770–476 BC), Zhou Xu, a prince of Wei, killed his elder brother Duke Huan, and usurped the throne. Born as a tyrant, Zhou Xu was cruel to his subjects and frequently started wars with neighbouring states, trying to divert the people's attention and reduce their dissatisfaction with him so as to consolidate his autocracy.

The ruler of Lu, knowing Zhou Xu had already usurped the throne of Wei and his greed of annexation, asked one of his ministers, "He wanted to conquer other states. Do you think he will fulfil his wild ambition?"

"No, absolutely no! Because he is such a tyrant, making his people lead miserable lives. He also had no trusted followers due to his capricious character. In addition, war is like fire. The more one plays with it, the more dangerous his situation will be. It is an absolute truth that whoever plays with fire will get burned."

The minister's words were proved right soon. In less than a year, the people of Wei, with the help of the State of Chen, overthrew Zhou Xu and killed him.

Later, people use it to mean that those who do evil will finally ruin themselves.

亡羊补牢

古时候有个人，养了几只羊。

一天早上，他去放羊，发现少了一只。原来羊圈破了个窟窿，夜里，狼从窟窿钻进去，把羊叼走了。

邻居劝他说："赶快把羊圈修一修，堵上那个窟窿吧。"

他叹着气说："羊已经丢了，还修羊圈干什么呢？"

第二天早上，他去放羊，发现羊又少了一只。原来狼又从窟窿钻进去，把羊叼走了。

他很后悔没有接受邻居的忠告，心想，现在修还不晚。于是便立刻去堵上了那个窟窿，把羊圈修得结结实实的。从此，他的羊再也没丢过。

Better Late than Never

In ancient China, a man raised several sheep in his yard.

One morning, when herding his sheep, he found one of his sheep lost. After careful check, he noticed a hole in his sheepfold. It must be a hole made by a wolf, through which the sheep was carried away.

One of his neighbors suggested him to mend the sheepfold, saying, "You'd better block the hole at once, or the wolf will come again."

However, the man didn't take the neighbor's advice, sighing, "The sheep is already lost. Why bother to block the hole."

The next day, when he went to herd his sheep in the morning, he found another sheep lost. It must be carried away by the wolf, once again, through the hole.

He then felt regretful to refuse the neighbor's suggestion, and thought it better to be late than never to block the hole in the sheepfold.

After mending the sheepfold, his sheep was never lost anymore.

望梅止渴

东汉末年，曹操带兵打仗，在行军的路上遇到了很大的困难，荒原百里，没有水源。将士们都干渴难忍，有的体弱的士兵，都干渴得晕倒了，曹操看到这样的情形觉得非常难办。

于是，曹操就急步登上前面的山头，查看前方的状况。当登上山头的时候，曹操失望了，放眼望去，依然是没有人烟，哪来的水源？不过，曹操灵机一动，想到了办法。

曹操下令：士兵行至前面的梅林休息。并且准许士兵尽量吃多汁的酸梅，不受约束。士兵们想着酸梅的味道，口渴就立刻缓和下来。

后人用成语“望梅止渴”来比喻用幻想来安慰自己。

To Quench One's Thirst by Thinking of Plums

In the late Eastern Han Dynasty(AD 25–220), Cao Cao, met great trouble when marching out his troops under the burning sun in a mountainous area. The soldiers felt so thirsty under the sun that some of them even fell into dizziness. However, it was a wild mountainous place without any water source within the 100 miles nearby.

In great anxiety, Cao Cao ascended a mountain to look into the distance, which made him disappointed because he saw no water source in his range of visibility. However, an idea jumped into his mind.

He summoned all his soldiers and gave out the following order: the troop should march to the nearby plum trees for a rest, where soldiers will be allowed to eat the juicy sour fruit as much as they desired. This order made the soldiers' mouths watery, because they thought of the juicy acid flavor of plums at once.

The phrase "to quench one's thirst by thinking of plums" was used as an idiom in China, which means consoling oneself with false hopes.

望洋兴叹

成语望洋兴叹出自《庄子·外篇·秋水第十七》。故事说：秋天的大水按着时令到了，无数支流的水都灌进了黄河。河面十分宽阔，水雾蒸腾，不论是河的两岸，还是河心的沙洲，隔岸望去，简直分不清岸上的是牛还是马。这时呀，河伯欣欣然自我陶醉起来，认为天下的美景，全都集中在自己身上了。

河伯顺着水势向东前行，到了北海，朝东一看，只见一片汪洋，无边无际。到这时，河伯才开始改变他那洋洋自得的神态，仰起头来对着北海神无限感叹地说："俗话说：'有的人懂得了一点道理，便以为没有谁能比得上自己。'这正是批评我这种人的啊。今天要不是我亲眼见到这浩瀚无边的北海，我还会以为黄河是天下无比的呢！那样，岂不被有见识的人耻笑。"

这个成语原指看到人家的伟大，才感到自己的渺小。后来人们用它比喻做事力量不够或条件不充分而感到无可奈何。

Lamenting One's Littleness Before the Vast Ocean

This idiom was excerpted from a story in the *Holy Canon of Nanhua*, a Taoist classic written by Zhuangzi. It is a story about the god of a river: with the coming of autumn, all water from its numerous tributaries flowed into the Yellow River, making itself wider. The river was very broad, and it was so misty that everywhere near the river was filled with vapour, making it almost impossible to identify the objects on the bank. Seeing this, the god of the river exclaimed with excitement and conceit, "No other river on earth can compare with it. And therefore I am the greatest river god."

He then walked along the river to the North Sea, the east end of the Yellow River, where he saw the boundless ocean. The ocean made him feel ashamed for his conceit, sighing, "as the saying goes 'people who think they know everything know nothing'. Actually I am one of such people. If I haven't seen the North Sea, how can I know the Yellow River is nothing compared with the ocean. If I remained like that, I would be laughed at by sensible people."

As the story shows, the phrase "lamenting one's littleness before the vast ocean" used to mean the shameful feeling like that of the god of the river when he see the vast ocean. However, it is nowadays mainly used to mean one's helplessness when feeling powerless in doing things.

W

为虎作伥

《太平广记》记载了一个传说，相传有一只老虎把人咬死以后，吃掉人身上的肉，却不让他的灵魂离开。这个灵魂下次还要帮着老虎去吃人，让老虎再把那个人咬死、吃掉，这样这个人的灵魂才能获得自由。

这个传说后来就变成了为虎作伥这个成语，用来比喻替恶人做帮凶，引诱或帮助恶人干坏事。

To Play the Jackal to the Tiger

There is a tale recorded in *Extensive Records Compiled in the Taiping Years*, telling that a hungry tiger devoured a man and forced the man's ghost to help look for people for the tiger to eat. Only by finding another poor guy for the tiger to eat, can the ghost get its freedom to leave the tiger for good.

From this ancient story, the idiom "to play the jackal to the tiger" was made, which means holding a candle for the devil.

味如鸡肋

公元 217 年，刘备派兵进攻汉中。经过激战，终于杀死守将夏侯渊，拿下了汉中。夏侯渊被杀，汉中失守的消息传到曹操军中，曹操立即率领大军从长安前往汉中。但大军开到汉中城外时，发现那里所有有利地形都已被黄忠等抢占，一时难以取胜。双方相持了几个月，曹军的处境越来越不妙。

Tasting like Chicken Ribs

In AD 217, Liu Bei's troop started its massive attack to the Hanzhong region and killed Xiahou Yuan, a famous general of Cao Cao's army. When the news that Hanzhong was captured by Liu Bei reached Cao Cao's army, Cao Cao immediately led his army to march from Chang'an to Han Zhong. However, they reached Hanzhong only to find that all the favorable terrains had already been occupied by Huang Zhong, a general of Liu Bei, and others, making it very difficult for Cao Cao to win the battle. A stalemate lasted for several months, making Cao's army in a more and more unfavorable condition.

一天晚上曹操用饭，发现菜中有一碗是鸡肋骨做的汤。他注视着鸡肋，若有所思。正好这时他的亲信夏侯淳来请示当夜口令，曹操随口说了“鸡肋”二字。夏侯淳听了有些奇怪，但也不再询问，照原话传达下去。在营中办理文章、事务的主簿杨修听到“鸡肋”的口令后，马上收拾行装，准备动身。大家见他这样，都问他怎么知道将要退军。杨修回答说：“你们都知道，鸡肋这东西丢弃它可惜，但吃起来又没有什么肉。以它来比喻汉中，不攻下来可惜，但攻起来又不那么容易。所以我知道魏王打算退军了。”众人听了将信将疑。第二天，曹操果然下令回师，大家这才信服。

现在，“味如鸡肋”大多用于形容价值很低或没有价值的事物。

One evening, when having dinner, Cao noticed there was a soup with chicken ribs. Looking at the chicken ribs, Cao was lost in thought. Just at that time, Xiahou Chun, one of his generals, came to ask for instructions, for which Cao spoke two words without thinking. The two words are nothing else but "chicken ribs". Although feeling strange with these two words, Xiahou didn't ask further but communicated the two words to the army.

Almost all the soldiers felt the two words strange except Yang Xiu, a secretary of Cao, who packed up at once, ready to leave for Chang'an. Seeing his behavior, everybody asked him what had happened, for which Yang Xiu answered, "We all know chicken ribs are tasteless when eaten but a pity to throw away. Our lord was actually using it to metaphorically refer to Hanzhong, which was difficult to take but a pity to give up. He had already made up his mind to give it up." Everybody was not sure about Yang's saying until the next day, when Cao Cao gave out the order to return to Chang'an.

Nowadays, the phrase "tasting like chicken ribs" is used a lot to refer to things which are of little or no value.

卧薪尝胆

春秋时期，吴国和越国之间进行了一场战争，吴王阖闾不幸受了重伤，不久就死了。他的儿子夫差作了吴国的新国王，他发誓要替父亲报仇。于是，他严格地操练他的士兵，把他们训练成了一支非常厉害的军队。三年以后，他对越国发动了战争，抓住了越王勾践，把他带回了吴国。

为了复仇，夫差让勾践住在他父亲墓旁的破石屋里天天看墓、喂马。勾践表面上服从，心里面却想着复仇。几年以后，勾践被放回越国。他立刻开始秘密聚集一支军队。为了提醒自己不要忘了报仇，他睡在柴上，还每天在吃饭睡觉前尝一尝苦胆。同时，他专心治理国家，大力发展农业，加强民众教育。几年后，越国又变得强大起来，然后，勾践抓住一个适当的机会消灭了吴国。

后来，人们用它来描述为实现目标而忍辱负重，克服困难。

Stoop to Conquer

In the Spring-Autumn Period (770–476 BC), a war broke out between two states, namely Wu and Yue. During the war, Helv, the King of Wu, was severely injured, leading to his death soon. His son Fuchai, after taking the throne, swore to avenge his father's death. He drilled his army rigidly until it was a perfect fighting force. Three years later, he launched the war against Yue, and caught Goujian alive.

Fuchai ordered Goujian to live in a stone cottage beside his father's tomb, guarding the tomb and feeding horses as revenge. Goujian obeyed the order, but under the apparent obedience lied his strong wish to revenge. Years later, approved of Goujian's obedience, Fuchai let go of Goujian, who returned to his own country at once. In his own country, Goujian built up an army secretly, and forced him to sleep on sticks and taste the gall every time before the meal, so as to remind him to keep the revenge in heart. At the same time he administered his state carefully, developing agriculture and educating the people. After a few years, his country became powerful again. Then Goujian seized a favorable opportunity to wipe off the State of Wu.

Later, a phrase "stoop to conquer" was made according to Goujian's experience, and nowadays people use this phrase to describe someone who endures self-imposed hardships to strengthen one's resolution to realize one's ambition.

下车泣罪

传说舜见禹治水有功，又深受百姓爱戴便把部落联盟领袖的位置让给了他。

有一次禹乘车出外巡视，见到有个犯罪的人被押着走过。禹吩咐把车停下，问：“这人犯了什么罪？”

押送的人回答说：“他偷了别人家的稻谷被抓住，我们把他送去治罪。”禹听了便下车，来到那罪人身旁，问：“你为什么要去偷别人家的稻谷呢？”

那罪人看出问话的是个大人物，以为要严办他，吓得低着头不吭声。禹对此并不生气，一面对他进行规劝，一面流下泪来。禹左右的人见了，都很不理解。其中一个问道：“这人偷了东西，该送去受惩罚。不知大王为什么痛苦得流下眼泪？”

禹擦了擦眼泪回答说：“我不是为这个罪人流泪，而是为自己流泪。从前尧和舜做领袖的时候，老百姓都和他们同心同德；如今我做了领袖，老百姓却不和我同心同德，做出这损人利己的事来，所以我内心感到非常痛苦！”

禹当即命侍从取出一块龟板，在上面刻写了“百姓有罪，在予一人”八个字，然后下令把那罪人放了。

To Turn Others' Crimes into One's Own Count

In Chinese legends, Shun and Yu are both respectable tribal alliance leaders. After serving as the leader for several years, Shun abdicated and handed over the crown to Yu.

One day when Yu was out for an inspection tour on a carriage, he saw a criminal being escorted by officers. He ordered to pull up and asked, "What crime has this man committed?"

"He was caught stealing other's millet. We are sending him to the court." One of the officers answered.

Hearing this, Yu got off to come close to the criminal and asked, "Why did you do that?"

Knowing Yu a big shot, the criminal thought Yu was going to punish him severely, so he kept silent with his head bowed.

Yu wasn't angry about it, and he cried as he admonished the criminal. People on site didn't understand Yu, and one of them asked, "This guy deserves punishment. I wonder why Your Majesty shed tears for him?"

"I am not crying for him. Instead, I am crying for myself. When Yao and Shun were leaders, people are of one heart and one mind. Now when I am the leader, some of my people do things that are detrimental to others. This made me feel so sad." Yu answered, wiping his tears.

Yu then ordered his attendants to take a turtle shell, on which several words were carved: "when people commit crimes, the leader should be punished". He then released the criminal.

相敬如宾

春秋时期，晋国大臣郤芮因罪被杀，儿子郤缺也被废为平民，务农为生。郤缺不因生活环境和个人际遇的巨大变化而怨天尤人，而是一面勤恳耕作以谋生，一面以古今圣贤为师刻苦修身，德行与日俱增。不仅妻子甚为仰慕，就连初次结识的人也无不赞叹。

一次郤缺在田间除草，午饭时间妻子将饭送到地头，十分恭敬地跪在丈夫面前，郤缺连忙接住，频致谢意。夫妻俩相互尊重，饭虽粗陋，倒也吃得有滋有味。

此情此景，感动了路过此地的晋国大夫胥臣。经过一番交谈，胥臣认为郤缺是治国之才，极力举荐他为下军大夫，后来郤缺立大功，升为卿大夫。

To Be Always Courteous Toward Each Other like Guests

In the Spring-Autumn Period (770–476 BC), Xi Rui, a nobleman in the State of Jin, was executed. His son Xi Que, was also degraded into a civilian who lived on farming. In spite of the huge changes in living environment and personal encounters, Xi Que maintained a positive attitude toward life. He not only worked hard on the farm but also cultivated his morality as the ancient sages did, which made him a venerable man admired not only by his wife but even by people who met him for the first time.

One day when Xi was weeding in the farm, his wife came to send meal for him. Seeing Xi, his wife fell on her knees with great respect and handed the meal to him, for which Xi felt grateful and took over the meal with great courtesy. They then ate the meal together with a good appetite, although the meal was simple.

Xu Chen, a high official of Jin, who happened to pass by and saw the couple's behavior, was deeply touched by what he saw. He regarded Xi as a talent and his later conversation with Xi proved his thinking. He then recommended Xi to the King. With Xu's help, Xi became an official and was later promoted to a higher position due to his achievement.

笑里藏刀

唐太宗时，有个名字叫李义府的人，因善写文章，被推荐当了监察御史。李义府还善于奉承，他曾写文章颂扬过唐太宗，因此博得太宗的赏识。唐高宗时，李义府又得到高宗的信任，任中书令。从此更加飞黄腾达。

李义府外表温和谦恭，同人说话总带微笑，但大臣们知道，他心地极其阴险，因此都说他笑里藏刀。李义府在朝中为所欲为，培植亲信，任意让妻儿向人索取钱财，还随意封官许愿。高宗知道这些以后，曾婉转地告诫过他，但李义府并不放在心上。

有一次，李义在宫中看到一份任职名单，回家后，让儿子把即将任职的人找来，对他说："你不是想做官吗？几天内诏书即可下来，你该怎样谢我？"那人见有官做，立刻奉上厚礼。之后，高宗得知了此事，觉得不能再容忍了，就以"泄露机密"为名，将李义府父子发配边疆。

A Wolf in Sheep's Clothing

During the reign of Emperor Taizong of Tang, a man named Li Yifu was nominated to be the supervisory censor, because he was good at writing, besides, flattering. In one of his writings, he ever flattered Taizong, which made him highly appreciated by Taizong. He was also appreciated by Gaozong, Taizong's son who took the throne when Taizong died. He then was appointed as the Chief of the Central Secretariat during Gaozong's reign.

However, although appearing to be modest and polite, Li was actually well-known as an insidious man by his peers, who secretly remarked him as a wolf in sheep's clothing.

His peers were not framing him up. In the court, he did numerous illegal things, such as nurturing his cronies, letting his wife and son accept bribes, and promising high posts and other favors for others who bribed him. Walls have ears and his deeds were more or less known by Gaozong, who warned him in an indirect way. However, he seemed not influenced by Gaozong's warning, which doomed his failure later.

His failure came when one day he saw a name list on which names of future officials were written. Back home, he asked his son to call for one of the future officials, and told him, "I know you wish to be one of us. I promise you will get the position, but I wonder what you will do to repay me?" That man, hearing his words, gave him bribe at once.

As it had been mentioned that "walls have ears", Gaozong soon knew what Li did and flew into rage. In a short time, Li, the "wolf in sheep's clothing", with his son, was exiled to the frontier as a punishment for his revealing secret.

胸有成竹

北宋画家文同，字与可。他画的竹子远近闻名，每天总有不少人登门求画。

文同在自己家的房前屋后种上各种各样的竹子。无论春夏秋冬，阴晴风雨，他都会去竹林观察竹子的生长变化情况，琢磨竹枝的长短粗细，叶子的形态、颜色，每当有新的感受就回到书房，铺纸研墨，把心中的印象画在纸上。

日积月累，竹子在不同季节、不同天气、不同时辰的形象都深深地印在他的心中，只要凝神提笔，在画纸前一站，平日观察到的各种形态的竹子立刻浮现在眼前。所以每次画竹，他都显得非常从容自信，画出的竹子，无不逼真传神。

当人们夸奖他的画时，他总是谦虚地说："我只是把心中琢磨成熟的竹子画下来罢了。"诗人晁补之写了一首诗评价文与可画竹，其中有两句："与可画竹，胸有成竹。"

A Well-regulated Mind

Wen Tong, whose literary name is Yuke, is a famous artist of Chinese painting in Song Dynasty (AD 960–1279). His painting of bamboos was so popular in China that lots of people came to visit him for his paintings everyday.

Wen was such a bamboo-lover that he had grown various types of bamboos around his house. He would look at the bamboos closely, observing their process of growth and appearance in different seasons. Whenever he had new reflections about the painting of bamboos, he would immediately go to his studio to paint it down.

This made him know bamboos so well that whenever he took out his painting brush, he had already had a picture of the bamboos in his mind. Therefore, he could always paint bamboos in a vivid and lively way.

Although people admired his paintings so much, he always kept a low profile, saying, "It's no big deal. I just paint the bamboos in my heart down." Chao Buzhi, one of his friends, ever wrote a poem about his painting, of which one sentence was like this, "when painting bamboos, Yuke had already had a well-regulated mind."

X

削足适履

汉朝有一本叫《淮南子》的书，讲述了一个故事：有一天一个愚人去买鞋，店主拿给他一双鞋，鞋小了，他不是让店主去换，而是打算把自己的脚削去一块，来适应鞋的大小。他去帽店买帽子，帽子小了，他又打算把自己的头皮削去一点，以适应帽子的大小。

“削足适履”比喻办事情不遵循实际情况，生拉硬套，牵强附会。

To Cut One's Feet to Fit the Shoes

In *Huainanzi*, a collection of various philosophical treatises compiled in Han Dynasty (220 BC–AD 8), there is a story about a fool: one day, the fool went to buy shocs. After trying on a pair of shoes the shopkeeper gave him, he found the shoes too small. To the shopkeeper's surprise, he cut his feet to fit the shoes, rather than ask the shopkeeper to change the shoes for another pair. The fool then went to a hat shop, where he meant to cut his head to fit into a hat that was not of his size.

People then use the phrase "to cut one's feet to fit the shoes" to refer to people like the fool who acts in a procrustean way and never considers the practical situation.

Y

掩耳盗铃

在战国时期，有一个小偷偷了一只钟。他准备把钟扛在背上带走。可是钟又大又沉，很难扛走。因此他想用锤子把钟敲成碎片，这样运起来就能轻松多了。可是，他敲了一下，那只钟便发出巨大的响声。他怕别人听到了钟声会发现他，于是他在用锤子敲钟时捂上了自己的耳朵。不过，即使他这样做，别人还是听得到钟声的。

所以“掩耳盗铃”是非常愚蠢的行为，就像把头埋在沙子中一样。后来，人们用此成语来形容那些自欺欺人之徒。

To Plug One's Ears While Stealing a Bell

In the Warring States Period (475–221 BC), a thief had stolen a bell and wanted to carry it away on his back. The bell was too bulky and heavy for him to carry, so he found a hammer to strike the bell with his all might, aiming to break it into pieces. The striking produced an enormous crashing sound, making the thief terribly frightened. For fear of the sound being heard by other people, he then plugged his ears when striking the bell, which, of course, led to his being caught on site.

From this story, we know "to plug one's ears while stealing a bell" is a rather ridiculous behavior. It is like what ostriches did when in danger. Later, people have used the phrase "plugging one's ears while stealing a bell" to refer to the ignorance and foolishness of the person who deceives himself as well as others.

偃旗息鼓

故事发生在三国时期。一次，曹操与刘备交战。刘备命令大将赵云去抢夺曹操的粮食。曹操带领大军追赶。赵云边打边退，一直退到营寨前，叫士兵打开营门，放倒军旗，停止擂鼓，在营外设好埋伏。

生性多疑的曹操追到寨门口，心想，寨门大开，必有伏兵，即匆忙下令撤退。就在曹操调头后退的时候，蜀军营里金鼓齐鸣，杀声震天，飞箭如雨般射向曹军。曹军惊慌失措，夺路逃命，自相践踏。赵云趁势夺了曹军的粮草，杀死了曹军大批兵马，得胜回营。

后来，“偃旗息鼓”这个成语就用来比喻停止攻击或者事情中止。

To Furl All the Banners and Silence All the Drums

In the Three Kingdoms Period (AD 220–280), a war broke out between Cao Cao and Liu Bei. Under Liu Bei's order, Zhao Yun, a general of Liu Bei, went to Cao Cao's camp to loot Cao's food supplies. Rather irritated by it, Cao Cao led on a large force against Zhao Yun, who then retreated swiftly as far as the gates of his camp. Zhao Yun gave out orders to open the gate widely, and to furl all the banners and silence all the drums, while secretly stationed his troops in ambush nearby.

Seeing this, Cao Cao, suspicious by nature, was afraid of falling into Zhao Yun's ambush and gave out an order to retreat his army. When Cao Cao was about to leave, Zhao Yun ordered his soldiers to unfurl all the banners and beat drums. At the same time, countless arrows flew to Cao's army, making the soldiers trample on each other in great panic when running for their lives. This provided a favorable situation for Zhao Yun to loot Cao Cao's food supplies.

From then on, this idiom "to furl all the banners and silence all the drums" has been used a lot to metaphorically indicate halting an attack or ceasing all activities.

Y

叶公好龙

叶公喜欢龙，衣带钩、酒器上都刻着龙，居室里雕镂装饰的也是一条条张牙舞爪的龙。他这样爱龙，被天上的真龙知道后，便从天上下降到叶公家里，龙头搭在窗台上探望，龙尾伸到了厅堂里。叶公一看真龙，转身就跑，吓得像失了魂似的，惊恐万状。由此看来，叶公并不是真的喜欢龙，他喜欢的只不过是那些像龙的东西。

人们用“叶公好龙”形容自称爱好某种事物，实际却害怕的人。

False Love of What One Actually Fears

Ye Gong was well-known for his fondness of dragons. In his house, dragons could be seen everywhere, up and down, front and back, each baring its teeth and brandishing its claws.

His love for dragon was later known by the real dragon, which lived in the heaven. The real dragon was so happy that one day, it flew to Ye's house, wishing to get acquainted with Ye. It landed on the roof of Ye's house, its head on Ye's window, looking inside eagerly for Ye, its tail toiled to the window, rocking and rattling the whole house.

Ye Gong, however, was frightened out of his wits by the unexpected coming of the real dragon, and ran for his life immediately. So it turned out that what Ye Gong really loved was not a real dragon, but something resembling a dragon.

People then use the phrase "false love of what one really fears" to refer to people who profess to love what they really fear.

夜郎自大

汉朝的时候，在西南方有个名叫夜郎的小国家，它虽然是一个独立的国家，可是国土很小，百姓也少，物产更是少得可怜。从没离开过国家的夜郎国国王却以为自己统治的国家是全天下最大的国家。

有一天，夜郎国国王与部下巡视国境的时候，他指着前方问道："这里哪个国家最大呀？"部下们为了迎合国王的心意，于是就说："当然是夜郎国最大！"走着走着，国王又抬起头来，望着前方的高山又问道："天底下还有比这座山更高的山吗？"部下们回答说："天底下没有比这座山更高的山了。"后来，他们来到河边，国王说："我认为这可是世界上最长的河川了。"部下们仍然异口同声回答说："大王说得一点都没错。"

从此以后，无知的国王就更相信夜郎是天底下最大的国家了。

有一次，汉朝派使者来到夜郎，骄傲又无知的国王因为不知道自己统治的国家只和汉朝的一个县差不多大，竟然不知天高地厚地问使者："汉朝和我的国家哪个大？"

后来人们就用成语夜郎自大来比喻本来没有什么能耐，却自以为很了不起而瞧不起别人的人。

Ludicrous Conceit of the King of Yelang

In Han Dynasty (220 BC–AD 220), there was a small country called Yelang on the southwest border of China. Independent as it is, it was small in size and population, and was poor in natural resources. However, its king, who had never seen the outside world, always regarded his kingdom as the largest country in the world.

One day, when patrolling his country with the officials, the King, in arrogance, asked his officials, "Which country is the biggest one in the world?" His officials replied: "Yelang, for sure!"

He then asked again, pointing to the mountain in front of them. "Is there a higher mountain than this one?" His officials once again replied, "of course not! This is the tallest one."

When coming close to a river, the King continued, "I think this is the longest river in the world. Don't you think so?" It's no doubt that the officials answered, "Yes, it is!"

After this patrol, the King became more and more proud of his country, thinking it big and powerful.

One day, a Han envoy visited Yelang. The self-conceited King, not knowing his country is of the same size as a county of Han, asked the envoy arrogantly, "Which is bigger, Han or my country?"

Later this idiom came to be used to refer to those who are capable of nothing yet are conceited.

Y

一鼓作气

春秋时代，齐国派兵攻打鲁国。鲁国的国王鲁庄公带着谋士曹刿指挥作战。

齐军第一次击鼓以后，鲁军准备发起进攻。曹刿说：“不行。”齐军三次击鼓以后，曹刿才说：“现在可以进攻了。”结果齐军大败。战斗结束后，鲁庄公问曹刿胜利的原因。曹刿说：“打仗要靠勇气。第一次击鼓，士气十分旺盛；第二次击鼓，士气有些衰落；第三次击鼓，士气就消耗尽了。敌人士气耗尽，我们趁机发起进攻，所以取得了胜利。”

此后，这个成语就被用来形容做事情时鼓足干劲，一口气把工作做完。

Rousing the Spirits with the First Drum Roll

In the Spring-Autumn Period (770–221 BC), the army of Qi launched a military attack against Lu. Zhuang Gong, the King of Lu, commanded the battle with the help of Cao Gui, one of his military advisers.

In the war, after the first roll of drums from the Qi side to summon Lu to battle, Zhuang Gong wanted to attack. However, Cao Gui suggested him to wait for the right chance, saying, "we should wait for Qi's third drum roll."

After Qi's army beat the drums for three rolls, Zhuang Gong gave out orders to attack, and they successfully beat the enemy.

After the battle, Zhuang Gong asked Cao Gui why he suggested starting the attack when hearing Qi's third drum roll, for which Cao Gui answered, "In a battle, spirits are needed. Their spirit was aroused by the first roll of the drums, but was depleted by the second. And it was completely exhausted by the third. When they are exhausted, it is a good opportunity for us to start the attack."

Now, the idiom refers to getting something done in a vigorous effort and without stop.

Y

一箭双雕

南北朝时，北周有个叫长孙晟的武将，善于射箭，又智谋超人。他曾被派遣护送公主到西北突厥去成婚。突厥国王摄图很器重他，把他留了下来，常让他随自己一起去打猎。一次，摄图看见两只大雕在空中争夺一块肉，便交给长孙晟两支箭，请他将雕射下来。长孙晟跨马前奔，拉开弓，只听嗖的一声，一箭竟穿过两只大雕的胸脯。雕顿时双双落下。

这个成语原指射箭技术高超。现指一举两得。

Kill Two Hawks with One Arrow

In the period of the Northern and Southern Dynasties (AD 420–589), there was an expert archer named Zhangsun Sheng in the Northern Zhou Dynasty. Due to his extraordinary skills in archery and his fast wits, he was ordered by the emperor to escort the princess to Turks, a nationality in the northwest border of ancient China, for imperial marriage.

Ishbara Qaghan, the Khan of the Turkic Khanate, also known as She Tu, regarded highly of Sheng, and made him stay in Turks as one of his subordinates. When going out for hunting, Qaghan often asked Sheng to accompany him.

One day, when out hunting, Qaghan saw two hawks fighting for a piece of meat in the air. He then handed two arrows to Sheng, asking him to shoot the two hawks. To everyone's amazement, Sheng, on horse back, killed the two hawks with only one arrow in an almost effortless way.

People then use the phrase "two hawks with one arrow" to describe one's proficient skills. Nowadays, it is used to mean achieving a dual purpose, an equivalent to another phrase "to kill two birds with one stone" in English.

一鸣惊人

战国时期，有一个大臣叫淳于髡，他身材矮小，但非常有头脑，齐威王继承王位已有三年了，可是他整天饮酒作乐，不理朝政。于是淳于髡想了个激励齐威王的办法。他说："大王，臣听说齐国北方有一只大鸟，三年来不飞也不叫，大王知道这是一只什么鸟？"齐威王知道淳于髡在暗喻自己，不由得大笑起来。笑过一阵后，他才说："此鸟不飞则已，一飞冲天；不鸣则已，一鸣惊人！"从此齐威王勤于朝政，励精图治，国威大振。

成语"一鸣惊人"比喻平时默默无闻，突然干出一番惊人的事来。

Startling the World with a Single Cry

In the Warring States Period (475–221 BC), there was an official named Chunyu Kun in the State of Qi. Although a man of small size, he was very intelligent.

King Wei of Qi, who had already taken his throne for 3 years, was indulged in drinking binges everyday, and ignored the state affairs.

To make King Wei concentrate on the state affairs, Chunyu told the king a funny story, "Your Majesty, I heard that in the north, there was a big bird dwelling in the hills. Although three years had passed, it neither flew nor cried. Could Your Majesty tell me the reason?"

Knowing quite clear that Chunyu was actually insinuating his indulgence, King Wei burst into laughter. Halting his laughter, King Wei said the following words seriously, "Once that bird starts to fly and sing, it will astonish the world." King Wei thereupon devoted himself to his duties and built his state up into a powerful one.

This idiom, which is equivalent to "to set the Thames on fire", is used to indicate that a person may rise from obscurity and achieve greatness astonishingly.

Y

一毛不拔

墨翟，是战国时期的大思想家，史称墨子，是墨家学派的创始人。他主张兼爱，反对战争。

同一时期，还有一位叫杨朱的哲学家，他反对墨子的兼爱，主张贵生、重己，重视个人生命的保存，反对他人对自己的侵夺，也反对自己对别人进行侵夺。

有一次，墨子的学生禽滑釐问杨朱道："如果拔下你身上一根汗毛，能使天下人得到好处，你拔不拔？"

杨朱回答："天下人的问题，绝不是拔一根汗毛所能解决得了的！"

禽滑釐又说："假使能的话，你愿意吗？"

杨朱默不作声了。

这个成语原指杨朱的极端为我主义。后形容为人非常吝啬自私。

Unwilling to Give Up Even a Hair

Mo Di, known as Mo-tse, was a very famous philosopher living in the Warring States Period (475–221 BC). He founded the school of Mohism, advocating universal love and non-aggression.

There was another school in his time, founded by Yang Zhu, another philosopher who was against Mo's idea, especially his idea of universal love, and was preaching his ideas of self-seeking and egoism. He also advocated an idea of "no trespass" between people, which, in some degree, was similar to Mo's idea of "non-aggression".

One day, Qingu Xi, one of Mo's disciples, asked Yang Zhu, "If you can benefit the people by pulling one your countless hair, will you do it?"

"It's nonsense. How can I benefit the people by pulling a hair?" Yang Zhu answered in contempt.

"I mean if. If it really can benefit the people, will you do it?" Qingu Xi asked again.

This made Yang Zhu quite embarrassed. He said nothing to the question, because if he indeed spoke his true idea out, he would be laughed at by people.

From this story, we know Yang Zhu's idea, compared with Mo's, was a rather selfish one. This idiom originally indicated extreme egoism. People now use the phrase "unwilling to give up even a hair" to refer to selfish ones, meaning they are very stingy.

Y

一丘之貉

汉朝汉宣帝时，有个很有名的人叫杨恽，他的父亲是汉昭帝时的丞相，母亲是史学家司马迁的女儿。他从小受到良好的教养，少年时在朝廷中的名气就很大，因为向汉宣帝举发大将霍光谋反，被封为平通侯。汉朝当时的社会贿赂风气很严重，有钱人用钱行贿，可以到处玩乐，没钱贿赂的人一年到头都要辛苦地工作。因此他大力革除了这些弊病，整顿了朝廷的不良风气，获得了人们的称赞。他自认为功劳很高，有时目中无人，得罪了太仆戴长乐。

有一次，杨恽听说匈奴的首领单于被人杀了，便说：这是不明是非的君王，忠心的臣子提议的治国策略不用，却听信小人的谗言，杀害忠良，结果性命不保，国家灭亡。秦朝如果不是因为这样，也许现在还存在，而不会被汉朝代替。自古以来，各朝代的君王都是如此，喜欢听信小人的谗言，就像从同一个山丘里出产的貉，没有什么差别。这话传到长乐的耳里，他连忙向汉宣帝报告，宣帝听到杨恽把自己和历代君王比作一丘之貉非常震怒，再加上长乐又说了许多杨恽的坏话，因此就下令革去杨恽的官职。

后来“一丘之貉”用来比喻那些臭味相投、不务正业的人。

Birds of the Same Feather

During the Reign of Emperor Xuan of Han Dynasty, there was a minister named Yang Yun. Yang was born in an aristocratic family, whose father was the Imperial Chancellor of Emperor Zhao's reign, mother the daughter of Sima Qian, a well-known historiographer. Well-bred, he made a name for himself in his boyhood days, and was conferred the title of Marquis of Pingtong later due to his meritorious service in exposing the revolt of Huo Guang. In his time, bribery was a common practice. By bribery, the rich could do whatever they want without being punished, while the poor led miserable lives because they had no money to bribe. Yang detested it so much that he took some measures to get rid of bribery, which won him reputation among people. However, he was kind of supercilious, making him envied by some of his peers, Dai Changle, for instance.

One day, when hearing the news that the leader of the Huns was killed, Yang remarked in this way, "He is a leader who listens to one-side story, so he deserves to be killed. It is the same thing in Qin Dynasty. If the Emperor of Qin hadn't acted like the Huns' leader, Qin might not have been replaced by Han. It's a pity that almost all emperors listen to one-side stories as the Huns' leader did. They are just like birds of the same feather!"

His words were later known by Dai Changle, who then reported it to Emperor Xuan, putting in many striking additions. Emperor Xuan then flew into rage and discharged Yang from his position.

This idiom is now used to refer to people of the same kind who do not attend to their proper work and have the same bad habits.

一饭千金

帮助汉高祖打天下的大将韩信，在未得志时，境况很是困苦。

那时候，他时常去城下钓鱼，希望碰着好运气，便可以解决生活。但是，这究竟不是可靠的办法，因此，时常要饿着肚子。幸而在他钓鱼的地方，有很多漂母（清洗丝棉絮或旧衣布的老婆婆）在河边作工。其中有一个漂母很同情韩信的遭遇，便不断地救济他，给他饭吃。韩信在艰难困苦中，得到那位勤劳善良仅能以双手勉强糊口的漂母的恩惠，很是感激，便对她说，将来必定要重重地报答她。那漂母听了韩信的话，很是不高兴，表示并不希望韩信将来报答她的。后来，韩信替汉王立了不少功劳，被封为楚王，他想起从前曾受过漂母的恩惠，便命从人送酒菜给她吃，更送给她黄金一千两作为答谢。

这句成语即出自这个故事，意思是比喻重重地报答对自己有恩的人。

To Bestow upon the Former Benefactor a Thousand Taels of Silver

Han Xin, a military officer of great contributions in battles, used to live a tough life before he won recognition from Liu Bang, the first emperor of Han Dynasty.

To feed himself, he usually went fishing in the suburb and wished a good luck to fill the belly. However, it was not a reliable way of living at all, and he often ended up a day in hunger.

Fortunately for him, there were lots of laundry workers by the river, one of whom was a kind-hearted old lady who often gave food to Han. It's worth mentioning that it was really a hard choice for the old lady to give material assistance to Han, for she herself was living from hand to mouth, with her hardworking as her sole income.

Han Xin was holding such a grateful attitude toward the old lady that he promised he would pay her back one day. The old lady, however, was not happy about what Han said, saying, "I didn't expect you to pay me back, so you can forget it."

Years later, Han became an excellent military officer of Liu Bang, and was conferred the title of "the Lord of Chu". He didn't forget the old lady, and thought it was time for him to pay the lady back. He then sent someone to bring delicious food to the lady, and gave her a thousand taels of silver in reward for the lady's help.

People then use the phrase to refer to someone who pays back a debt of gratitude with rich rewards.

一厢情愿

从前，有个农夫偶然在国都看见了公主，顿时被她的美貌倾倒。回家后，天天思念，不久就生病了。

他的亲人和朋友都来看他。他们知道农夫想娶公主后，觉得事情很难办。因为国王是不会把女儿嫁给一个农夫的。可这个农夫叫道："得不到公主我会死的。"朋友们说服不了他，只好想了一个办法骗他。

几天后，他们又来看农夫，并告诉他他们去见过公主，但公主拒绝了他们的请求。其实，他们根本没见过公主。农夫相信了朋友们的话，可他并不死心。他认为如果他亲自去，公主一定会答应。

后来，人们就用"一厢情愿"来比喻一个人只顾自己的想法，不管当时的客观情况，也不理会别人的看法。

One's Own Wishful Thinking

In ancient China, there was a farmer living in the suburb of the capital city. One day, when sightseeing in the capital, he saw the princess, and lost his heart to her at the first sight. From then on, he missed the princess day and night, making himself fall ill soon.

When his relatives and friends came to see him, he told them he wanted to marry the princess. This made his relatives and friends quite puzzled, for they knew it was impossible for the king to consent his daughter's marrying a poor farmer. Then they determined to help the farmer, because the farmer insisted that he would die of lovesickness if he couldn't marry the princess.

Days later, they came back to see the farmer again, telling him he was refused by the princess. It was, of course, a white lie. They hoped the farmer would stop his fantasy and go back to his normal life. Contrary to their expectation, the farmer, instead, believed the princess would accept his love if he could meet her in person.

From then on, people in China use the phrase "one's own wishful thinking" to describe the man who only considers his own aspiration, ignoring the objective situation and other's opinions.

一言为重

古时候秦国有个相国叫商鞅，秦王很器重他。公元前 359 年，他打算在秦国实行变法，但他怕百姓们不相信官府，就决定做件事以取得他们的信任。

有一天，他把一根 10 米长的竿子竖在都城南门外，然后告诉百姓如果谁把这根竹竿拿到城边北门，就赏给他 10 两银子。开始，大家听到这个消息都很吃惊，没人敢试。于是商鞅又提高声音说："谁把这根竹竿拿到北门，赏 50 两银子。"这时，有一个胆子挺大的人愿意去试一试。当他把竹竿拿到北门时，商鞅立刻赏给他 50 两银子。其他人看见了，都非常后悔自己没去试。

经过这件事，大家都相信了官府。后来商鞅的变法进行得很成功，秦国因此成为当时最强大的国家。宋代王安石就作诗纪念："自古驱民在信诚，一言为重百金轻。"

后来，人们就用"一言为重"来比喻一个人信守诺言。

To Keep One's Promise

In the Warring States Period (475–221 BC), Shang Yang was highly appreciated by the King of Qin, and was nominated as the Prime Minister. With the King's support, Shang decided to implement a political reform in Qin in 359 BC. To show the government's resolution in carrying out the reform, he thought of an idea to win citizens' trust.

The idea was to have a 10-meter long pole erected at the south gate outside the capital, and to ask the crowd to carry it to the north gate. He told the crowd that anyone who made it would be awarded 10 ounces of silver. People were shocked by what Shang said, yet it was hard for them to believe it. Seeing this, Shang raised his voice to say, "Anyone who carries it to the north gate will be awarded 50 ounces of silver, and for this I promise you!" Out of curiosity, a man did carry it to the north gate, for which he was indeed awarded the money promised, making the others very regretful for not believing Shang's words.

In this way, Shang Yang achieved his aim successfully. Soon the state of Qin became the strongest country. Wang Anshi, a poet living in Song Dynasty wrote a poem in honor of Shang Yang, "Getting trust from people is important for ruling, while keeping promise is more valuable than 100 pounds of gold."

Later, people use it to praise the man who keeps his promise.

一字之师

唐代僧人齐己，对诗文很有兴趣，常带着自己写的诗稿，前来拜会诗人郑谷。

一天，齐己把诗稿一首一首地拿出来请郑谷看。郑谷读到《早梅》这首诗时，不由得沉思起来。郑谷吟道："前村深雪里，昨夜数枝开……"郑谷对齐已说："梅开数枝，就不算早了。"郑谷又沉吟了一会，说："不如把'数'字改为'一'字。"齐己听了，惊喜地叫道："改得太好了！"恭恭敬敬地向郑谷拜了一拜。文人们知道了，就把郑谷称为齐己的"一字之师"。

A Teacher of "One" Word

In Tang Dynasty (AD 618–907), there was a monk whose monastic name was Qi Ji. He had great interest in writing poems and often called on Zheng Gu, a poet of his time, with his poems.

One day, Qi Ji was showing his poems one by one to Zheng Gu. Zheng lost in thought when a poem entitled *Plum Blossoms in Early Spring* came into his sight. The poems had two sentences reading like this, "in the snowfield near the village, several plum blossoms appeared last night", for which Zheng remarked, "if several plum blossoms appeared, it is no longer early spring." Pondering over it for another while, Zheng then suggested, "how about changing the word "several" into "one"?"

This suggestion made Qi enlightened. He then bowed to Zheng, saying delightedly, "You are so right. The word makes my poem perfect."

From then on, Zheng was well-known as the "one word teacher" of Qi.

Y

以管窥天

春秋时期，齐国神医扁鹊经过虢国听说虢太子猝死，就问中庶子太子的症状，认为虢太子只是假死可以救活。中庶子不信，扁鹊认为他是以管窥天、孤陋寡闻，就在太子的穴位上扎针，太子就苏醒过来，再经汤药调解，20 天后就完全康复。

这个成语比喻见闻狭隘或看事片面。

Being of a Narrow Vision

In the Spring-Autumn Period (770–476 BC), there was a great physician named Bian Que in the State of Qi. One day, when passing by the State of Guo, Bian Que heard of the sudden death of Guo's crown prince. He then asked one of the courtiers about the syndromes of the prince, and in accordance with the syndromes, he asserted that the prince was actually not dead but in a state of syncope.

The courtiers, of course, didn't believe Bian Que's words and refused to let him cure the prince. In anger, Bian Que cursed them as people of a narrow vision, while at the same time gave an acupuncture treatment to the prince's body. It was hard for the courtiers to believe that the prince regained consciousness with Bian Que's treatment. The revived prince then took the medicine prescribed by Bian Quan and recovered 20 days later.

Nowadays, this idiom is used to describe people who are short-sighted and have no comprehensive view toward things.

Y

以邻为壑

禹是中国历史上著名的治水专家。到了战国初，有个叫白圭的水利专家，也非常出名。什么地方河堤有了裂缝、漏洞，他一到就能修好。

后来，他被魏国请去当相国，魏国的国君对他很信任。有一次，孟子来到魏国，白圭在会见他的时候，表露出自己有非凡的治水本领，甚至自我吹嘘说："我的治水本领已经超过大禹了！"孟子是位非常有学问的人，当场驳斥他说："你说的话错了。大禹治水是把四海当作大水沟，顺着水性疏导，结果洪水都流进大海，与己有利，与人无害。如今称治水，只是修堤堵河，把邻国当作大水沟，结果洪水都流到别国去，与己有利，与人却有害。这种治水的方法，怎么能与大禹的相比呢？"

后来，人们用这个成语来比喻只图自己一方的利益，把困难或祸害转嫁给别人。

Benefiting Oneself at the Expense of Others

Yu, one of the greatest tribal chiefs in Chinese history, was also known as an excellent expert in regulating water conservancy. In the Warring States Period (475–221 BC), there was another water conservancy expert named Bai Gui. He was famous for being able to repair any water-leaking dams.

Due to his great reputation, he was invited to work as the prime minister of Wei, and won an unconditional trust from the King of Wei.

One day, Mencius, a great philosopher of China, visited Wei and was received by Bai Gui, the prime minister. Bai Gui was so proud of his own achievement in regulating water conservancy that when meeting Mencius, he couldn't help lavishing praise on himself like this, "It is no exaggeration to say that my capability in water conservancy has surpassed that of Yu's."

However, to his surprise, Mencius, one of the greatest philosophers and scholars in China, contradicted him in this way, "As far as I can see, Yu regulated water in a completely different way from you, as he was actually taking the sea to be the spillway, leading the flood into it, which benefited his own state, while doing no harm to the neighbouring states. On the other hand, nowadays, when regulating flood, experts choose to take the neighbouring states as the spillway by building high dams to halt the flood from his own state, which benefits his own state at the expense of the neighbouring states. So how can you compare yourself with Yu?"

Nowadays, the phrase is often used to mean considering only one's own profits and transferring crisis to others.

Y

以貌取人

春秋时期，孔子的弟子子羽相貌丑陋，孔子对他很冷淡，认为他不会成才。然而子羽品德极好，继续自修。后来，子羽成为有名的学者，声誉很高，各国诸侯都很敬重他。而弟子宰予长得很好且巧言善辩，起初孔子对他很有好感，但他既无仁德又无学识。宰予后来做了齐国的大夫，因与人合谋作乱，被齐王处死。

孔子听说后感慨地说："我凭人说话来衡量人，在宰予身上犯了错误；凭相貌衡量人，在子羽身上犯了错误。看来是不能以貌取人啊！"

Judge People by Their Appearance

In thc Spring and Autumn Period (770–221 BC), Confucius had quite a number of students, one of whom was called Zi Yu. Confucius always held an indifferent attitude toward Zi Yu, because Zi Yu was as ugly as a stick. Although being treated by his teacher in that way, Zi Yu was always a diligent learner and later became a well-known scholar. He enjoyed a great prestige and every duke deeply respected him. It happened that Confucius had another student named Zai Yu, who was a nice-looking guy but good for nothing. Confucius liked him because he struck an attitude of a gentleman, but he was not a man of virtue. Later, Zai Yu became a senior official in the State of Qi. In the end, he was executed by the King of Qi because he conspired to stage an armed rebellion.

Confucius sighed, "I judged people by their appearance and made a mistake on Zi Yu; I judged people by their words and made a mistake on Zai Yu. It's unwise to judge people by their appearance."

The idiom means judging people by their appearance and words.

以卵击石

墨子是战国时期有名的思想家。有一年，墨子前往北方的齐国。途中遇见一个算命先生，他对墨子说："您不能往北走啊，今天天帝在北边杀黑龙，你的皮肤很黑，去北方是不吉利的呀！"墨子说："我不相信你的话！"说完，他继续朝北走去。但不久，他又回来了，因为北边的淄水泛滥，无法渡过河去。

算命先生得意地对墨子说："怎么样？我说你不能往北走嘛！遇到麻烦了吧？"墨子微微一笑，说："淄水泛滥，南北两方的行人全都受阻隔。行人中有皮肤黑的，也有皮肤白的，怎么都过不去呀？"算命先生听后支吾着说不出话来。墨子又说："假如天帝在东方杀了青龙，在南方杀了赤龙，在西方杀了白龙，又在中央杀了黄龙，岂不是让全天下的人都动弹不得了吗？所以，你的谬论是抵挡不过我的道理的，就好比拿鸡蛋去碰石头，把普天下的鸡蛋全碰光了，石头还是毁坏不了。"

算命先生听后羞愧地走了。

Like an Egg Trying to Crush a Stone

Mo-tse is a famous philosopher who lived in the Warring States Period (475–221 BC).

One year, he was heading for the State of Qi in the north. On the way, he came across a fortune-teller, who told him, "You can not go north, because the Lord of Heaven is now slaughtering a black dragon there. It's unlucky for you to go there because you are dark in color." Mo-tse didn't believe the fortune-teller's words and kept heading for north. However, he went back soon, for the river on the north was in flood, making it unable to cross.

Seeing Mo-tse coming back, the fortune-teller said triumphantly, "I told you it is unlucky to go north! Do you believe it now?" Mo-tse, with smile on his face, then said, "I came back because the river in north was in flood, not because I met the Lord of Heaven. What's more, all the people who wanted to cross the river were unable to do it, including me. We are of different colors, some light, and some dark. Why are the light-skinned people unable to cross the river either?" Mo-tse's answer made the fortune-teller faltered, without giving any reasonable explanation. Mo-tse then continued, "If the emperor killed the blue dragon in the east, the red dragon in the south, the white dragon in the west, and the yellow dragon in the middle, wouldn't it make all the people in the world unable to move? So your fallacy means nothing to me. When you tell me your fallacy, it is like throwing an egg to crush a stone, which is a mission impossible."

The fortune-teller then left in shame.

以逸待劳

西汉末年，陇甘军阀隗嚣脱离刘秀，去投靠在四川称帝的公孙述。刘秀大怒，派兵去攻打隗嚣，结果反被隗嚣打败。

刘秀再派征西大将军冯异前去占领栒邑。隗嚣得到消息，命令部将行巡立刻去栒邑抢占有利地形。冯异的部将们知道后，都劝冯异不要和行巡大军作战。冯异斩钉截铁地说："我们必须抢占栒邑'以逸待劳'。"冯异命令部队急行军，抢在行巡之前，占领了栒邑。冯异严密封锁消息，紧闭城门，偃旗息鼓，让将士们休整。行巡的部队刚急匆匆地赶到城下，城楼上突然鼓声大作，亮出了冯异的帅旗。毫无防备的行巡军队，吓得四下逃窜。冯异打开城门，领兵冲出城来，大败敌军。

让自己的军队养精蓄锐，以等候从远方赶来的敌军，以达到消灭敌人的目的，称为"以逸待劳"。

To Wait at One's Ease for an Exhausted Enemy

In the late Western Han Dynasty (202 BC–AD 8), Wei Ao, a warlord in Longgan region, claimed to break away from Liu Xiu, and became a subordinate of Gongsun Shu, who ruled in Sichuan. In great anger, Liu Xiu launched a battle toward Wei Ao but was defeated.

Liu Xiu then sent another troop led by Feng Yi to take the city of Xunyi. Xunyi was such a critical place for the battle that Wei also sent one of his troop led by Xing Xun to take it.

Feng's military officers suggested avoiding the enemy, for which Feng was firmly against, saying, "We must take Xunyi before the enemy arrive, so as to make us wait at our ease for an exhausted enemy." He then ordered his troop to make a rapid march and finally took Xunyi before the enemy.

In Xunyi, Feng gave out orders to withhold information from the enemies, and to make his troop rest and reorganize, so as to wait for the enemy troop at ease.

When Xing's troop arrived in a hurry, they didn't know their enemies had been waiting for them for a long time, so when Feng's troop unfurled all the banners and started beating drums, they fled in panic, thus were defeated.

As is shown in the story, ordering one's own troop to rest and reorganize to wait for the enemy troop in order to eliminate enemy is called "to wait at one's ease for an exhausted enemy".

异军突起

秦朝末年，秦二世荒淫无道，天下百姓怨声载道，陈胜、吴广率先揭竿而起，各地纷纷响应。这时，东阳县有个狱吏名叫陈婴，他在县中一向很有威信，东阳的百姓都很尊敬他。东阳县的年轻人见到全国起义浪潮风起云涌，也杀了东阳县令，聚集了几千人，宣布起义。他们一致请陈婴做他们的首领。县中的老百姓听说陈婴做了起义军的首领，纷纷前来投军。没多少时间，东阳的义军便壮大到两万多人。东阳的年轻人又想拥戴陈婴为王，并独树一帜；所有士兵一律用青色头巾裹头，显示他们是一支新起的与众不同的军队。

A Sudden Rising of a New Force

In the late Qin Dynasty (221–206 BC), during the Reign of Hu Hai, Emperor Qin II, people were leading miserable lives, and complaints were heard everywhere. After Chen Sheng and Wu Guang's rising up in arms, revolting appeared all over the country, greatly threatening the reign of the Qin Emperor. Following the trend, people in Dongyang killed the county magistrate and claimed to revolt. Chen Ying, a warder respected a lot in his county at that time, was invited to be their chief.

Due to his prestige in his county, people came to join his army, making the army reach an amount of more than 20 thousand soldiers. The army wanted to set Chen as their emperor and was so special that all the soldiers were wearing a blue headdress, their flags also distinctive from those of other armies. It was well-known at that time that Chen Ying's army was a sudden-rising new force.

Y

但是，陈婴的母亲对陈婴说：“自我嫁到陈家，从没听到你家的祖先有什么大贵的人，现在你的名气一下子这么大，不是什么好兆头。你不如率众归顺于什么人，将来起义成功，还可获得封侯。万一起义失败；也没有人会责怪你。”于是，陈婴便不敢称王，他对部下说：“项梁是楚将项燕的儿子，很有名声。将来带兵灭亡秦国的，一定是项氏。我决定率兵归附他。”这时，正好项梁率兵过江，陈婴便归顺了项梁。

后来，人们用此成语来比喻与众不同的新派别或新力量一下子崛起。

Chen Ying's mother, however, believed his son was keeping a quite high profile, which might lead to his failure one day. She then told his son, "I have been married to your father for years. To my knowledge, you have already been the greatest and most famous one in your family, which I believed may bring you bad luck. I hope you can pay allegiance to other's army, because whether you can overthrow the reign of Qin or not, you will at least not die an unnatural death."

Chen Ying, quite a filial son to his mother, accepted his mother's advice finally, and led his army to join that of Xiang Liang's, because he believed Xiang Liang, the son of Xiang Yu, was destined to be the new emperor. Although he joined other's army, Chen Ying was stilled remembered as a special one due to his special force.

People in China nowadays use the phrase "a sudden rising of a new force" to refer to the uprising of a new power or a new school.

异曲同工

西汉时期有名的文学家司马相如和扬雄都是以词赋见长。司马相如是汉景帝时期的人，作品有《子虚赋》《上林赋》，辞藻华丽；扬雄是汉成帝时期的人，作品有《甘泉赋》《河东赋》，主张修政。唐朝文学家韩愈评价说“子云相如，同工异曲。”

此成语比喻不同时代、不同人的文章、言论一样精彩，或不同的事情产生相同的效果。

Different in Approaches but Equally Satisfactory in Result

Sima Xiangru and Yang Xiong were both well-known writers in the Western Han Dynasty (202 BC–AD 8), both being good at Han Fu, a rhymed literary form of sentimental or descriptive composition. Although they were of different era, Sima of the age of Emperor Jing (188–141 BC), Yang of the age of Emperor Cheng (51–7BC), they were often mentioned in the same breath. They both had their own masterpieces, *ShangLin Fu* and *Zixu Fu* for Sima, and *Ganquan Fu* and *Hedong Fu* for Yang, about which, Han Yu, one of the greatest writer in Tang Dynasty, remarked, "Their masterpieces are different in approaches but equally satisfactory in result."

People in China then use Han Yu's remark as a phrase to refer to different writings and sayings which are equally fantastic. This phrase can also be used to refer to different things which can have the same effect.

Y

易如反掌

战国时期大思想家孟子主张推行“仁政”“王道”，他的弟子公孙丑问他到齐国去能否像管仲、晏婴一样有所作为。孟子很不高兴，说：“管仲辅佐齐桓公，晏婴辅佐齐景公，是因为齐国地广人多，推行王道、统一天下就像翻转手掌那样容易。”

As Easy as Turning One's Hand over

Mencius was a great philosopher living in the Warring States Period (475–221 BC). He developed a philosophy of "benevolent governance" and "kingly way", which he advocated to carry out in the states of his time. Gongsun Chou, one of his students, asked him whether he could truly make a difference in the State of Qi as Guan Zhong and Yan Ying did. Gongsun's question made Mencius unhappy, saying, "Guan Zhong and Yan Ying, when they were assisting the governance, were in Qi's heyday with vast territory and large population. It was as easy as turning one's hand over for them to put "kingly way" into force."

Chinese people then use the phrase "as easy as turning one's hand over", which is equivalent to "a piece of cake" in English, to refer to something easy to be done.

Y

引狼入室

有个牧羊人在山谷里放羊。他看见远远地有只狼跟着，就时刻提防着。几个月过去了，狼只是远远地跟着，并没有靠近羊群，更没有伤害一只羊。牧羊人渐渐地对狼放松了戒心。后来，牧羊人觉得狼跟在羊群后面有好处，不用再提防别的野兽了。再后来，他索性把狼当成了牧羊狗，叫它看管羊群。牧羊人见狼把羊管得很好，心里想，人们都说狼最坏，我看不见得。

有一天，牧羊人有事要进城去，就把羊群托狼看管，狼答应了。狼估计牧羊人已经进城了，就冲着山林中大声嚎叫了几声。它的嚎叫声引来了许许多多、大大小小的狼。那群羊全被狼吃掉了。牧羊人不了解狼的本性，才被狼的伪善欺骗了。

To Set a Wolf to Keep the Sheep

One day, a shepherd, when herding sheep in a valley, saw a wolf following them in a distance. He then was on guard against the wolf for months, only to find the wolf never came close to his sheep for once. Gradually, he let his guard against the wolf down, and even thought it an advantage to have the wolf following them, because with the wolf following, no other beast would come close to them any more. He later set the wolf to keep the sheep, thinking, "They say wolves are all bad, but my wolf is definitely a good one. How fortunate I am."

However, one day, things changed. When the shepherd had things to deal with in the town, he left all the sheep to the wolf by itself. The wolf, making sure the shepherd had already left, howled at the mountain. Its howling was actually signals for other wolves, informing them to come at once for the unguarded sheep. The sheep, of course, were all devoured by the wolves. It was a pity that the shepherd was cheated by the wolf dressed in sheep's clothing.

引锥刺股

苏秦，战国人，少有大志。但由于学识浅薄，得不到重用，甚至家里的人都瞧不起他。这使他很难过，并受到很大刺激。他决心发愤读书，增长学识。苏秦经常读书到深夜，疲倦了，难免打瞌睡。为了振作精神，他拿了一把锥子，一打瞌睡，就猛刺大腿。后来，他终于成为一个政治家、军事家，游说齐、楚、燕、韩、赵、魏六国合纵抵抗秦国。

“引锥刺股”形容学习勤奋刻苦。

To Keep Awake by Pricking One's Own Thigh with a Needle

Su Qin was a man who lived in the Warring States Period (475–221 BC). He dreamed to make a difference in his time when he was still in his boyhood. However, with limited knowledge, he couldn't get a proper position in his country, and was even looked down upon by his family. Although feeling sad and frustrated, he made up his mind to be a man of knowledge. Therefore, he often stayed up to read. Whenever he felt tired and sleepy, he would prick his own thigh with a needle to keep himself awake. Owing to his diligent study, he finally became a well-known politician, as well as an excellent strategist, who succeeded in making his theory of vertical alliance be well accepted by the six States, and putting it into force.

People then use the phrase to refer to diligent study.

饮鸩止渴

霍谞是东汉有名的“小才子”。他有个在郡里当官的舅舅，叫宋光。由于宋光为人正直、秉公执法，所以成了一些权贵的眼中钉。后来，权贵们联合起来诬告宋光篡改诏书，皇帝信以为真，就把宋光逮捕，押到京都洛阳，关进了监狱。这时，霍谞才十五岁。

霍谞不相信舅舅会篡改诏书。宋光入狱以后，霍谞十分着急，日夜思考解救舅舅的方法。最后，他决定给当时掌管朝廷大权的大将军梁商写一封信，为舅舅申冤。

他在信中说：宋光出身官宦之家，现已位居地方首长的高位。他为人正直、秉公守法，从而得到了朝廷的重用。这样的一个人，即使对于皇上的诏书有所疑虑，也会采用一种稳当的方式来解决，怎么可能冒着死罪私下更改诏书？这样的行为好比是一个人为了解渴而去饮鸩（“鸩”的羽毛泡过的毒酒）。这样的话，食物刚到咽喉，还没进到肠胃里人就已经断气了，怎么可能会有人这样做呢？

梁商读了这封信，觉得霍谞说得很有道理，又听说他只有十五岁，对他的胆识颇为赞赏。后来，梁商不仅重审此案，还亲自到皇帝那里替宋光辩白。案件终于真相大白，宋光也被无罪释放。

To Quench a Thirst with Poison

Huo Xu was a famous young prodigy in the Eastern Han Dynasty (AD 25–220). When he was 15 years old, his uncle Song Guang was convicted of the crime of tempering with the imperial verdict and was thrown into prison. As a matter of fact, Song was a candid and upright man. It was his uprightness that made him the most hated man by the bigwigs, who then framed Song up.

Huo Xu knew his uncle so well that he firmly believed Song innocent, so he was anxious to think about how to save his uncle. He at last determined to write a letter to Liang Shang, the Grand General, who was in charge of the court at that time. In the letter, he asked for Liang to redress an injustice for his uncle.

In the letter, he said, "Song Guang was born in an official family and was now already the highest administrator in his region. He got promoted due to his uprightness in administration. It is unbelievable that such an upright man with a promising future would temper with the verdict. If he really did so, it was kind of like quenching a thirst with poison, a suicidal behavior, rather than a way to solve problems."

Having read the letter, Liang thought what Huo said was reasonable. When he was told Huo was only a boy of 15 years age, he couldn't believe it but admire Huo's great courage. He then started a retrial for Song's case and judged Song innocent.

Y

郢书燕说

楚国首都郢都有个人给燕国宰相写信。书信是在夜晚书写的，因为灯火不够亮，于是写信人对拿蜡烛的人说："举烛。"一边说一边把"举烛"写到信上。

燕国宰相得到书信便阅读，高兴地说："举烛的意思是崇尚光明,崇尚光明的意思就是举荐贤能并任用他们。"燕国宰相告诉国王，国王非常高兴，国家得到很好的治理。

治理是得到了治理，但并不是书信的意思。

Distorted Interpretation

One day, the Grand Chancellor of Yan received a letter from Ying, the capital of Chu. The letter was written at night and when writing it, the writer asked the candle holder to hold the candle higher, because it was so late at night that he could not see the words clearly. What he told the holder was three words “raise the candle”. It was funny that after saying three words, he subconsciously wrote them down on the letter.

When reading the letter, the Grand Chancellor, however, mistook the three words as an implication for him to uphold righteousness, so he gladly said, “he was asking me to recommend talents to the King and to promote them in important positions. What a wise man he is!”

He then told what the letter said to the King, who was glad to accept it too. They then ran the country quite well.

Although the three words were well-accepted by the King and the Grand Chancellor, it was actually a distorted interpretation.

Y

游刃有余

战国时，有一个熟练的厨师，其解牛的技艺之高超为梁惠王所叹服。问其所以如此，厨师回答说：“我这把刀用了十九年了，解杀的牛也有几千头了，可是你看这刀刃还像是刚磨出来一样锋利。因为那牛体的骨节有空隙，刀口却薄得像没有厚度，把没有厚度似的刀口插入有空隙的骨节，宽宽绰绰的，它对于刀的运转必然是大有余地的了。”

“游刃有余”形容做事富有技巧，毫不费力。

To Do a Job with Skill and Ease

In the Warring States Period (475–221 BC), there was a cook who was so skilled in dismembering oxen that even King Hui, the King of Wei, admired him so much and wondered how he did it so skillfully.

The cook then answered, "I beg Your Majesty to look at my cleaver. I have been using it for dismembering no less than several thousand oxen for 19 years, but it is still as sharp as a new one. That's because there are gaps in the bones of oxen, which provide enough space for the cleaver to go through, which enables me to do the job with skill and ease."

People then use the phrase to describe a job done with skills.

余音绕梁

战国时有一位善歌者韩娥，韩国人。一次她经过齐国，因路费用尽，便在齐国都城（临淄，今属山东）的雍门卖唱筹资。韩娥声音清脆嘹亮，婉转悠扬，十分动人。这次演唱，轰动全城。唱完以后，听众还聚在雍门，徘徊留恋，不肯散去。

The Tune Lingering in the House

In the Warring States Period (476–221 BC), there was a good singer named Han E in the State of Han.

Once when she was passing through the State of Qi, she had to sing to raise money for her tour. She chose to give performance in the Gate of Yong in Linzi, the capital of Qi. Her songs sounded melodious and attracted many passers-by, making her quite popular in the city. After her performance, people refused to leave because they found the tune still lingering in the Gate of Yong. Some even believed that Han E might have never left the gate, otherwise, why would there still be the echo of her singing in their ears?

Nowadays, the phrase is used to refer to wonderful music or singing. It can also be used to refer to good writings.

鱼目混珠

《玉清经》里记载，从前有一个人叫满愿，他有一次到外地去，碰巧遇见一个卖珍珠的人。满愿看到那颗珍珠又大又明亮，真是爱不释手，就花大价钱买下来，把珍珠带回家。他用最好的材料做了一个精巧的盒子，把珍珠放在里面。每天晚上，夜深人静的时候，满愿就把珍珠拿出来，独自欣赏把玩。后来，有人知道满愿有一颗珍贵的珍珠，就想去观赏一下，满愿一概婉言谢绝。

满愿有一个叫寿量的邻居，恰好也有一颗大珍珠在家里，那是他从路上捡来的。寿量想："满愿的珍珠有什么了不起，我也有啊。"后来满愿和寿量同时得了一种病，医生诊断后说得用珍珠粉配药，满愿和寿量没办法，只得拿出各自藏着的珍珠。医生看到寿量的珍珠后笑着说："你这颗不是珍珠，是鱼的眼睛啊！"

To Pass Off the Sham as Genuine

According to the *Yuqing Jing*, there was a man named Man Yuan, who bought a pearl when he was on a tour. The pearl was so big and luminous that it attracted his attention at the first sight and he paid a high price for it. Back home, he made a delicate case for keeping it. Everyday in the midnight, he would took out the pearl from the case, delighting in appreciating it and touching it. When his neighbors wanted to see his pearl, he would reject it.

Shou Liang, one of Man Yuan's neighbors, also had a big pearl, which he found on the way. Shou Liang also was so proud of his own pearl that in his mind, the pearl of Man was nothing.

Later, Man and Shou were both in a same serious illness, for which the doctor suggested to cure by medicine made from pearl powders. Without choice, they two had to take out their beloved pearls. Seeing their pearls, the doctor laughed, pointing to Shou's pearl and saying, "this is not a pearl at all. It is just an eye of a certain fish."

The phrase "to pass off the sham as genuine" was thus coined.

愚公移山

《列子·汤问》载，古时候有两座大山，一座叫太行山，一座叫王屋山。那里的北山住着一位老人名叫愚公，快90岁了。他每次出门，都因被这两座大山阻隔，要绕很大的圈子，才能到南方去。所有他决定率领子孙挖掉这两座大山。

有个名叫智叟的老人得知这件事后，嘲笑愚公说："你这样做太不聪明了，凭你这有限的精力，又怎能把这两座山挖平呢？"愚公回答说："你这个人太顽固了，简直无法开导，即使我死了，还有我的儿子在这里。儿子死了，还有孙子，孙子又生孩子，孩子又生儿子。子子孙孙是没有穷尽的，而山却不会再增高，为什么挖不平呢？"

天帝被愚公的精神所感动，派了两个大力神下凡，把两座山背走。从此，这里不再有高山阻隔了。成语"愚公移山"形容赢得胜利的决心和克服困难的勇气。

The Foolish Old Man Who Removed the Mountains

According to the *Liezi*, the The Foolish Old Man of the North Mountain, nearly ninety years of age, lived behind two high mountains. He was unhappy about the fact that the mountains blocked his way to the south, so he called the whole family to level the two mountains. While they were working, the Wise Old Man at the River Bend stopped the old man. He laughed and said, "How unwise you are! At your age, old and feeble as you are, you cannot even remove one hair on the mountain, let alone so much earth and so many rocks!"

The Foolish Old Man had a long sigh and said, "You are not even as clever as a child. Though I'm about to die, there will be my sons, who will have their sons and grandsons. Generation after generation, my offspring are endless while the mountain can not get higher. With more and more stones being removed, smaller and smaller will the mountain become. Why is it impossible to level them?"

The Wise Old Man, who thought himself clever, had no more words to say.

The Foolish Old Man then led his family digging the mountains continually from early morning till late night. Finally, a god of the mountains was touched by their actions and he helped them finish the job quickly.

Nowadays, the phrase is used a lot to indicate the determination to win victory and the courage to surmount every difficulty.

Y

与虎谋皮

传说有一个人非常喜欢穿皮衣服，还爱吃精美的饭食。他打算缝制一件价值昂贵的狐狸皮袍子，于是就与狐狸商量说："把你们的毛皮送给我几张吧"，狐狸一听，全逃到山林里去了。他又想办一桌肥美的羊肉宴席，于是去找羊说："请帮帮我的忙，把你们的肉割下二斤，我准备办宴席"，没等他说完，羊就吓得狂呼乱叫，互相报信，一齐钻进树林里藏了起来。这样，那人十年也没缝成一件狐狸皮袍子，五年也没办成一桌羊肉宴席。

这个故事原来叫"与狐谋皮"，后来转化成"与虎谋皮"，比喻跟恶人商量要他牺牲自己的利益，那是绝对办不到的。

To Borrow a Skin from the Tiger

Legend has that a man was very fond of living an extravagant life, dreaming to feast every day on the most delicate dishes and wear the most costly clothes.

One day, he planned to make a robe from fox skin. Instead of buying it from the market, he turned to a fox, asking, "Could you give your skin to me?" His words frightened the fox far away into the forest.

Unable to make the robe, he had another idea to hold a feast with lamb. Again, he turned to a sheep for help, saying, "I beg you to do me a favor by cutting some of your meat for me. Could you?" Hearing his words, the sheep and other sheep, of course, ran for their lives into the forest too.

It was a funny story that the man never gave up his stupid idea of turning to sheep and foxes for their meat and skin. People then, from his story, coined an idiom "to borrow a skin from the fox" to indicate that it is impossible to earn one's profit by asking an evil to sacrifice. Later, the phrase was changed into "to borrow a skin from the tiger", which has the same meaning.

鹬蚌相争

一只河蚌张开蚌壳，在河滩上晒太阳。有只鹬鸟，从河蚌身边走过，就伸嘴去啄河蚌的肉。河蚌急忙把两片壳合上，把鹬嘴紧紧地钳住。鹬鸟用尽力气，却怎么也拔不出嘴来。蚌也脱不了身，不能回河里去了。河蚌和鹬鸟就争吵起来。鹬鸟说："一天、两天不下雨，没有了水，回不了河，你总是要死的！"河蚌也说："假如我不放你，一天、两天之后，你的嘴拔不出去，你也别想活，总要饿死！"河蚌和鹬鸟吵个不停，谁也不让谁。这时，恰好有个打鱼的人从那里走过，就把它们两个一起捉去了。

现在用来比喻双方相持不下，结果两败俱伤，让第三者得利。

A Struggle Between a Snipe and a Clam

One day, a clam opened its shells to sunbathe on a beach. A snipe, when passing by, pecked at the clam with its beak. To protect itself, the clam closed its shells, clamping the snipe tightly, making it unable to take its beat back. They two were involved in a deadlock, having nothing to do but curse the other.

The snipe said, "You can not go back to the water, if you don't let me go. I promise you will die in one or two days!"

"You will die of hunger if I won't let you go." The clam also refused to admit its being inferior.

They two then remained in the deadlock, each refusing to give way.

Finally a fisherman came close and took both of them away.

Nowadays, the phrase was used to indicate a fact that if two sides contend, a third party may benefit.

Y

欲盖弥彰

春秋时代，邾国有一个人，名字叫黑肱，为国家做事。他偷偷地把邾国一块土地送给鲁国，希望鲁国收留他。他以为没人知道自己做的这件事，就悄悄地搬到鲁国去了，没想到鲁国却把这件事清清楚楚地记录下来。

后来，邾国人发觉黑肱搬走了，纷纷打听，才知道黑肱做了对不起国家的事。黑肱没想到不想让别人知道的事，很多人都知道了。

后人多用“欲盖弥彰”一词来形容一个人做错了事，越想掩盖，结果所做的错事就越明显。

The More Concealed, the More Conspicuous

In the Spring-Autumn Period (770–221 BC), there was a man named Heigong in the State of Zhu. As a public official, Heigong had chances of making use of public power for private interest. One day, he secretly gave a piece of land to the State of Lu, a more powerful state in his time, hoping that he would become a citizen of Lu. The State of Lu, though indeed took him in as a citizen, secretly recorded what he did to his own country, thinking him a faithless man. Heigong himself was unconscious of this, and personally believed what he did was not known by anyone in his own country.

However, it was impossible to cover his disloyal actions, especially when people found he had already moved into Lu. It was his moving to Lu that made his actions known by everyone in his country.

People in China then use the phrase "the more concealed, the more conspicuous" to refer to the fact that a person who tries to cover up his mistakes will make them expose more.

越俎代庖

在中华民族的历史传说中，有一位杰出的领袖叫唐尧。

在唐尧的领导下，人民安居乐业。可是唐尧很谦虚，当他听说隐士许由很有才能的时候，就想把领导权让给许由。

唐尧对许由说："日月出来之后还不熄灭烛火，它和日月比起光亮来，不是太没有意义了吗？及时雨普降之后还去灌溉，对于润泽禾苗不是徒劳吗？您如果担任领袖，一定会把天下治理得更好，我占着这个位置还有什么意思呢？我觉得很惭愧，请允许我把天下交给您来治理。"许由说："您治理天下，已经治理得很好了。我如果再来代替你，不是沽名钓誉吗？我现在自食其力，要那些虚名干什么？鹪鹩在森林里筑巢，也不过占一棵树枝；鼹鼠喝黄河里的水，不过喝饱自己的肚皮。天下对我又有什么用呢？算了吧，厨师就算不做祭祀用的饭菜，管祭祀的人也不能越位来代替他下厨房做菜。"

To Exceed One's Duties and Meddle in Others' Affairs

Yao, a legendary monarch in ancient China, made people in his time lead peaceful and safe lives. One day, he heard of a recluse named Xu You. Yao, as a man of high moral standard, developed an idea of handing over the crown to Xu.

According to the *Zhuangzi*, to make Xu accept his idea, Yao said, "It's said that when the Sun or the Moon rises, it is not necessary to keep the candle on. It is just like when in rainy days, it is not necessary to irrigate the crops. Compared with you, I was just like the candle or the irrigation water. So please allow me to hand over the crown to you! I believe you will make our country better."

However, despite Yao's sincerity, Xu showed no interest in taking over the crown. He responded to Yao in this way, "The country is in its prosperous state under your lead, Your Majesty. If I take over the crown now, it seems like I am stealing your achievement, with which any upright man would disagree. I am a person living on my own and do not have the power to shoulder great responsibilities. It is my view of life that a contended mind is a perpetual feast. For a man like me, isn't it useless to hold the crown? So I beg your pardon. Please don't force me to exceed my duties and meddle in your affairs!"

运斤成风

楚国的郢都有个勇敢沉着的人，他的朋友石是个技艺高明的匠人。有一次，他们表演了这样一套绝活：郢人在鼻尖涂上像苍蝇翅膀一样薄的白粉，让石匠用斧子把这层白粉削去。只见匠人不慌不忙地挥动斧头，呼的一声，白粉完全被削掉了，而郢人的鼻尖却丝毫没有受到损伤，郢人也仍旧面不改色，若无其事地站在那里。

这件事被宋国的国君知道了，他非常佩服石的绝技和郢人的胆量，很想亲眼看一看这个表演。于是，国君就恭恭敬敬地把匠人石请来，让他再表演一次，石说："我的好友已经去世，我失去了唯一的搭档，再也没法表演了。"

根据这个故事，后人将"运斤成风"引为成语，比喻手法熟练，技艺高超。

To Create a Gust by Wielding the Axe

In the Warring States Period (475–221 BC), there was a very brave man living in Ying, the capital of Chu. The man had a good friend named Shi, who was a skilled craftsman. One day, they worked as partners to give audience a fantastic performance, which is to chip off a film of lime from the brave man's nose by Shi, the skilled craftsman. Under the close look of the audiences, Shi calmly shipped off the lime from the nose of his friend, who, due to his brave disposition, had been keeping a calm face from the beginning to the end. They finished their performance amid the gasp of the audiences, the brave man in perfect physical condition, his friend Shi keeping a straight face.

People thought the performance so amazing that it was told from mouth to mouth, quickly to the ears of the King. The King also thought it unbelievable, and he couldn't wait to ask the brave man and Shi to come to the imperial court to give him the performance. However, it was a pity that the brave man had already passed away. In a very sad tone, Shi told the King, "I can't do the show once again, because without my dear friend, I am nobody."

However, from their story, a phrase "to create a gust by wielding the axe" was made, indicating that someone was highly skilled when doing things.

凿壁偷光

匡衡是西汉人，出生在一个穷苦的农民家庭。他从幼年起就酷爱读书。白天要劳动，没有多少空余时间，晚上很想读书，却穷得点不起灯，他为此很苦恼。后来，他发现邻居家夜夜有灯光，就想了个办法。

因为邻家点灯的房子和他的住室之间，只隔着一堵墙，于是，他便在墙上凿了个小孔。灯光果然从小孔里透过来了。他高兴得跳了起来。从此以后，他每夜蹲在墙脚，借着这一线亮光读书，直到邻居家熄了灯，他才心满意足地去睡觉。

这样日积月累，匡衡终于成了著名的大学者。

人们用“凿壁偷光”形容勤奋刻苦的学习者。

A Light Stealer

Kuang Heng was born in a poor farmer's family in Western Han Dynasty (202 BC–AD 8). He developed his great interest in reading when he was in his boyhood. However, his family was too poor to afford him to go to school, and he had to find a job to help his father feed his family. In daytime, he had to work hard at his job, and at evening, when a day's job was over, he would read books at home although he was exhausted. His family was so poor that they had no money to buy candles, which made reading a mission almost impossible. One night, when seeing the light from the window of his neighbor's cottage, he came up with an idea.

The idea was to steal light from the neighbor's by boring a hole on the wall between his room and the neighbor's. When the hole was made, the light indeed came though it, which made him as cheerful as a lark, because he then was able to read by the light.

From then on, he would read by the hole night after night, and with his diligent study, he finally became a famous scholar of his time.

People then use the phrase "a light stealer" to refer to a diligent learner.

曾参杀人

过去曾参的家在费地，费地有个跟曾参同名同姓的人杀了人，有人向曾子的母亲报告说“曾参杀人了”时，曾子的母亲说：“我的儿子是绝对不会去杀人的。”没隔多久，又有一个人跑到曾子的母亲面前说：“曾参真的在外面杀了人。”曾子的母亲仍然不去理会这句话，她还是坐在那里不慌不忙地穿梭引线，照常织着自己的布。又过了一会儿，第三个报信的人跑来对曾母说：“曾参的确杀了人。”曾母心里骤然紧张起来，急忙扔掉手中的梭子，端起梯子，越墙逃走了。虽然曾参贤德，他母亲对他很信任，但有三个人怀疑他（杀了人），慈爱的母亲也不相信他了。

后来人们用这个成语，来比喻流言可畏。

Rumors are Dreadful

Zeng Shen, known as Zeng Zi, used to live in Fei, a county in north China. It was a coincidence that there was another man named Zeng Shen in Fei too, who murdered someone else. Although Zeng was quite innocent, rumors came out that he had been a murderer. A friend of his even went to his mother's place to tell her the rumor.

Zeng's mother, however, knew her son so well that she regarded the rumor as nonsense, telling the friend, "My son will definitely not do that."

In a short time, another friend came to Zeng's mother and said, "Zeng has been a murderer", for which Zeng's mother still took an indifferent attitude, busy weaving by threading her needles into the cloth.

It was hard to expect that there came a third friend, telling his mother the rumor for the third time. This time, his mother started to feel anxious, thinking it might be a truth because so many people had told her the same story. She felt so worried that she took out a ladder and used it to help her cross the wall and ran away.

From this story, we know that rumors are so dreadful, even when they were about Zeng Zi, a well-known and intelligent sage in the history.

Nowadays, this phrase is a commonly-used phrase about the harm of rumors.

枕戈待旦

西晋人祖逖和刘琨，都是性格开朗、仗义好侠的志士。年轻时不但文章写得好，而且都喜欢练武健身，决心报效祖国。当时，晋朝表面上还管辖着中原大地，但实际上已是内忧外患、风雨飘摇了。祖逖和刘琨一谈起国家局势，总是慷慨万分，常常聊到深夜。

To Maintain Combat Readiness

Zu Di and Liu Kun were both young men of lofty ambitions and knight spirits in the Western Jin Dynasty (AD 266–316). They not only wrote excellent articles, but also were fond of practising martial arts to keep fit, in order to render meritorious service to the country. In their time, although in appearance the Jin Dynasty had jurisdiction of China, it was actually in a state of flux, threatened by domestic strife and foreign aggression. They often talked till late night about state affairs passionately, concerning about the future of their country.

一天，祖逖又和刘琨谈得十分兴奋，刘琨不知什么时候睡着了，祖逖却久久沉浸在谈话的兴奋之中，不能入睡。“喔，喔，喔——”荒原上的雄鸡叫了起来，祖逖一跃而起，踢醒了刘琨：“听，这雄鸡啼鸣多么振奋人心呀，快起来练剑吧！”于是，两人操起剑来，在高坡上对舞。从此，他俩每天清早听到头一声鸣叫，一定来到荒原上抖擞精神练起剑来。

刘琨被祖逖的爱国热情深深感动，决心献身于国家。一次他给家人的信中写道：“在国家危难时刻，我经常‘枕戈待旦’，立志报国，常担心落在祖逖后边，不想他到底走到我的前头了！”

“枕戈待旦”形容强烈的报效祖国的愿望。

One day, again, when talking about sate affairs, they were in a very excited mental state. It was Liu Kun who first calmed down and fell asleep. Zu Di, on the other hand, kept in a high spirit the whole night. "Cock-a-doodle-doo"came the crow of rooster in the wasteland. Hearing the crow, Zu Di jumped up and kicked Liu Kun awake, saying, "Listen, how inspiring the rooster's crow is! Let's get up to practice sword playing!" They then got up and practiced sword playing on a slope, both feeling exalted in mind. From then on, they kept practising sword playing vigorously and energetically in the wasteland every day when they heard the first crow in the morning.

Deeply touched by Zu Di's patriotic passion, Liu Kun was determined to devote himself to his homeland. He once wrote to his family, "At the time when the country is in dire peril, I am resolved to dedicate myself to the service of my country. I often fear that I might lag behind Zu Di in rendering service to the country, and, in fact, I am behind him. So, let me work harder and always maintain combat readiness. Only in this way, can I keep pace with him."

People nowadays use the phrase "to maintain combat readiness" to refer to one's strong will to devote to his country.

郑人买履

从前，郑国有个人想买双鞋。他量好了自己脚的尺码，把它放在了椅子上。可当他赶往市集时，却忘了带量好的尺码。他要买鞋时，才想了起来。

他说："我忘带尺码了。"

他回家去取量好的尺码。等他赶回来时，市集已经关了，他还是没能买到鞋。

有人问："为什么不用你自己的脚去量鞋子呢？"

他说："我宁愿相信尺码也不相信我自己的脚。"

"郑人买履"的故事非常深刻地讽刺了那些只相信教条而不顾客观实际的人。

To Buy Shoes Like the Man from Zheng Did

According to the *Hanfeizi*, a man of the State of Zheng wanted to buy a pair of shoes. He measured his feet and put the measurement on a chair. When he set out for the market he forgot to bring it along, which occurred to him after he had found the pair he wanted.

"I forgot to bring the measurement. I will go back to fetch it." said he.

He did go back to get his measurement. However, when he arrived at the market again, it had already been closed.

"Why didn't you try on the shoes with your feet?" he was asked.

"Why? I have the measurement. I'd rather trust the measurement than trust my feet." he answered.

From this ridiculous story, people made the phrase "to buy shoes like the man from Zheng did", which ironically refers to people who behave in dogmatic ways without considering practical situations.

纸上谈兵

战国时，赵国名将赵奢的儿子赵括，喜欢看兵书。他把兵书背得滚瓜烂熟，谈起打仗来头头是道。一次，秦国派兵攻打赵国，赵王派赵括率领四十万大军去抵抗。由于他只知道死抠书本而不会在实际中灵活运用，最后指挥失策，以致全军覆灭，他自己也中箭身亡。

人们根据这一历史故事，把死抠书本，没有实际经验，只会夸夸其谈称为“纸上谈兵”。

Being an Armchair Strategist

In the Warring States Period (475–221 BC), the State of Zhao had a famous general called Zhao She, whose son, Zhao Kuo, was very fond of reading books on military science and discussing strategies. He could recite military texts by heart, and when discussing warfare he spoke so clearly and logically that it seemed that even his father was not his match.

One day, Zhao was under the attack of the State of Qin. Well-known for his excellence in military strategies, Zhao Kuo was nominated as the commander in chief for the army against Qin, leading 400,000 soldiers. Although high expectation was placed on him by the king, Zhao Kuo was defeated and lost his life, because he had no practical experience of battle.

People in China then use the phrase "being an armchair strategist" to refer to people who are only good at theorizing, but lack of practical experience.

Z

指鹿为马

秦二世时，丞相赵高野心勃勃，日夜盘算着要篡夺皇位。可朝中大臣有多少人能听他摆布，有多少人反对他，他心中没底。于是，他想了一个办法，准备试一试自己的威信，同时也可以摸清敢于反对他的人。

一天上朝时，赵高让人牵来一只鹿，满脸堆笑地对秦二世说："陛下，我献给您一匹好马。"秦二世一看，笑着对赵高说："丞相搞错了，这是一只鹿，你怎么说是马呢？"赵高面不改色心不跳地说："请陛下看清楚，这的确是一匹千里马。"然后，一转身，用手指着众大臣，大声说："陛下如果不信我的话，可以问问众位大臣。

Calling a Stag a Horse

During the reign of Emperor Qin II, Imperial Chancellor Zhao Gao, obsessed with ambitions, was thinking about usurping the crown all the time. Not sure about the fact how many officials would be ordered about by him, he thought out a sinister plan to find out who were not on his side.

One day when court was held, Zhao led a stag into the court, and asked the emperor, grinning from ear to ear, "Here is a steed for you, Your Majesty! How do you think about it?"

The emperor smiled, saying, "It is not a horse, but a stag. Isn't it?"

Remaining calm, Zhao Gao said, "Will your Majesty please see more clearly? This really is a horse that covers a thousand li a day." He then turned his back against the emperor, and pointed his fingers to the officials, asking in a loud voice, "Our Majesty don't believe me. How about you? Do you think it a horse or a stag?"

大臣们都被赵高的一派胡言搞得不知所措，私下里嘀咕：这个赵高搞什么名堂？是鹿是马这不是明摆着吗！当看到赵高脸上露出阴险的笑容，两只眼睛骨碌碌轮流地盯着每个人的时候，大臣们忽然明白了他的用意。

一些胆小又有正义感的人都低下头，不敢说话，因为说假话，对不起自己的良心，说真话又怕日后被赵高所害。有些正直的人，坚持认为是鹿而不是马。还有一些平时就紧跟赵高的奸佞之人立刻表示拥护赵高的说法，对皇上说，“这确是一匹千里马！”

事后，赵高通过各种手段把那些不顺从自己的正直大臣纷纷治罪，甚至满门抄斩。

人们用“指鹿为马”形容颠倒是非。

The nonsense of Zhao Gao made the officials totally at a loss, and they whispered to themselves, "What tricks are Zhao Gao playing? Was it not obvious whether it was a stag or a horse?" However, when they saw the sinister smile on Zhao Gao's face and his two rolling eyes which were gazing at each of them, they suddenly understood his evil intentions.

Some of the ministers who were timid and yet had a sense of right consciousness did not dare to say anything, because to tell lies would make their conscience uneasy while to tell the truth would mean that they would be persecuted by Zhao Gao later. Some ministers with a sense of justice persisted that it was a stag and not a horse. There were still some crafty and fawning ministers who followed Zhao Gao closely in ordinary times approving of Zhao Gao totally.

After the event, Zhao Gao punished by various means those officials with a sense of justice who were not obedient to him, even with whole families of some of those ministers executed.

People then use the phrase to refer to people who call black white.

纸醉金迷

唐朝时有一个高明的医生叫孟斧。当时他住在国都长安，经常被请到宫中帮皇帝和妃子们治病。因为经常出入皇宫，所以他对皇宫的一切很熟悉，对皇宫里荒淫奢侈的华丽生活更是向往。后来黄巢领导的起义军攻打长安，他吓得急忙逃出长安，躲到四川。

在四川，孟斧因为想念皇宫中的生活，就根据记忆，模仿皇宫的装饰布置自己的家。他把家中布置得跟皇宫一样华丽，其中有一间光线很好的房间，孟斧把房间里所有东西的表面，全部都糊上一层黄金做成的薄纸。在阳光的照射下，满屋子金光闪闪，让人觉得像是住在金子做成的屋子里。所有到过这屋子的人都说："在这个屋子里休息一会儿，就会沉迷陶醉在满屋的金纸里。"

后人用此成语来形容奢侈豪华、腐朽享乐的生活。

To Lead a Voluptuous Life

In Tang Dynasty (AD 618–907), Meng Fu, a very capable physician, lived in Chang'an, the capital city. He was often asked to enter the imperial palace to cure diseases for the emperor and the concubines. Impressed a lot by the luxurious lives of the royal family, he dreamed of indulging himself in luxury and excessive pleasure one day. Unfortunately, he was destined not to be able to achieve his dream, especially when one day, a rebel army led by Huang Chao launched a war toward the government force in Chang'an, making him flee for safety to Sichuan, a district far away from Chang'an.

He didn't give up his dream of living a voluptuous life in Sichuan, where he decorated his house according to his memory about the royal palace. To resemble it, he decorated a well-lit room with wall paper made of gold, and covered all the furniture and wares in the room with the same gold paper. Every day when the sun rose, everything in the room, including the four walls, glistened and sparkled, giving everyone in the room an illusion of living in palace. "What a voluptuous life it is!" they would exclaim.

Since then, the phrase "to lead a voluptuous life" was made to describe excessive luxurious life.

趾高气昂

春秋时，楚国有个叫屈瑕的将军，是个只重视外貌却不学无术的人，只要稍有点成就，就很骄傲、自满。

有一次，他打败了剽悍的绞国，凯旋后骄傲自得，不把其他的朝臣放在眼中。第二年，屈瑕又奉命去打罗国，有一个叫作斗伯比的将军前往送行。当斗伯比回来时，悄悄地对车夫说：“屈将军这次一定会打败仗；因为我看他走路的样子，脚步一昂一翘的，便知道他的心并没有真正地用在作战上，而是去吓唬敌人的，这样子怎么能打胜仗呢？”斗伯比说完，沉思了一下，就进宫去见楚王，要楚王立刻派兵去接应。楚王不相信，回到后宫将这件事告诉了宠妃邓曼，邓曼认为斗伯比的见解很对，应该派兵救援。楚王听了，立即派大军前去，希望能够挽回局势。但是，战事已经发生，屈瑕因为轻敌而不设防，被罗国和卢国两面夹攻而一败涂地，只好自杀谢罪。

从此以后，这件事情就被后人流传着，而屈瑕走路的姿态也被引申成“趾高气扬”这句话，比喻一个人傲慢自得而不把任何人放在眼中。

Swollen with Arrogance

In the Spring-Autumn Period (770–221 BC), there was a general named Qu Xia in the State of Chu. Although a man good for nothing, Qu was flatulent and arrogant all day.

After beating the troop of Jiao, Qu felt even more proud and arrogant, looking down upon almost everybody around him. One year later, he was ordered to lead the army to start a war against the State of Luo. On the day they set off, another general named Dou Bobi was asked to hold them a send-off party. When they departed, Dou told his cart driver, "I have a strong feeling that Qu will be defeated in this war. That's because I noticed his proud way of walking with self-satisfied steps. His walking told me that he was not treating the war seriously, so he is doomed to fail."

Dou then went to the palace to tell his idea to the King, and asked the King to send another troop to come to Qu's aid. The King was at first doubtful about Dou's idea. However, after telling the idea to Concubine Deng Man, who agreed with what Dou said, the King started to feel it a serious thing to send another troop to the front line.

However, it was too late. The arrogant general Qu had already started his attack toward the enemy, and was defeated soon, still due to his arrogance. Having lost the battle, Qu felt so ashamed that he killed himself immediately.

Nowadays, people in China use the phrase "swollen with arrogance" to describe the way Qu walked, as well as his proud attitude toward others. He himself even became a symbol of arrogance. This idiom is used to describe an arrogant man who looks down upon others.

自相矛盾

楚国有个卖兵器的人，在市场上卖矛和盾。为了让人家愿意买他的货，他先举起盾向人们夸口道："你们看，我的盾是世上最坚固的盾，任何锋利的东西都不能刺穿它。"接着又举起他的矛，向人吹嘘说："你们再看看我的矛，它锋利无比，无坚不摧，无论多么坚硬的盾，都挡不住它，一刺就穿！"人群中有人问道："依你的说法，无论怎样坚硬的盾你的矛都能将其刺穿，而无论多么锋利的矛也不能把你的盾刺穿。那就拿你的矛来刺你的盾吧，看看结果怎么样？"卖兵器的人听了张口结舌，无从回答，只好拿着矛和盾走了。

"自相矛盾"用来比喻做事、说话前后不一致，自相抵触。

Self-contradiction

In the Spring-Autumn Period (770–221 BC), a man of the State of Chu was putting his weapons on sale in a market. He took out his shield first and said, "Look! This is the strongest shield in the world. It definitely can fend against anything sharp, even the sharpest spear in the world!" He then took out his spear and said loudly, "now look at the sharpest spear in the world, which can of course pierce into the strongest shield."

"What happens if you pierce your shield with your own spear?" a voice was heard from the audience.

Realizing he was actually making a self-contradiction when selling, the weapons seller felt very embarrassed, unable to say anything but to escape in great shame from the audience, leaving the audience in laughter.

Then, self-contradiction means paradox.

作壁上观

秦朝末年，大将章邯领兵攻打赵，赵军大败，逃到巨鹿死守，等待救援。各路反秦大军却按兵不动，只有项羽率军把秦军包围，项羽力能扛鼎，冲入敌阵，斩杀敌将苏角，大败秦军。巨鹿之战，消灭秦军主力，原来作壁上观的人纷纷投靠。

这则成语原指双方交战，自己站在壁垒上旁观。后多比喻站在一旁看着，不动手帮助。

To Be an Onlooker

In the late Qin Dynasty (221–207 BC), Zhang Han, a general of Qin, led his troop to start a war with the State of Zhao. They defeated the Zhao army, and forced them to retreat to Ju Lu, a city favorable for defence. The Zhao army was then besieged by the enemy, having no choice but wait for the help from their allies. However, no ally came to Ju Lu for their rescue. Instead, they all chose to be onlookers except Xiang Yu, a very brave and powerful general of that time. Xiang Yu led his army to attack the camp of Qin, where he killed General Su Jiao of Qin, and won the battle.

After the battle, the main force of Qin were destroyed, making the onlookers choose to join the side of Xiang Yu.

The phrase is now used mainly to refer to people who choose to stand by and do nothing when others are in need.

Z

坐怀不乱

春秋时期，鲁国的贤士柳下惠夜里在城门借宿时，遇到一无家可归的女子，当夜寒风呼啸，大雪纷飞。柳下惠怕她冻伤，让她坐在自己的怀中取暖，用衣服裹住她抱着她坐了一夜，没有发生不正当的淫乱行为。

柳下惠从此成为了正人君子的代名词。“坐怀不乱”也被人们用来形容男子的正派。

To Wear Joseph's Coat

In the Spring-Autumn Period (770–221 BC), Liu Xiahui, a well-respected man of virtue in Lu, met a homeless girl when he was staying overnight one day at the city gate. It was a cold night of a big snowfall and howling wind. To protect the girl from the harsh weather, Liu asked the girl to sit in his arms and covered the girl with his own clothes. What is more commendable is that during the whole night, no licentious behavior happened between Liu and the girl.

People then use the phrase "to wear Joseph's coat" to describe the uprightness of men, and Liu also became a model of upright men.

债台高筑

战国时代已经是周朝的后期，周赧王虽然是天子，却没有实权。当时称为战国七雄的齐、楚、燕、韩、赵、魏、秦七国，都很有势力。尤其是强大的秦国，秦王老是想吞并其他六国，将来自己当天子。

有一天，楚孝烈王听说魏国信陵君打败了秦国，就向周赧王说，现在是最好的时机，大家联合起来消灭秦国吧！周赧王早就知道秦国想侵犯周朝的野心，就一口答应派兵支援。军队需要马匹和武器，但是当时军费不够，只好向国内有钱的人借，并且说明等打胜仗回来，再加上利息还给大家。

谁知道，他们出兵以后，只有楚、燕两国兵马来会合，其他诸侯国并没派兵。仗没打，钱却花光了。债主天天在宫门口吵着还钱。赧王只好躲到一个高台上去。

当一个人欠了很多债却无力偿还时，就可以用“债台高筑”来形容。

With the Debt Platform Built up High

During the Warring States Period (475–221 BC), a period in the late Zhou Dynasty, King Nan, the King of Zhou, was a figurehead who had no real power. There were seven powerful states at that time, namely Qi, Chu, Yan, Han, Zhao, Wei and Qin, of which Qin was the most powerful one. The King of Qin was so ambitious that he always dreamed of swallowing up the other six states and becoming Tianzi, the ruler of the whole of China.

One day, King Nan was informed by the King of Chu that the army of Qin had been defeated by the army of Wei, under the leading of Lord Xinling. They then both thought it a good opportunity to unite all other states to conquer Qin together. However, although a consensus was made between King Nan and the other lords, the court did not have enough money to pay for the horses and weapons his troops would need. King Nan then borrowed money from the rich people of his country, promising to pay the money back with high interest after they won the war.

Unfortunately, it was out of the king's expectation that no states joined their group except Wei and Chu.The war was never fought, but the money had been completely spent. The creditors gathered at the palace gates every day to demand their money, and King Nan was forced to hide up atop his high platform.

Thus, when a person, like King Nan, owes a great debt, it is impossible for him to pay it all back. In this sense, we can say that "the debt platform is built up high".

朝三暮四

从前，宋国有一个老人，他在家中养了许多猴子。老人每天都会给每只猴子八颗栗子，早晚各四颗。后来，猴子越来越多，老人也越来越穷，所以他想每天只给猴子七颗栗子，于是他就和猴子们商量:“从今天开始，我每天早上给你们四颗栗子，晚上给你们三颗栗子，行不行？”猴子们想了一想，晚上怎么少了一颗呢？于是大叫起来，非常不愿意。老人一看，连忙说:“那么我早上给你们三颗，晚上再给你们四颗，可以了吧？”猴子们听了，以为晚上的栗子已经由三个变成四个，跟以前一样，就高兴地同意了。

“朝三暮四”原意是指实质不变，用玩弄手段、改换名目的方法使人受骗上当。后引申为说话、办事反复无常不负责任。

Three at Dawn and Four at Dusk

According the *Zhuangzi*, in the State of Song, there was an old man who raised many monkeys at his home. Every day early in the morning, the old man would feed each monkey 4 chestnuts, and every day at the dusk, he would feed them again with 4 other chestnuts. Days passed until he fed so many monkeys that he had not enough chestnuts gradually. So he wanted to feed monkeys seven chestnuts each day.

He then discussed it with the monkeys, "From today, each of you will get four chestnuts for breakfast. At dusk, you will get three only. What do you say to it?"Hearing this, all the monkeys got angry. How come one more too short in the evening? Then the old man changed to say, "what about three in the morning and four in the evening?" The monkeys accepted the idea with joy for they thought there were still four in the evening.

From this funny story, an idiom "three at dawn and four at dusk" was coined, originally meaning fooling others by playing tricks. It nowadays indicates changing one's mind frequently or not being responsible. It also means playing fast and loose or chopping and changing.

终南捷径

唐朝时，书生卢藏用考取进士，为快速入朝为官，便和哥哥卢征明隐居在京城长安附近的终南山，以此扩大影响，后来朝廷终于让他出来做官。

司马承祯和卢藏用交好多年，可是他们二人在兴趣志向上相差很多。有一天，司马承祯奉唐睿宗之命前往长安宫中谈道说法。临别之际，卢藏用以朋友的身份来给他送行。司马承祯向其表明了自己想退隐天台山的意愿，而卢藏用建议他隐居终南山，并说："这座山里有很多好地方，你何必远走他乡呢？"司马承祯立刻就明白了卢藏用的意思，当即正色说道："在我看来，终南山只不过是通向官场的一条便捷之道罢了。"

卢藏用闻言，面露愧色，感到很尴尬，甚至都不知道该说什么了。

A Short-cut to a High Office

Lu Cangyong, a scholar of the Tang Dynasty (AD 618–907), used to live in Mount Zhongnan as a recluse with his brother Lu Zhengming. Although a recluse, he actually took his reclusive life in Zhongnan Mountian as a short-cut to offialdom, for he knew so well that it was a fashion for the imperial family in his time to invite recluses to work as ministers. His purpose was indeed achieved one day.

Sima Chengzhen, though a friend of Lu's, is of a different personality and interest with Lu. One day, Sima was invited by Emperor Ruizong to the royal palace to talk about natural law and God's will, after which Sima developed an idea of leading a reclusive life in Tiantai Mountain, a place very far away from the capital city. When Lu Cangyong came to see him off, Sima told his plan to Lu, for which Lu believed it not necessary to go that far to be a recluse. He believed, instead, it was more convenient for Sima to lead a reclusive life in Mount Zhongnan, the mountain in the suburb of the capital city where he used to live.

Sima, however, knew what Lu actually meant, and replied at once, "What I want is a real reclusive life, instead of a short-cut to a high office."

Sima's words made Lu shameful and embarrassed.

Z

炙手可热

唐玄宗李隆基年轻时是一个很有作为的皇帝，但是，唐玄宗后来任用李林甫为丞相，政治开始腐败。公元 745 年，他封杨玉环为贵妃，纵情声色，奢侈荒淫，政治越来越腐败。杨贵妃有个堂兄叫杨钊，由于杨贵妃得宠，杨钊也平步青云，做了御史，唐玄宗还赐名“国忠”。不久，李林甫死了，唐玄宗便任命杨国忠做丞相，把朝廷政事全部交给杨国忠处理。一时之间，杨家兄妹权势熏天，他们结党营私，把整个朝廷搞得乌烟瘴气，以致不久以后就爆发了安禄山、史思明的叛乱（安史之乱），出现民不聊生的局面。可当时，杨家兄妹仍过着花天酒地、穷奢极欲的生活。

Hot Enough to Scald One's Hands

Emperor Xuanzong is an emperor of great achievement in Tang Dynasty (AD 618–907). In his early years, he used to arouse all his efforts to make the country prosperous. However, since he nominated Li Linfu as the Imperial Chancellor, political corruption started to become a very serious problem in his reign. The problem got worse and worse since he conferred the title of the highest-ranking imperial concubine to Yang Yuhuan, a famous beautiful lady in Chinese history. Since then, Xuanzong completely indulged himself in luxury and excessive pleasure.

Due to the glory of Yang Yuhuan, Yang Zhao, a cousin of Yuhuan, had a meteoric rise in position too. He was later nominated as the censor of the central government, and was given the name "Guozhong" by Xuanzong. Ironically, although the name "Guozhong" means "being patriotic and loyal to the throne", Guozhong was actually a very crooked and evil official.

Yuhuan and Guozhong reached the top of their power after Li Linfu died, because Guo Zhong was nominated as the prime minister soon. Their being in power made Tang Dynasty lose her heyday. Years later, local warlords like An Lushan and Shi Siming launched a revolting war against the central government, making people lead miserable lives. However, turning a blind eye to the misery of ordinary people, Yuhuan and Guozhong still led a voluptuous life.

公元 753 年 3 月 3 日，杨贵妃等人到曲江边游春野宴，让水深火热中的百姓感到极度愤懑。诗人杜甫对杨家兄妹这种只顾自己享乐、不管人民死活的行为极为愤慨，写出了著名的《丽人行》一诗，大胆揭露和深刻讽刺了杨家兄妹生活的奢侈和权势的显赫。“炙手可热势绝伦，慎莫近前丞相嗔！”便是诗中的两句。这两句诗的意思是：杨家权重位高、势焰大，没有人能与之相比；你千万不要走近前去，以免惹得丞相发怒生气。

现在，人们用“炙手可热”形容气焰很盛，权势很大。

On the third day of the third lunar month in AD 753, Yuhaun and her relatives went to Qujiang River for a spring-outing. They set a big banquet on the river bank of Qujiang, making people in war feel extreme anger and disappointment. Du Fu, the most excellent poet in Chinese history, wrote a famous poem entitled *The Beauty's Springouting* satirizing the Yang Family out of anger. In the poem, there are two lines like this, "I suggest, my dear friend, not going near the Prime Minister. For he is burning hot, he might scald your hands."

These two sarcastic lines, together with the phrase "hot enough to scald one's hands", were memorized by later generations.

Nowadays, people in China often use the phrase to describe the supreme arrogance of a person with great power.

助纣为虐

刘邦进入咸阳城后，见宫殿巍峨，珍宝无数，美女成群，就想留在宫中享受一番。

当时的武将樊哙劝他不要因小失大，可是他不听。张良又劝他说："我们之所以能够来到咸阳，主要是因为秦君残暴无道。我们应该替天行道，消灭残余势力，改变秦朝的奢侈和淫乐，提倡艰苦朴素来号召天下。现在您才占领了秦国，就要享受秦王所享受的快乐，这是'助纣为虐'的行为。"刘邦认为张良的话有道理，于是撤出咸阳，把军队驻扎在霸上。

To Hold the Candle to the Devil

In the late Qin Dynasty (221–207 BC), Liu Bang's force conquered Xianyang, the capital of Qin. Impressed by the magnify-cent palace, the dazzling jewellery and the gorgeous ladies, Liu developed a new idea to stay at the palace to lead a luxurious life.

Fan Kuai, one of his military officers, suggested him not to be penny-wise and pound-foolish, but in vain. Zhang Liang, one of his think-tank, suggested him to stay out of the palace too. Zhang said to Liu, "The reason why we can be here is that the emperor of Qin was leading a brutal reign, making the people live in dire straits, and providing us an opportunity to win support from the people to overthrow Qin's reign. If you my lord stay in the palace, you are actually choosing a life resembling the Emperor Qin's. It is like holding the candle to the devil. People then will be against us too."

Zhang Liang's words made sense to Liu Bang. He then withdrew his troop from Xian Yang and stationed in Bashang.